GASTRIC SLEEVE BARIATRIC COOKBOOK

500 Everyday Bariatric-Friendly Recipes to Become Who You Always Wanted To Be. Eat Right, and Win Against Food Addiction with The Included Easy 8+1 Meal Plan

RACHEL AMY MEYER

IPH BOOKS
Healthy Lifestyle

...to My Dear Daddy, with love!

447 Chocolate Almond Ginger Mousse

INTRODUCTION

Gastric sleeve bariatric surgery is a permanent weight loss operation that has been shown to produce lasting weight loss. The operation involves the surgeon placing silicone sleeves around the top of the stomach. If you want to know what you need to do to prepare for this procedure, take a few hours and read below!

Why do I need preparation for gastric sleeve bariatric surgery?

- The operation does not always produce ideal results, so it pays off in advance to learn your options and choose which one will be best for your body type.
- Many factors, including your diet, level of physical activity, and even your emotional state, will influence how the result will turn out, so it is best to do everything you can before the operation.
- The medical staff is reluctant to perform the procedure if they feel you might not be able to handle it. Most people who prepare the pre-operation are ready for this operation and then get approval.

What should I start with?

The first thing you should start with is a complete medical examination that considers your general health, and most physicians recommend starting with an exercise routine as soon as possible. Many weight loss patients find out the hard way that it is easier to start this routine before the operation than after. Some physicians even recommend waiting until 3–6 months after surgery before starting a new diet and exercise program.

What should I eat before the surgery?

- To lose weight while still on solid food, you must start with a low glycemic index diet and avoid processed foods and sweetened drinks. It is best to visit a registered dietician and get help to make this switch gradually instead of trying it all at once.
- Many bariatric surgery patients find eliminating certain foods easier, simplifying the process. The dietician should be able to help you with this, or you can visit a support group that discusses various diets.
- Ideally, you need to cut out all the foods that contain unhealthy fats and start eating more vegetables and lean meats. Also, do not forget about flaxseed! It is very important to get enough fiber in your diet, so try eating a lot of vegetables, whole grains, and fruits with a low glycemic index.

What supplements should I take?

- Many people like taking vitamin C and fish oil, but they recommend consulting a doctor about doing this. As for calcium, you can get plenty of it from dairy products or by drinking soy milk.

What should I avoid before the surgery?

- Some patients find it easier to reduce their caffeine intake because this can increase the symptoms of gastric sleeve surgery. As for smoking, this is definitely something you should try avoiding. You are cutting out a lot of calories when you quit smoking, so if you are serious about losing weight, do not smoke!
- As for the mood-altering substances, you should probably finish them off at least 2 weeks before your surgery date. The operation does not necessarily provide extra energy, but it will allow you to sleep more easily, so if alcohol is ruining your sleep schedule even after stopping, just get rid of it.

The genuine work towards weight loss starts after the surgery has been conducted. Participants must eat smaller and more frequent meals for the rest of their lives. Of course, the stomach can only accommodate small portions, but they would be used up fast, and the dieter has to eat more often.

The Gastric Sleeve Diet is multiphase. It is aimed at helping people prepare for the surgery, recover after the surgery, and transition to eating healthy for the rest of their lives. You can undertake the Gastric Sleeve Surgery Diet if you think that the surgery itself is overwhelming. A Gastric Sleeve diet might be your answer if you want to implement lifestyle changes and eat healthily. You can follow the strict rules of eating that it offers without actually pulling out your stomach. If you are considering undergoing surgery but have not decided yet, you can try the diet instead.

Gastric Sleeve Diet Phases

The Gastric Sleeve diet has four phases. It has been designed to carry the surgery recipient through preparation to recovery and life after that. It can stop overeating for recipients of the surgery and anyone who is committed to the process. Achieving success with your Gastric Sleeve diet requires your total commitment.

The four phases of the diet are transitionary, and they build upon each other so that the stomach does not experience shock. At first, the now delicate stomach would be unable to receive anything substantial. Using the diet, you can carry it steadily to its new normal state by building up what you eat. The Gastric Sleeve diet has made this easy by telling you precisely what you should eat.

In addition, if you are undergoing Gastric Sleeve surgery, your surgeon may require you to go through a special pre-operation diet. It is aimed to keep you in a healthy enough state for the surgery. You should deliberate a pre-operation diet with your surgeon ahead of the surgery. The diets each person should take during the pre-operation stage can vary, so you want to know all the details from your surgeon well ahead of time.

Phase 1

Phase 1 of the diet is the first week after surgery. You are expected to take only clear liquids at this stage. Your new stomach needs a lot of hydration to heal, which is very important. Proper hydration can speed up healing and reduce symptoms like nausea and vomiting.

It may be hard to stick to a liquid diet, but it is relatively easy for people who undertake the surgery because they will hardly feel hungry. You are expected to take only clear liquids during phase one. Avoid taking sugary drinks, caffeinated drinks, carbonated drinks, and soda. So, you want to avoid beverages, coffee, and tea.

You should replace this with drinks that contain no sugar. You should maintain your regular 8 glasses of water a day. Some clear liquids you can take at phase one of your diet include broth, jelly, sugar-free popsicles, and decaffeinated tea and coffee. This phase of the diet is preoccupied with helping your stomach to heal.

Phase 2

This phase of the diet begins after 1 week of taking surgery. It starts when the recipient of the surgery begins to get hungry. At this stage, they can now take a protein-rich diet. You can quickly achieve this by including a sugar-free protein powder in your diet.

You should take a healthy diet full of nutrients and avoid sugary foods and anything with little or no nutritional value. You should not take sugary and high-fat foods at this phase. You should take up to 20 grams of protein each day. You should also maintain your regular water intake each day.

Some foods you can take include thin soups, diluted juice, low-sugar applesauce diluted with water, and so on. You can start taking dense food as you reach the end of the second week of your surgery. Depending on how hunger manifests, you can take this when the third week begins. Some food suggestions for this period include mashed potatoes, scrambled eggs, smoothies, puréed whitefish, and so on.

In this latter part of phase 2, your goal should be to take between 60 g to 80 g of protein every day. Taking only half a cup of liquids with every meal would be best, and you can start with the proteins first. You will have to take many small meals in phase two of your diet.

Phase 3

In phase 3 of your diet, you should take soft foods. Your food should include 60 g to 80 g of protein and enough water. You can eat puréed foods but make sure that they are sugar-free. You should avoid other foods: bread, fatty foods, rice, white pasta, raw vegetables, skin and seeds of vegetables and fruits, and anything that is not soft.

Concentrating on high-protein foods and maintaining a nutrient-filled diet would be best. It can hasten recovery after surgery, and it can also provide a full feeling. Some foods on this list include eggs, soups, soft fish, low-fat deli meat, softened vegetables, and low-fat cheese.

You should also continue to take your protein each day. If you must take caffeine, limit it to no more than 2 cups of coffee per day.

Phase 4

Phase 4 usually begins after 4 weeks have elapsed from the surgery date. If you are not willing to undertake the surgery but would love to take the diet, you must begin at phase four. Phase 1 to 3 is aimed at causing the body to adjust to its new stomach size and carry the stomach through recovery.

Since you have not undertaken the surgical procedure, you would not need to go through those stages. You can skip them and start in phase four. Everyone taking phase four of the Gastric Sleeve diet is expected to continue taking protein shakes and giving the body up to 60 to 80 grams of protein per day. You must also stay hydrated.

However, you must not drink anything within 30 minutes of each meal. During this phase, your doctor can recommend a bariatric multivitamin that you must take daily. Avoid sugar, low-fiber, and processed foods and snacks.

It means that you should focus on taking foods that give you the nutritional value you need. You want to avoid the deficits caused by taking calorie-filled drinks. You also want to avoid taking fried foods, sodas, bread, and grains. You can safely eat lean meats, vegetables, low-fat cottage cheese, fish, and fruits at this stage. Remember that whatever you are taking will be in small quantities. You want to adjust to having a smaller stomach size; you want to refrain from shocking your stomach with too much.

444 Chia Raspberry Pudding

ABOUT THE AUTHOR

The book's author has always been a sportswoman with a healthy lifestyle. She was a competitive athlete for her school until she had to give it all up due to a cancer diagnosis.

Fortunately, she overcame it, but the psychological pain led her to a full-blown addiction to junk food.

Thanks to her professional chef boyfriend, now her current husband, she rediscovered her love of healthy cooking for herself and her family.

Unfortunately, a few years ago, her father started suffering from obesity-related cardiovascular issues, which led him to surgery, and it was the cause that led her to passionately study a dietary regimen suitable for people who have undergone bariatric surgery like her father.

After truly losing weight with bariatric surgery, her father could take back his life and do simple things previously precluded, such as long walks, carefree vacations, and playing with his grandchildren.

Her father's success was a strong motivation for her, who went on to study with great luminaries in the field, even going so far as to publish books to help as many people as possible.

All of us and Rachel are very proud to have founded IPH BOOKS Healthy Lifestyle (a brand of Ichnos Publications) through which we will publish books on daily health and wellness and new lifestyles that make you feel good, quickly and easily.

Follow her on facebook and other social to receive news and special offers dedicated exclusively to her followers

To stay in touch with the author, you can email

rachelamy.meyer.author@ichnospublications.com

or follow this page to learn about all upcoming publications.

https://www.amazon.com/Rachel-Amy-Meyer/e/B09NXBMHNY

If you have enjoyed this book, she would appreciate you sharing your experience with others by leaving an honest review on amazon. By all means, write directly to Rachel to find out what we can improve. Believe us, we will know how to be grateful.

We look forward to reading a message from you (or review). Thank you!

Ichnos Author's Team

176
Southwest
Deviled Eggs

175
Asian Cabbage
Salad

243
Crispy Zucchini
Wedges

225
Tempeh and
Avocado
Lettuce Wraps

361
Cheesy Turkey
Calzone

299
Delicious
Chickpea and
Mushroom Bowl

OVERVIEW OF GASTRIC SLEEVE BARIATRIC SURGERY

Gastric sleeve bariatric surgery is a weight loss surgery where the surgeon removes up to 75% of the stomach and leaves a narrow tube, or "sleeve," that can hold approximately 1 ounce of food. The procedure reduces the stomach size, so patients feel full more quickly and for a shorter time. It means they eat less and have fewer cravings for sweets and high-calorie foods.

Gastric sleeve surgeries are designed to be safer than some other weight-loss surgeries because there is no cutting involved in this type of surgery. The procedure also allows patients to 'reverse' the surgery later if their weight increases.

Gastric sleeve bariatric surgery is performed by a general surgeon specializing in the procedure and has performed hundreds of gastric sleeve surgeries. No open incisions, no hospital stays, and no intra-operative problems can occur in the stomach.

Many patients have tried varying diets and medications with little to no success, so they are willing to try something new if it provides better results. Gastric sleeve surgery is proven to provide patients with long-term results while preserving their health, allowing them to stay healthy while they lose weight.

The Gastric Sleeve Procedure is designed to remove 70% of the stomach, and the surgeon leaves a small tube (less than 1 ounce) that can hold approximately 1 ounce of food. It's like having only a small stomach with the ability to eat smaller amounts at once. Once your body adjusts to eating less food, your appetite will decrease. You will also typically feel full quickly after eating, and you will be able to make smaller meals more often. The gastric sleeve procedure lasts between 2 and 3 years, but you may be able to get a 'reverse' gastric sleeve surgery which removes part of the stomach. If your weight increases, you can make the sleeve smaller. It will allow you to lose the weight again and keep it off successfully..

Recommendations Before and After Bariatric Surgery

Weeks Before Bariatric Surgery

It is recommended before surgery (3–4 weeks before) and at least 2 weeks before it: HYPOCALORIC DIET (opt source plus 3 packages distributed throughout the day) and free intake of caloric liquids (vegetable broths or of defatted meat, infusions, skimmed dairy ...).

Supplementary medication: Supradyn or Multi-centrum effervescent: 1 tablet per day, and Omeprazole 20 mg: 1 tablet per day.

Postoperative Recommendations Bariatric Surgery

1. Make frequent meals, at least 5-6 shots a day in small quantities, and chew food well.
2. The time you dedicate to meals should last between 20-30 minutes.
3. Do not mix liquid and solid foods; do not drink liquids during meals, but drink small amounts about (30 minutes before) or after (one hour later) and do not exceed the volume of 150 ml of liquid per intake.
4. Drink water, sugar-free soft drinks, and infusions.
5. Avoid carbonated and sugary drinks (juices, soft drinks) and alcohol.
6. Avoid flatulent foods.
7. Stop eating before being very satiated, as soon as you feel full.
8. Do not take simple sugars (sugar, honey, jam, chocolate...).
9. Gradually introduce milk and dairy products, starting with yogurt and soft cheese. If the patient has an intolerance, they should not consume it.
10. If you feel full before eating, it is better to drink liquids than solids to avoid gastric discomfort.
11. If you don't tolerate food, accept it forever. Try to try it again in 3-4 weeks.
12. Medications must be taken crushed or in liquid format.
13. Avoid eating whole foods.

Diet After Bariatric Surgery

FIRST WEEK: Liquid Diet

In this first week after bariatric surgery, you can take:

Water and sugar-free liquids as infusions (in volumes of 50 ml). If the patient has an adequate tolerance for these foods, it can include skimmed milk or liquid yogurt, defatted vegetable or meat broths, juices without added sugars, and infusions. Always at least 6 daily intakes and in small sips.

It will include Optisource plus (3 packages per day distributed in small shots). The total daily liquid volume will be at least 2500 ml.

AT 15–30 DAYS: CRUSHED DIET

From 15–30 days, if the patient has good tolerance, it can take:

Scrambled eggs, passed by water or tortilla, cooked ham, turkey, fresh, low-fat cheeses, mashed vegetables, crushed carbohydrate, and protein, you can also take fruit porridge or piece of boiled or baked fruit, and yogurts skimmed.

Keep some Optisource supplements up to date.

Example menu of 5 types of mashed potatoes:

- Zucchini puree, cooked potato, and cooked chicken.
- Mashed carrots, onions, potatoes, and chicken.
- Pureed chard, chickpeas, and cooked egg.
- Pureed broccoli, carrot, rice, and fish.
- Zucchini puree, pasta soup, and lean veal.

FROM 4–8 WEEKS

You can eat a normal and healthy diet.

What are the benefits

We tell ourselves that health is all about what we put in our bodies. However, many of us are still caught up with the idea that weight loss is just a matter of what you eat. Even if you are trying to lose weight, it's not always easy, and there are often moments when, for various reasons, the health benefits of weight loss can seem elusive. In those cases, there is a birth alternative option called the Vertical Sleeve Gastrectomy, which may help you reach your goal and offer other health improvements beyond a simple fat percentage reduction.

Generally, this type of surgery is performed under sedation and lasts about 2 hours. Drastic weight loss can result directly from the surgery, but other benefits to consider.

Benefits of Gastric Sleeve Bariatric Surgery

Many people are considering gastric sleeve gastric bypass surgery due to the potential for weight loss, improved health markers, and better quality of life. Gastric Sleeve Bariatric Surgery is an operation in which a surgeon makes a small incision in the abdomen and pulls up part of the stomach. The operation induces weight loss by reducing the amount of food that can be ingested at once.

A patient can experience bodyweight changes ranging from 6–15% at 6 months to 20–30% over 2 years. Weight loss is usually sustained only after 3–5 years, with gradual weight regain. Patients with a history of diabetes or metabolic syndrome, as well as those with a body mass index over 50 or those who do not lose weight after other types of bariatric surgery, should consider Gastric Sleeve Bariatric Surgery as the only surgery available for morbidly obese individuals.

Gastric Sleeve Surgery has been shown to reduce the risk of death from all other causes by 40%. Gastric Sleeve also reduces the risk of death from other diseases such as stroke, diabetes, congestive heart failure, and cancer.

Gastric Sleeve Surgery is a safe operation with a mortality rate of 0.2%. There is also a low risk of complications such as surgical leaks and infection, requiring only minor surgery after the operation. Additionally, Gastric Sleeve reduces the risk of hernias by 50% or more.

Patients who undergo Gastric Sleeve Bariatric Surgery are more likely to comply better with their medications. Gastric Sleeve Surgery can also help improve glycemic control in people with diabetes by lowering the insulin required to maintain normal blood sugar levels after surgery by 25–45%. Glycemic control usually improves within the first day following surgery.

Because gastric bypass surgery provides a larger stomach, patients who have it tend to be able to eat as much as they need, as well as take more medications. Gastric bypass surgery also allows patients who normally have difficulty eating to eat as much as they want and do so without becoming sick with the "portion distortion syndrome," which occurs after these surgeries.

What to Know and What to Expect

It is natural to have concerns about the operation as the body reacts to unfamiliar and stressful surgeries. Many patients experience increased anxiety or even depression during the operation, further complicating their recovery. Here are some tips for you to consider before and after surgery to be able to get over anxieties:

- Upon entering your surgical suite, ask for someone you trust who has had this surgery before for mentoring or support.
- To avoid being too scared during your surgery, you need a clear understanding of what will occur.
- Make sure that one's lifestyle does not aggravate one's anxiety levels.
- Try to find an optimal balance between work and life, as demanding jobs tend to increase stress levels which could make your recovery period more difficult.
- Avoid caffeine intake as this can cause a lot of anxiety for some people.
- Consult with an ear, nose, and throat doctor if you have problems controlling anxieties or any other mental health issues that may be causing you distress during your surgery.
- Make sure to get at least 7–8 hours of sleep every night before the operation for your body to recuperate from daily stress and be ready for recovery.
- Participate in your pre-operative instructions by following the given diet recommendations and by taking vitamins needed after surgery.
- Make sure to take the leftover painkillers and antibiotics for 3 days.
- If you are a smoker, you might smoke "before" or "after" surgery, but try not to smoke excessively as it could make your recovery more difficult.
- Try to keep busy and do not think too much about the operation that is about to happen.
- Try not to eat too much sugar before or after going under anesthesia.
- Consult a doctor who is an expert in plastic surgery if you have doubts about the surgery procedure.
- Make sure that one's body does not get too cold under anesthesia, especially in patients who are obese.
- Try to keep a positive attitude and focus on the future rather than the past.
- Take some deep breaths and try to believe that you will soon be rid of this surgery.
- Talk about your fears with someone you trust before and after surgery, and try not to be too afraid of what others might think.
- Be sure to discuss the risks of possible complications with your plastic surgeon during or after the surgery.
- Keep a journal of one's anxiety levels while under anesthesia to help understand them and strategize how to handle them better.
- If you feel that your level of anxiety is too high, ask if you can be sedated to relax before the surgery.
- If you are a physician or a medical professional, learn how to control your stress levels so as not to give them to your patients.
- Ensure one's body temperature does not fall under 37-38°C during and after the surgery.

Different Phases

Bariatric surgery, typically, is a weight loss procedure that involves altering the digestive tract to make it smaller; it is a common option for those who are morbidly obese and suffering from obesity-related health conditions. Since it's a surgical procedure, some planning is required before the operation takes place. In this post, you'll learn what to expect from gastric sleeve bariatric surgery and understand all the steps and food typically needed for each phase of bariatric surgery!

Start by learning about what gastric sleeve bariatric surgery entails! Gastric Sleeve Bariatric Surgery can be performed laparoscopically or with an open abdominal procedure. This procedure affects the stomach by decreasing size to make you feel full sooner.

Phase 1: Preparation phase

The first stage of the procedure starts about a week after your surgery. In this phase, you will have a feeding tube inserted into your stomach through a tube attached to your stomach muscle. This feeding tube is usually surgically placed in a vein branching from the inside of your wrist or hand, depending on surgeons' preferences. The feeding tube allows for the intravenous infusion of fluids and nutrients and oral nutritional supplements to make up for any deficiencies from lack of food during this phase!

The gastric sleeve bariatric surgery is a weight loss surgery that removes most or all of the stomach so that the person's food intake is limited. Considering this procedure for yourself or someone you know, it is important to know what diet to follow during the preparation phase. Here are some suggestions.

1. Avoid large amounts of food in one sitting: Everyone should take smaller portions and eat more throughout the day rather than eating large amounts at one time, which can cause severe gastrointestinal problems. It also goes for fluids because diarrhea can occur if too much liquid comes into contact with your digestive tract at one time after an operation like gastric sleeve bariatric surgery.
2. Avoid stimulants, including caffeine, recreational drugs, alcohol, cigarettes, and food additives.
3. Avoid foods that are very high in fat.
4. Eat protein-rich foods such as meat, poultry, fish, cheese, soy products, and egg whites to help maintain blood sugar levels.
5. Stress should be avoided as much as possible during the preparation phase of gastric sleeve bariatric surgery to keep the body healthy by removing toxins from your system, which can lead to illness if not removed.
6. Avoid foods that will block wound healing, such as hard cheese, cooked or raw shellfish, and foods high in sugar, such as highly sweetened foods and sodas.
7. Avoid saturated fats like those found in meats and butter.
8. Avoid high-fat dairy products such as those high in butterfat, ice cream, and mayonnaise because they can cause abdominal fat to increase after gastric sleeve bariatric surgery by releasing a substance called butyrate which can induce inflammation of the intestines.
9. Avoid foods that can cause water retention, which is also called edema. These foods include green beans, beets, soybeans, and cauliflower because they contain saponins.
   Avoid heavy foods like fatty meats, bacon, and other types of meat; too much red meat or fatty fish like salmon or tuna that contain heme iron which could increase the chance of bruising after gastric sleeve bariatric surgery by putting too much pressure on the vessels surrounding your stomach which may cause an increased risk of bleeding during the healing time after the operation.
10. Avoid sugar at all costs during the preparation phase of gastric sleeve bariatric surgery, even if it is hidden in natural food products such as fruit juice. Look at the label and ensure it does not have added sugar.
11. Stay away from carbonated beverages because they can cause gas in the stomach.

Phase 2: Transition phase

In this stage, all the incisions and the tubes inserted into your body will heal. You will still have a feeding tube inserted through your wrist or hand, which you will need to use to consume adequate water and IV fluids. In addition, IV pain medications will help alleviate any discomfort from this stage of the surgery and the post-surgery healing process.

During this phase, you will also have protein drinks and supplements to help jumpstart metabolism. It is because, during gastric sleeve bariatric surgery, the first part of the stomach has been removed along with some intestinal tissue. The protein shakes, and supplements provide a source of protein for your body to digest first and then absorb into your system since the new stomach size limits absorption from food eaten.

The transition phase of gastric sleeve bariatric surgery is when your stomach's post-op size and function will be much different than before the procedure, and there are certain foods you should eat to make the time easier. Read on to learn more.

Many people struggle with what they can and cannot eat after gastric sleeve bariatric surgery. However, there are some things that everyone needs to know about before getting this weight loss procedure done; those things include what to eat during the transition phase.

The transition phase of gastric sleeve bariatric surgery is not easy for anyone. Your stomach has been sized down so much that little to no food can come through. Additionally, your body is still healing while adjusting to new eating habits and reducing the amount of food the sleeve can eat.

Tips for what to eat during the transition phase of gastric sleeve bariatric surgery:

- Start with softer foods, like soups and mashed potatoes. These items are okay on your first day back home after gastric sleeve bariatric surgery.
- Stick with clear liquids for the first 48 hours, introducing only puréed foods afterward. Avoid carbonated or caffeinated beverages.
- Soft foods are best for the stomach during the first few days after gastric sleeve bariatric surgery. Protein shakes are okay, however.
- Adding fat makes food easier to swallow and digest. Butter, oil, margarine, mayonnaise, and cream are good fat sources; however, do not overdo it during gastric sleeve bariatric surgery since fat slows down digestion even further.
- Make sure your portions are small; do not go back for seconds right away.
- Only drink fluids, no more than 8 oz. at each meal.
- Eat small meals 6 to 8 hours apart.
- Eating small meals will make you feel fuller more quickly and help prevent overeating due to nausea and pain. Consuming only 200–400 calories at each meal will also help you manage your food intake for the rest of your life.
- Always avoid high-fat foods high in saturated fats while on the post-surgical diet while recovering from gastric sleeve bariatric surgery.
- Avoid foods that contain high amounts of salt and sugar.
- Do not eat solid foods within 2 hours of taking your pain medication.
- Do not eat meals that are very high in fiber.
- Stop eating when you feel full; do not overeat, even if you really like a certain food or want to finish everything on your plate. It will help to prevent nausea and vomiting while recovering from gastric sleeve bariatric surgery.
- Stop eating an hour before bedtime.
- Do not eat for at least a few hours after a meal. It will help prevent overeating and food from going through the digestive system too quickly, leading to nausea.
- Drink plenty of fluids throughout the day. Avoid tea, coffee, and soda since they cause digestive issues and cause dehydration. Drink water only; fruit juices are okay, but add a bit of water if you add ice cubes to your drinks.
- To avoid feeling full, slowly eat while sitting up.

If there is one thing that everyone knows about gastric sleeve bariatric surgery, it is that you need to follow the post-surgical diet to avoid problems while recovering from this weight loss procedure.

Phase 3: Recovery phase

Once all the tubes and stitches have been removed, you can return to normal eating habits and consume food as normal. If you're like most bariatric surgery patients, your portions will be much smaller than you're accustomed to, as well as what is recommended by the ADA. Bariatric surgery patients typically eat 4-6 times per day, with each meal containing 2-3 ounces of lean protein, fresh or steamed vegetables, and whole grains.

Also, during this phase, your doctor may recommend a vitamin and mineral supplement containing vitamins and minerals commonly found in foods following bariatric surgery. These supplements can ensure that your body gets the nutrients it needs following the restrictive nature of bariatric surgery and may help you stave off any nutrient deficiencies.

How to Eat During Recovery

Every time a person undergoes bariatric surgery, they will have a specific period of recovery that lasts between 2-4 weeks after the procedure has been completed. The time will vary depending on the individual and how much weight they have lost, but once the stomach sleeve procedure is complete, many changes will occur in the body.

Taste Changes: Losing weight can be very hard for some people. One of the things that may occur is they may lose their sense of taste. I have had many patients tell me that they cannot taste certain foods or sweetness anymore and may not eat food until they realize it is a "must" they must eat for health reasons. It is common in bariatric surgery patients and needs to be checked by a doctor.

Digestion Changes: Another issue that may occur post-surgery is a change in the way the digestive system works. As you lose weight, your body will naturally want to store fat in places already difficult to access. It can strengthen stomach acids and make the digestive process much more active in absorbing nutrients from food consumed.

Fat Absorption: This is another issue that occurs post-bariatric surgery. During weight loss, fat must diffuse from the weight loss area of the stomach into other parts of the body, such as muscles, blood, the liver, and bone marrow. If this does not happen, people can get very sick from their bodies being unable to absorb fat nutrients.

What to Eat During Recovery

You must get the right amount of protein and calories when you have a gastric sleeve procedure to maintain good health. This process will change based on each individual, but some general guidelines exist.

Protein: You should consume a specific amount of protein daily following your bariatric surgery, usually between 50-80 grams daily. Protein heals tissue and helps build muscle mass, which will not only help reduce the weight loss from the surgery but also increase the chance that you will maintain your weight loss in the future.

Carbohydrates: The amount of carbohydrates you should consume each day following the surgery is very specific. The average person needs around 120-250 grams of carbohydrates daily to stay healthy and lose weight post-surgery.

1. Almond Tea

Preparation Time: 1 minute
Cooking Time: 5 minutes **Servings:** 2–3
Ingredients:

- 1 cup water
- 1 tsp. cinnamon
- 5 tbsp. almond powder

Directions:

1. Bring out a pan and place it on some high heat. Add the water with the rest of the ingredients.
2. Bring it to a boil and take it off the heat when boiling.
3. Serve warm and enjoy.

Nutrition: Calories: 40 kcal; **Carbs:** 1.4 g; **Fat:** 3 g; **Protein:** 1.5 g

2. Kiwi Sorbet

Preparation Time: 5 minutes
Cooking Time: 5 minutes; **Servings:** 2–3
Ingredients:

- .5 lb. kiwi fruit, chopped
- 4.5 cups ice cubes, crushed

Directions:

1. Add all of the ingredients above into a blender.
2. Blend them for half a minute, and then serve and enjoy.

Nutrition: Calories: 105 kcal; **Carbs:** 26 g; **Fat:** 0.3 g; **Protein:** 0.6 g

3. Chicken Bone Broth

Preparation Time: 5 minutes
Cooking Time: 2 hours; **Servings:** 2–3
Ingredients:

- 1 oz. chicken bones, cleaned
- 2 tbsp. apple cider vinegar
- 1 onion, sliced
- 5–6 garlic cloves
- 1 tbsp. cooking oil
- ½ tsp. salt
- ½ tsp. white pepper
- 1-inch ginger slice
- 6 cups water

Directions:

1. Add chicken bones with water, onion, garlic, ginger, oil, vinegar, salt, and pepper in a large skillet. Cover with lid.
2. Leave to cook on low heat for 2 hours.
3. Strain the broth and discard residue.
4. Serve hot and enjoy.

Nutrition: Calories: 147 kcal; **Total Fat:** 5 g; **Carbohydrate:** 9 g; **Protein:** 10 g

4. Pineapple and Mango Water

Preparation Time: 5 minutes + 1-hour chilling time
Cooking Time: 0 minute
Servings: 2–3
Ingredients:

- 1 cup pineapple slices
- 1 cup ripe mango, chunks
- 10 cups water
- ½ tsp. protein powder
- 1-inch ginger sliced, peeled

Directions:

1. Transfer all ingredients into a pitcher and place to chill for at least an hour.

2. Pour into serving glasses and serve.

Nutrition: Calories: 10 kcal; **Total Fat:** 0.0 g; **Carbohydrate:** 12 g; **Protein:** 0.0 g

5. Honeydew & Kiwi Infused Water

Preparation Time: 5 minutes + 1-hour chilling time
Cooking Time: 0 minute; **Servings:** 2–3
Ingredients:

- 1 kiwi, peeled and sliced
- 2 cups honeydew melon, chopped
- 10 cups water

Directions:

1. In a pitcher, combine the fruits.
2. Fill to the top with water.
3. Refrigerate for 1 hour before serving.

Nutrition: Calories: 12 kcal; **Total Fat:** 0.0 g; **Carbohydrate:** 4.4 g; **Protein:** 0.0 g

6. Sweet and Sour Lychee Infused Water

Preparation Time: 5 minutes + 1-hour chilling time
Cooking Time: 0 minute; **Servings:** 2–3
Ingredients:

- 1 cup lychees, peeled, seeded
- 1 tbsp. ginger powder
- 10 cups water
- 3 tbsp. lemon juice

Directions:

1. Combine all your ingredients in a pitcher.
2. Refrigerate for 1 hour before serving.

Nutrition: Calories: 2 kcal; **Total Fat:** 0.0 g; **Carbohydrate:** 31 g; **Protein:** 0.0 g

7. Kiwi and Kale Detox Water

Preparation Time: 5 minutes + 1-hour chilling time
Cooking Time: 0 minute
Servings: 2–3
Ingredients:

- 4 kiwis, sliced
- 5 kale leaves
- 10 cups cold water

Directions:

1. Combine all your ingredients in a pitcher.
2. Refrigerate for 1 hour before serving.

Nutrition: Calories: 1.7 kcal; **Total Fat:** 0.0 g; **Carbohydrate:** 8 g; **Protein:** 17 g

8. Watermelon and Lemon Water

Preparation Time: 10 minutes
Cooking Time: 0 minute; **Servings:** 2–3
Ingredients:

- 3 cups watermelon, chunks, seeded
- 3 tbsp. lemon juice
- 1 pinch salt
- 10 cups water

Directions:

1. Combine all your ingredients in a pitcher.
2. Refrigerate for 1 hour before serving.

Nutrition: Calories: 105.1 kcal; **Total Fat:** 1.4 g; **Carbohydrate:** 24.6 g; **Protein:** 2.1 g

9. Mango and Ginger Infused Water

Preparation Time: 5 minutes + 3 hours chilling time
Cooking Time: 0 minute; **Servings:** 2–3
Ingredients:

- 1 cup mango, diced
- 1-inch ginger, peeled and sliced
- 2 cups ice
- Water, to top off

Directions:

1. Peel and slice the ginger in 3–4-coin size slices.
2. Transfer the ginger into a pitcher along with mango.
3. Top with 2 cups of ice and fill with water.
4. Refrigerate for 3 hours.
5. Serve.

Nutrition: Calories: 1.3 kcal; **Total Fat:** 0.0 g; **Carbohydrate:** 0.4 g; **Protein:** 0.0 g

10.Lavender and Blueberry Infused Water

Preparation Time: 5 minutes + 1-hour chilling time
Cooking Time: 0 minute
Servings: 2–3
Ingredients:

- 8 cups water
- 1 pint fresh blueberries
- 1 tbsp. lavender flowers

Directions:

1. Mix all your ingredients in a large pitcher.
2. Stir gently and refrigerate for 1 hour.
3. Strain and serve with ice.

Nutrition: Calories: 1.3 kcal; **Total Fat:** 0.0 g; **Carbohydrate:** 0.4 g; **Protein:** 0.0 g

11. Piña Colada Infused Water

Preparation Time: 5 minutes + chilling time
Cooking Time: 0 minute; **Servings:** 2–3
Ingredients:

- 1 cup pineapple, peeled and thinly sliced
- 2 cups ice
- 6 cups coconut water

Directions:

1. Pour out your pineapple into a large pitcher.
2. Top with ice.
3. Pour in water to the top and cover.
4. Refrigerate for 1 hour before serving.

Nutrition: Calories: 1.3 kcal; **Total Fat:** 0.0 g; **Carbohydrate:** 0.4 g; **Protein:** 0.0 g

12. Watermelon Juice

Preparation Time: 5 minutes
Cooking Time: 0 minute; **Servings:** 2
Ingredients:

- 1 watermelon, peeled, deseeded, cubed
- 1 tbsp. date sugar
- ½ key lime, juiced, zest
- 2 cups soft-jelly coconut water

Directions:

1. Place watermelon pieces in a high-speed food processor or blender, add lime zest and juice, add date sugar and then pulse until smooth.
2. Take 2 tall glasses, fill them with watermelon mixture until ⅔ full, and then pour in coconut water.
3. Stir until mixed, and then serve.
4. Storage instructions:
5. Divide the drink between 2 jars or bottles, cover with a lid and then store the containers in the refrigerator for up to 3 days.

Nutrition: Calories: 55 kcal; **Fat:** 1.3 g; **Protein:** 0.9 g; **Carbohydrate:** 9.9 g; **Fiber:** 7 g

13. Ginger Tea

Preparation Time: 5 minutes
Cooking Time: 5 minutes;**Servings:** 2–3
Ingredients:

- 3 cups boiling water
- 3 tsp. ginger root, grated

Directions:

1. Combine all ingredients together before allowing them to sit and rest for 10 minutes or so. Serve and enjoy.

Nutrition: Calories: 1.3 kcal; **Total Fat:** 0.0 g; **Carbohydrate:** 0.4 g; **Protein:** 0.0 g

14. Beetle Juice

Preparation Time: 10 minutes
Cooking Time: 5 minutes; **Servings:** 2–3
Ingredients:

- 6 medium beetles; peeled, seeded, and pieced
- 1 cup of water

Directions:

1. In a juicer, add beetle pieces and extract the juice according to the manufacturer's directions.
2. Transfer into 2 glasses and serve immediately.

Nutrition: Calories: 259 kcal; **Fat:** 0.1 g; **Cholesterol:** 0 mg; **Carbohydrate:** 64.9 g; **Fiber:** 13.3 g; **Protein:** 5.3 g

15. Key Lime Tea

Preparation Time: 5 minutes
Cooking Time: 5 minutes; **Servings:** 2–3
Ingredients:

- 1 sprig dill weed
- $^1/_{16}$ tsp. cayenne pepper
- 1 tbsp. key lime juice
- 2 cups spring water

Directions:

1. Take a medium saucepan, place it over medium-high heat, pour in water, and then bring it to a boil.
2. Boil for 5 minutes, and then strain the tea into a bowl.
3. Add lime juice, stir until mixed, and then stir in cayenne pepper.
4. Divide tea between 2 mugs and then serve.

Nutrition: Calories: 2.4 kcal; **Fat:** 0 g; **Protein:** 0 g; **Carbohydrate:** 0.5 g; **Fiber:** 0 g

16. Strawberry Juice

Preparation Time: 10 minutes
Cooking Time: 5 minutes; **Servings:** 2
Ingredients:

- 2 cups fresh strawberries, hulled
- 1 tsp. fresh key lime juice
- 2 cups spring water, chilled

Directions:

1. In a high-powered blender, put all ingredients and pulse well.
2. Through a strainer, strain the juice and transfer it into 2 glasses.
3. Serve immediately.

Nutrition: Calories: 46 kcal; **Fat:** 0 g; **Cholesterol:** 0 mg; **Carbohydrate:** 11.1 g; **Fiber:** 2.9 g; **Protein:** 1 g

17. Grape Juice

Preparation Time: 10 minutes
Cooking Time: 5 minutes; **Servings:** 2
Ingredients:

- 2 cups red grapes, seedless

- ½ lime
- 2 cups spring water

Directions:

1. In a blender, put all ingredients and pulse well.
2. Through a strainer, strain the juice and transfer it into 2 glasses.
3. Serve immediately.

Nutrition: Calories: 63 kcal; **Fat:** 0.1 g; **Cholesterol:** 0 mg; **Carbohydrate:** 16.2 g; **Fiber:** 0.9 g; **Protein:** 0.6 g

18. Mango Juice

Preparation Time: 10 minutes
Cooking Time: 5 minutes; **Servings:** 4
Ingredients:

- 4 cups mangoes; peeled, pitted, and chopped
- 2 cups spring water

Directions:

1. In a blender, put all ingredients and pulse well.
2. Through a strainer, strain the juice and transfer it into 4 glasses.
3. Serve immediately.

Nutrition: Calories: 99 kcal; **Fat:** 0.2 g; **Cholesterol:** 0 mg; **Carbohydrate:** 24.7 g; **Fiber:** 2.6 g; **Protein:** 1.4 g

19. Apple and Kale Juice

Preparation Time: 10 minutes
Cooking Time: 5 minutes; **Servings:** 2
Ingredients:

- 2 large green apples, cored and sliced
- 4 cups fresh kale leaves
- ¼ cup fresh parsley leaves
- 1 tbsp. fresh ginger, peeled
- 1 key lime, peeled and seeded
- 1 cup spring water, chilled

Directions:

1. In a blender, put all ingredients and pulse well.
2. Through a strainer, strain the juice and transfer it into 2 glasses.
3. Serve immediately

Nutrition: Calories: 196 kcal; **Fat:** 0.1 g; **Cholesterol:** 0 mg; **Carbohydrate:** 47.9 g; **Fiber:** 8.2 g; **Protein:** 5.2 g

20. Watermelon and Strawberries Drink

Preparation Time: 5 min;
Cooking Time: 0 min; **Servings:** 2
Ingredients:

- 1 cup strawberries
- 1 cup watermelon, chunks
- 1 tsp. date
- 1 cup soft jelly coconut water

Directions:

1. Plug in a high-speed food processor or blender and add all the ingredients into its jar.
2. Cover the blender jar with its lid and then pulse for 40 to 60 seconds until smooth.
3. Divide the drink between 2 glasses and then serve.

Nutrition: Calories: 110 kcal; **Fat:** 0 g; **Protein:** 0 g; **Carbohydrate:** 28 g; **Fiber:** 6 g

21. Clear Vegetable Stock

Preparation Time: 10 min
Cooking Time: 15 min; **Servings:** 4–5
Ingredients:

- 1 tbsp. olive oil
- 1 onion
- 1 stalks celery
- 1 carrot
- 1 bunch green onions, chopped
- 2 garlic cloves, minced
- 2 sprigs parsley, fresh
- 2 sprigs thyme, fresh
- 2 bay leaves
- 1 tsp. salt
- 2 quarts water

Directions:

1. Chop scrubbed vegetables into 1-inch chunks.
2. Heat oil in a soup pot. Add onion, celery, carrots, green onions, bay leaves, thyme, parsley, and garlic. Cook over high heat for 5–10 min, stirring frequently.
3. Add salt and water and bring to a boil. Simmer for 30 min on low.
4. Strain, discard vegetables and enjoy.

Nutrition: Calories: 123 kcal; **Fat:** 2 g; **Carbs:** 14 g; **Protein:** 6 g; **Sodium:** 321 g

22. Strawberry Limeade

Preparation Time: 5 min
Cooking Time: 0 min; **Servings:** 2–3
Ingredients:

- ½ cup ice cubes
- ¼ tsp. strawberry extract
- 1 ½ cup cold water
- ½ lime juice

Directions:

1. Add all ingredients into a serving glass and stir well.
2. Serve and enjoy.

Nutrition: Calories: 9 kcal; **Fat:** 0 g; **Carbohydrate:** 2 g; **Sugar:** 0.5 g; **Protein:** 0.1 g; **Cholesterol:** 0 mg

23. Refreshing Watermelon Pops

Preparation Time: 15 min
Cooking Time: 4–5 hours to chill; **Servings:** 2–3
Ingredients:

- 1 tbsp. fresh lime juice
- 4 cups watermelon cubed, remove seeds

Directions:

1. Add lime juice and watermelon into the blender and blend until smooth.
2. Pour the blended mixture into the popsicle molds and place in the refrigerator for 4–5 hours.
3. Serve and enjoy.

Nutrition: Calories: 23 kcal; **Fat:** 0.1 g; **Carbohydrate:** 5.7 g; **Sugar:** 4.7 g; **Protein:** 0.5 g; **Cholesterol:** 0 mg

24. Raspberry Watermelon Pops

Preparation Time: 10 min
Cooking Time: 4 hours to chill; **Servings:** 2–3
Ingredients:

- 1 cup raspberries
- 2 cups watermelon, cubed and remove seeds

Directions:

1. Add raspberries and watermelon into the blender and blend until smooth.
2. Pour the blended mixture into the popsicle molds and place in the refrigerator for 4 hours.
3. Serve and enjoy.

Nutrition: Calories: 26 kcal; **Fat:** 0.2 g; **Carbohydrate:** 6.3 g; **Sugar:** 4 g; **Protein:** 0.6 g; **Cholesterol:** 0 mg

25. Raspberry Grapefruit Ice Pops

Preparation Time: 10 min
Cooking Time: 5 min; **Servings:** 2–3
Ingredients:

- 8 drops liquid stevia
- 1 ½ cup fresh grapefruit juice
- 4 cups raspberries, frozen

Directions:

1. Add all ingredients into the blender and blend until smooth.
2. Pour the blended mixture into the popsicle molds and place in the refrigerator for 4 hours.
3. Serve and enjoy.

Nutrition: Calories: 190 kcal; **Fat:** 0.3 g; **Carbohydrate:** 48.3 g; **Sugar:** 40.3 g; **Protein:** 1.5 g; **Cholesterol:** 0 mg

26. Delicious Cherry Lime Pops

Preparation Time: 10 min
Cooking Time: 4 hours to chill; **Servings:** 2–3
Ingredients:

- 1 lime juice
- ½ tsp. lime zest, grated
- 1 ¼ cup water
- 2 ½ cups cherries, pits removed

Directions:

1. Add all ingredients into the blender and blend until well combined.
2. Pour the blended mixture into the popsicle molds and place in the refrigerator for 4 hours.
3. Serve and enjoy.

Nutrition: Calories: 39 kcal; **Fat:** 0 g; **Carbohydrate:** 9 g; **Sugar:** 8 g; **Protein:** 0.9 g; **Cholesterol:** 0 mg

27. Watermelon Sorbet

Preparation Time: 10 min
Cooking Time: 3–4 hours to chill; **Servings:** 2–3
Ingredients:

- 6 cups watermelon, cubed and remove seeds
- ½ tbsp. honey
- ½ lemon juice

Directions:

1. Add watermelon into the blender and blend until smooth.
2. Add honey and lemon juice into the blender and blend to combine.
3. Pour the blended mixture into the container and place in the refrigerator for 3–4 hours or until set.
4. Serve and enjoy.

Nutrition: Calories: 9 kcal; **Fat:** 0 g; **Carbohydrate:** 2 g; **Sugar:** 0.5 g; **Protein:** 0.1 g; **Cholesterol:** 0 mg

28. Apple Basil Lime Infused Water

Preparation Time: 10 min
Cooking Time: 5 min; **Servings:** 2–3
Ingredients:

- ½ green apple, sliced
- ½ lime, sliced
- 6 fresh basil leaves
- 2 cups water

Directions:

1. Add basil, apple, and lime into a glass jar.
2. Pour water into the jar and stir well.
3. Close with lid and place in the fridge for 1 hour.
4. Serve and enjoy.

Nutrition: Calories: 34 kcal; **Fat:** 0.1 g; **Carbohydrate:** 9.5 g; **Sugar:** 6.1 g; **Protein:** 0.3 g; **Cholesterol:** 0 mg

29. Cinnamon Tea

Preparation Time: 1 minute
Cooking Time: 5 min; **Servings:** 2–3
Ingredients:

- 1 tsp. cinnamon
- 1 cup water
- ½ lemon

Directions:

1. Add the water to a pan and bring to a boil. Add the cinnamon and stir to help it dissolve.
2. Squeeze the lemon into the tea and stir well. Serve hot.

Nutrition: Calories: 9 kcal; **Carbs:** 2.5 g; **Fat:** 0.1 g; **Protein:** 0.2 g

30. Turmeric Tea

Preparation Time: 1 minute
Cooking Time: 5 min; **Servings:** 2–3
Ingredients:

- 1 tbsp. raw honey
- 2 cups water
- ¼ tsp. turmeric
- ¼ tsp. ginger powder

Directions:

1. Add the water into a pan and let it heat up to boil. When boiling, take off the heat.
2. Add the turmeric and ginger and let it rest for a bit.
3. After 5 min, strain the tea and pour it into cups. Stir in pepper and honey and serve hot.

Nutrition: Cal: 35 kcal; **Carbs:** 8 g; **Fat:** 0 g; **Prot:** 0.1 g

31. Basil Tea

Preparation Time: 5 min
Cooking Time: 5 min; **Servings:** 2–3
Ingredients:

- 1 tsp. honey
- 1 cup water
- 1 tbsp. basil, dried

Directions:

1. Add your basil to some boiling water and let it rest there for 10 min.
2. When that time is up, strain it out and add honey. Stir well and serve it nice and hot.

Nutrition: Cal: 20 kcal; **Carbs:** 4 g; **Fat:** 0 g; **Prot:** 0.1 g

32. Strawberry-Infused Water

Preparation Time: 10 min
Cooking Time: 0 min; **Servings:** 2–3
Ingredients:

- 5 thyme sprigs
- 1 cucumber, sliced
- 4 cups water
- ½ cup strawberries, sliced

Directions:

1. Add the strawberries, cucumber, and thyme to a jar and add in the water.
2. Let it sit for a bit, and then serve.

Nutrition: Calories: 21 kcal; **Carbs:** 5 g; **Fat:** 0.2 g; **Protein:** 1 g

33. Peanut Tea

Preparation Time: 1 minute
Cooking Time: 5 min , **Servings:** 2–3
Ingredients:

- 1 cup water
- 1 tsp. cinnamon
- 5 tbsp. peanuts, ground

Directions:

1. Use a saucepan to heat the water and get it nice and warm.
2. Stir in the rest of the ingredients, and then serve hot.

Nutrition: Calories: 40 kcal; **Carbs:** 1.4 g; **Protein:** 1.5 g; **Fat:** 3.5 g

34. Beef Bone Broth

Preparation Time: 5 min
Cooking Time: 2–3 hours; **Servings:** 2–3
Ingredients:

- Water
- 1 ginger slice
- ½ tsp. white pepper
- ½ tsp. salt
- 1 tbsp. cooking oil
- 6 garlic cloves
- 1 onion, sliced
- 2 tbsp. apple cider vinegar
- 1 oz. beef bones

Directions:

1. Take a skillet and add the pepper, salt, vinegar, oil, ginger, garlic, onion, and water.
2. Cover with the lid, and let it cook on a low setting for 2–3 hours.
3. After this time, strain the broth and remove the residues before serving it warm.

Nutrition: Calories: 37.8 kcal; **Carbs:** 8.2 g; **Fat:** 0.2 g; **Protein:** 1 g

35. Carrot and Red Apple Tea

Preparation Time: 5 min
Cooking Time: 5 min; **Servings:** 2–3
Ingredients:

- 2 cups water
- ½ cup lychee, seeded
- 2 carrots, sliced
- 1 cup red apples, chopped

Directions:

1. Blend the lychee, water, carrots, and apple.
2. Take out a pan and mix all the ingredients, allowing them to boil.
3. After this, take them off the heat and give them 5 min to rest and cool down.
4. Strain out the juice, and then serve.

Nutrition: Calories: 184 kcal; **Carbs:** 45 g; **Fat:** 0 g; **Protein:** 1 g

36. Banana Pops

Preparation Time: 5 min
Cooking Time: 15 min to freeze; **Servings:** 2–3
Ingredients:

- 1 cup plain yogurt
- 1 banana
- 1 flavored jelly package
- 1 cup boiling water

Directions:

1. Add all of the above ingredients and then place them inside a blender. Turn it on and mix to make it nice and creamy.
2. Add to a popsicle mold and then place in the freezer until it is hard and ready to go.

Nutrition: Calories: 93 kcal; **Carbs:** 22 g; **Fat:** 0.4 g; **Protein:** 2.2 g

37. Fennel and Ginger Herbal Tea

Preparation Time: 10 min
Cooking Time: 5 min**; Servings:** 2
Ingredients:

- 2 cups spring water
- 1 tbsp. fennel seeds, crushed slightly
- 1 (½-inch) piece fresh ginger, peeled and crushed slightly
- 2 tsp. agave nectar

Directions:

1. Add water over medium heat in a small saucepan and bring to a rolling boil.
2. Stir in the fennel seeds and ginger and remove from the heat.
3. Strain the tea into 2 serving cups and stir in the agave nectar.
4. Serve immediately.

Nutrition: Calories: 33 kcal; **Fat:** 0 g; **Cholesterol:** 0 mg; **Carbohydrate:** 7.5 g; **Fiber:** 1.6 g; **Protein:** 0.5 g

38. Ginger and Cinnamon Herbal Tea

Preparation Time: 10 min
Cooking Time: 10 min ; **Servings: 1**
Ingredients:

- 1 cup spring water
- 1 (1-inch) piece fresh ginger, cut into pieces
- 1 cinnamon stick
- 1 tsp. agave nectar

Directions:

1. In a saucepan, add water, ginger, and cinnamon over high heat and bring to a boil.
2. Now, adjust the heat to low and simmer for about 5 min.
3. Remove the tea saucepan from the heat and strain it into a serving cup.
4. Stir in the agave nectar and serve immediately.

Nutrition: Calories: 40 kcal; **Fat:** 0.1 g; **Cholesterol:** 0 mg; **Carbohydrate:** 9.6 g; **Fiber:** 1.3 g; **Protein:** 0.5 g

39. Ginger and Lime Herbal Tea

Preparation Time: 10 min
Cooking Time: 15 min; **Servings:** 2
Ingredients:

- 2 cups spring water
- 2 tbsp. fresh ginger root, cut into slices
- 1 tbsp. fresh key lime juice
- 1 tbsp. agave nectar

Directions:

1. In a saucepan, add water, ginger, and cinnamon over high heat and bring to a boil.
2. Now, adjust the heat to low and simmer for about 10 min.
3. Remove the tea saucepan from the heat and strain it into serving cups.
4. In the cups, stir in the lime juice and agave nectar and serve immediately.

Nutrition: Calories: 34 kcal; **Fat:** 0 g; **Cholesterol:** 0 mg; **Carbohydrate:** 8.6 g; **Fiber:** 0.6 g; **Protein:** 0.1 g

40. Linden Herbal Tea

Preparation Time: 5 min
Cooking Time: 6 min ; **Servings:** 1
Ingredients:

- 2 tsp. fresh linden flowers
- 1 cup spring water
- 1 tsp. agave nectar

Directions:

1. In a saucepan, add water over medium heat and bring to a boil.
2. Stir in the linden flowers and cook for about 1 minute.
3. Remove from the heat and set aside, covered for about 10 min.
4. Strain the tea into a serving cup and stir in the agave nectar.
5. Serve immediately.

Nutrition: Calories: 20 kcal; **Fat:** 0 g; **Cholesterol:** 0 mg; **Carbohydrate:** 5.3 g; **Fiber:** 0.3 g; **Protein:** 0 g

41.Raspberry Herbal Tea

Preparation Time: 5 min
Cooking Time: 5 min
Servings: 2
Ingredients:

- 1–2 tsp. red raspberry leaf tea
- 1 cup boiling spring water
- 1 tsp. agave nectar

Directions:

1. In the teapot, place the raspberry leaf tea and top it with boiling water.
2. Cover the pot and steep for 3–5 min.
3. Strain the tea into 2 serving cups and stir in the agave nectar.
4. Serve immediately.

Nutrition: Calories: 20 kcal; **Fat:** 0 g; **Cholesterol:** 0 mg; **Carbohydrate:** 5.3 g; **Fiber:** 0.3 g; **Protein:** 0 g

42. Anise and Cinnamon Herbal Tea

Preparation Time: 5 min
Cooking Time: 15 min; **Servings:** 2
Ingredients:

- 7-star anise
- 1 (2-inch) cinnamon stick
- 2–3 cups water

Directions:

1. Add water over medium heat in a saucepan and bring to a rolling boil.
2. Add star anise and cinnamon stick and boil for about 10 min.
3. Remove from heat and steep, covered for about 3 min.
4. Strain the tea into 2 serving cups and stir in the agave nectar.
5. Serve immediately.

Nutrition: Calories: 20 kcal; **Fat:** 0 g; **Cholesterol:** 0 mg; **Carbohydrate:** 4.4 g; **Fiber:** 2.3 g; **Protein:** 0.7 g

43. Piña Colada Smoothie

Preparation Time: 10 min
Cooking Time: 8 min to chill; **Servings:** 2–3
Ingredients:

- ½ cup pineapple chunks, canned and drained
- 4 oz. coconut milk, unsweetened
- ½ cup nonfat plain Greek yogurt
- ½ tsp. coconut extract

Directions:

1. Combine the pineapple, coconut milk, yogurt, and coconut extract with a blender.
2. Blend until smooth or until your desired consistency is reached. Pour into glasses and enjoy.
3. Alternatively, refrigerate for 10 to 15 min to chill before sipping.

Nutrition: Protein: 13 g; **Calories:** 148 kcal; **Fat:** 3 g; **Carbohydrate:** 19 g; **Fiber:** 1 g; **Total Sugar:** 17 g; **Added Sugar:** 0 g; **Sodium:** 46 mg

44. Green Mango Smoothie

Preparation Time: 10 min
Cooking Time: 2 min; **Servings:** 1
Ingredients:

- ⅓ avocado, peeled and pitted
- ⅓ cup fresh spinach
- ½ cup canned mango chunks, drained
- ½ cup nonfat plain Greek yogurt
- ½ cup nonfat milk
- 1 tsp. honey or sugar-free vanilla syrup

Directions:

1. Combine the avocado, spinach, mango, yogurt, milk, and honey in a blender.
2. Blend until smooth or until your desired consistency is reached. Pour into a glass and enjoy.

Nutrition: Protein: 21 g; **Calories:** 261 kcal; **Fat:** 8 g; **Carbohydrate:** 30 g; **Fiber:** 5 g; **Total Sugar:** 24 g; **Added Sugar:** 6 g; **Sodium:** 117 mg

45. Peachy Greek Yogurt Panna Cotta

Preparation Time: 10 min
Cooking Time: 5 min and 2–8 hours to chill
Servings: 4
Ingredients:

- ½ cup nonfat milk
- 1 ½ tbsp. honey
- 1 tbsp. unflavored powdered gelatin
- 1 ½ cup nonfat plain Greek yogurt
- ½ tsp. vanilla extract (optional)
- ½ cup peaches, no-sugar-added, sliced, canned, and drained

Directions:

1. In a small saucepan over low heat, heat the milk for 2 to 4 min until lukewarm. Add the honey and gelatin. Cook for 3 to 5 minutes, stirring, until the honey and gelatin dissolve. (Do not bring to a boil.) Remove from the heat.
2. In a small bowl, whisk the yogurt until smooth. Add the warm gelatin mixture and vanilla (if using). Whisk well to combine. Pour into 4 small jars, glasses, or ramekins. Refrigerate for at least 2 hours or overnight for best results.
3. Before serving, put the canned peaches into a blender or food processor and purée until smooth.
4. Top each panna cotta with 2 tablespoons of puréed peach and enjoy.

Nutrition: Protein: 12 g; **Calories:** 106 kcal; **Fat:** 1 g; **Carbohydrate:** 13 g; **Fiber:** <1 g; **Total Sugar:** 13 g; **Added Sugar:** 7 g; **Sodium:** 48 mg

46. Nutty Creamy Wheat Bowl

Preparation Time: 5 min
Cooking Time: 5 min
Servings: 2–3
Ingredients:

- 4 oz. nonfat milk
- 1 tbsp. wheat cream, uncooked
- Salt
- 1 tsp. almond butter
- cinnamon, ground, for seasoning
- ½ banana, mashed

Directions:

1. In a small saucepan or pot, stir together the milk and Cream of Wheat until combined. Place the pot over medium-high heat and bring the mixture to a boil, frequently whisking to keep lumps from forming.
2. Reduce the heat to low and simmer the cereal for 1 to 2 minutes until it thickens. Season with salt to taste, and pour the cereal into a bowl.
3. Add the almond butter and season with cinnamon. Top the cereal with mashed banana before enjoying.

Nutrition: Protein: 10 g; **Calories:** 167 kcal; **Fat:** 3 g; **Carbohydrate:** 26 g; **Fiber:** 2 g; **Total Sugar:** 11 g; **Added Sugar:** 0 g; **Sodium:** 127 mg

47. Baked Cinnamon-Apple Ricotta

Preparation Time: 10 min
Cooking Time: 8 min; **Servings:** 2–3
Ingredients:

- ½ cup part-skim ricotta
- ¼ cup no-sugar-added applesauce
- 1 tsp. cinnamon, ground
- Nutmeg, ground, for seasoning (optional)

Directions:

1. Preheat the oven to 375°F.
2. Spoon the ricotta into a 6-ounce ramekin. Top with the applesauce and sprinkle with the cinnamon and nutmeg (if using) to taste.
3. Bake for 15 minutes or until hot. Remove and let cool slightly before enjoying warm.

Nutrition: Protein: 14 g; **Calories:** 202 kcal; **Fat:** 10 g; **Carbohydrate:** 15 g; **Fiber:** 2 g; **Total Sugar:** 6 g; **Added Sugar:** 0 g; **Sodium:** 123 mg

48. Decadent Tomato-Basil Soup

Preparation Time: 10 min
Cooking Time: 10 min
Servings: 2–3
Ingredients:

- 2 tbsp. olive oil
- ¼ cup purple onion, diced
- 1 (15-oz.) can low-sodium whole tomatoes, or tomatoes diced, with their juices
- 8 oz. low-sodium chicken broth or vegetable broth
- 1 tsp. basil, dried
- 2 tsp. honey
- 1 tsp. aged balsamic vinegar (optional)
- Salt
- black pepper, freshly ground
- 8 tbsp. nonfat plain Greek yogurt

Directions:

1. In a medium saucepan over medium heat, heat the oil. Add the onion and sauté for about 5 min until golden.
2. Stir in the tomatoes with their juices, chicken broth, and basil, and bring the soup to a boil. Reduce the heat to low, cover the pan, and simmer the soup for 10 to 15 min. Remove from the heat.
3. Carefully pour the soup into a blender and blend at high speed until smooth. Add the honey and vinegar (if using). Season with salt and pepper to taste. Pour into glasses or bowls. Top each serving with 2 tablespoons of yogurt for extra protein and enjoy.

Nutrition: Protein: 4 g; **Calories:** 121 kcal; **Fat:** 7 g; **Carbohydrate:** 9 g; **Fiber:** 1 g; **Total Sugar:** 7 g; **Added Sugar:** 3 g; **Sodium:** 164 mg

49. Easy Green Pea and Ham Soup

Preparation Time: 10 min
Cooking Time: 10 min
Servings: 2–3
Ingredients:

- 1 tbsp. olive oil
- 1 (10-oz.) package frozen peas
- 4 oz. ham, cut into ¼-inch cubes
- 1 ½ cup low-sodium chicken broth or vegetable broth
- ⅓ cup nonfat plain Greek yogurt
- Black pepper, freshly ground
- Fresh parsley, chopped, for garnish

Directions:

1. In a medium saucepan over medium-high heat, heat the oil.
2. Add the peas, ham, and chicken broth and bring to a boil. Cook for about 10 min, or until the peas are very soft. Remove from the heat.

3. Carefully pour the soup into a blender and purée until smooth. Pour into bowls or cups. Top each serving with 1 tablespoon of yogurt and season with pepper to taste. Garnish with parsley and enjoy.

Nutrition: Protein: 11 g; **Calories:** 116 kcal; **Fat:** 4 g; **Carbohydrate:** 9 g; **Fiber:** 3 g; **Total Sugar:** 4 g; **Added Sugar:** 0 g; **Sodium:** 327 mg

50. Clam Chowder

Preparation Time: 10 min
Cooking Time: 5 min
Servings: 2–3
Ingredients:

- ½ onion, chopped
- 1 carrot, diced
- 1 stalk celery, diced
- 1 garlic clove, minced
- ½ tbsp. Creole seasoning
- Sea salt and black pepper, ground, to taste
- 1 cup seafood stock
- 1 ripe tomato, puréed
- 1 tbsp. tomato paste
- 1 bay leaf
- ½ lb. (227 g) clams, chopped
- 1 tbsp. flaxseed meal

Directions:

1. Heat a pan.
2. Now, sauté the onion, carrot, celery, and garlic
3. Add the remaining ingredients to the pan, except the chopped clams.
4. Add the lid and cook for 4 min at high heat. Once cooking is complete, carefully remove the lid.
5. Stir in the chopped clams and flaxseed meal.
6. Let it simmer for 2 to 3 minutes at medium heat or until everything is heated.
7. Serve in individual bowls topped with the reserved bacon. Bon appétit!

Nutrition: Calories: 264 kcal; **Fat:** 9.4 g; **Protein:** 20.8 g; **Carbs:** 26.2 g; **Net Carbs:** 20.2 g; **Fiber:** 6.0 g

51. Potato Mash

Preparation Time: 5 min
Cooking Time: 8 min
Servings: 2–3
Ingredients:

- 2 cups russet potatoes, peeled, diced (2½ medium potatoes)
- 1 cup Cheddar cheese, part-skim, shredded
- 1 cup nonfat plain Greek yogurt

Directions:

1. Fill the bottom of a medium saucepan with a couple of inches of water and insert a steamer basket. Place the potatoes in the steamer basket, bring the water to a boil, and cover; steam for about 15 minutes until softened. Remove from the heat.
2. Add the potatoes, Cheddar cheese, and yogurt to a blender or food processor. Blend the mixture on low for about 2 min or until smooth. Enjoy.

Nutrition: Calories: 144 kcal; **Fat:** 7.0 g; **Protein:** 11.0 g; **Carbs:** 10.0 g; **Net Carbs:** 9.0 g; **Fiber:** 1.0 g

52. Shrimp and Parsnip Bisque

Preparation Time: 10 min
Cooking Time: 5 min
Servings: 2–3
Ingredients:

- 1 tbsp. butter
- ⅓ cup white onion, chopped
- ½ celery rib, chopped
- 1 parsnip, chopped
- ½ carrot, chopped
- 1 tbsp. all-purpose flour
- ¼ cup sherry wine
- Sea salt and black pepper, ground
- ½ cup tomato purée
- 1 ½ cup chicken bone broth
- 8 oz. (227 g) shrimp, deveined
- ½ cup heavy whipping cream

Directions:

1. In a pan, melt the butter. Once hot, add the onion, celery, parsnip, and carrot until softened.
2. Add the flour and cook for 3 minutes until everything is well coated. Pour in sherry wine to deglaze the pot.
3. Now, add the salt, pepper, tomato purée, and broth.
4. Place the lid and cook for 5 min at high heat. Once cooking is complete, carefully remove the lid.
5. Now, add the shrimp and heavy cream and cook on medium heat for a further 2 to 3 min or until everything is heated through. Bon appétit!

Nutrition: Calories: 362 kcal; **Fat:** 18.9 g; **Protein:** 29.6 g; **Carbs:** 20.3 g; **Net Carbs:** 17.5 g; **Fiber:** 2.8 g

53. Salmon Curry

Preparation Time: 10 min
Cooking Time: 5 min
Servings: 2–3
Ingredients:

- 1 tbsp. butter
- 3 curry leaves
- ½ onion, chopped
- 1 garlic clove, crushed
- 1 (1-inch) piece fresh ginger, grated
- ½ dried Kashmiri chili, minced
- ½ cup tomatoes, canned and crushed
- ½ tsp. turmeric powder
- ½ tsp. coriander, ground
- ½ tsp. cumin, ground
- kosher salt and black pepper, ground, to taste
- 5 oz. (142 g) can coconut milk
- ¾ lb. (340 g) salmon fillets
- 1 tbsp. lemon juice

Directions:

1. In a pan, melt the butter. Once hot, cook the curry leaves for about 30 seconds.
2. Stir in the onions, garlic, ginger, and Kashmiri chili and cook for 2 minutes more or until they are fragrant.
3. Add the tomatoes, turmeric, coriander, cumin, salt, and black pepper. Continue to sauté for 30 seconds more.
4. Add the coconut milk and salmon.
5. Place the lid and cook for 2 minutes at low heat. Once cooking is complete, remove the lid.
6. Spoon the fish curry into individual bowls. Drizzle lemon juice over the fish curry and serve. Enjoy!

Nutrition: Calories: 363 kcal; **Fat:** 18.8 g; **Protein:** 35.1 g; **Carbs:** 10.5 g; **Net Carbs:** 8.2 g; **Fiber:** 2.3 g

54. Coconut and Cornmeal Porridge

Preparation Time: 15 min
Cooking Time: 6 min
Servings: 2–3
Ingredients:

- 6 cups water
- 1 ¼ cup coconut milk
- 1 ¼ cup yellow cornmeal, fine
- 2 ½ sticks cinnamon
- 1 ¼ tsp. vanilla extract
- ¾ tsp. coconut flakes
- ¾ cup sweetened condensed milk

Directions:

1. Add 5 cups of water and all the coconut milk to a pan.
2. Mix the cornmeal with 1 cup of water and add the mixture to the pot.
3. Stir in vanilla extract, coconut flakes, and cinnamon sticks.
4. Place the lid.
5. Cook for 6 min at high heat, stirring occasionally.
6. Remove the lid.
7. Stir in sweetened condensed milk.
8. Serve and enjoy.

Nutrition: Calories: 253 kcal; **Fat:** 3.1 g; **Protein:** 6.9 g; **Carbs:** 46.2 g; **Net Carbs:** 46.2 g; **Fiber:** 0 g

55. Coconut Pudding

Preparation Time: 5 min
Cooking Time: 5 min
Servings: 2–3
Ingredients:

- 1 cup coconut milk
- ¾ cup water
- ½ cup coconut cream
- 2 tbsp. maple syrup
- A pinch sea salt
- Whipped cream and coconut flakes for garnishing

Directions:

1. Add all the listed ingredients except whipped cream and coconut flakes to a pan.
2. Place the lid.
3. Cook for 15 min at medium heat, stirring occasionally.
4. Remove the lid.
5. Stir the prepared pudding and serve in a bowl.
6. Add the whipped cream and coconut flakes on top.

Nutrition: Calories: 476 kcal; **Fat:** 27.9 g; **Protein:** 18.6 g; **Carbs:** 36.5 g; **Net Carbs:** 35.1 g; **Fiber:** 1.4 g

56. Pimento Berry and Cornmeal Porridge

Preparation Time: 10 min
Cooking Time: 6 min
Servings: 2–3
Ingredients:

- 6 cups water
- 1 ¼ cup milk
- 1 ¼ cup yellow cornmeal, fine
- 2 ½ sticks cinnamon
- 5 pimento berries
- 1 ¼ tsp. vanilla extract
- ¾ tsp. nutmeg, ground
- ¾ cup sweetened condensed milk

Directions:

1. Add 5 cups of water and the milk to the Instant Pot.
2. Mix the cornmeal with 1 cup of water and add it to the pot.
3. Stir in vanilla extract, pimento berries, nutmeg, and cinnamon sticks.
4. Secure the lid of the cooker and press the Manual function key.
5. Adjust the time to 6 min and cook at high pressure.
6. After the beep, release the pressure naturally and remove the lid.
7. Stir in sweetened condensed milk.
8. Serve and enjoy.

Nutrition: Calories: 247 kcal; **Fat:** 5.4 g; **Protein:** 6.9 g; **Carbs:** 43.5 g; **Net Carbs:** 40.5 g; **Fiber:** 3.0 g

57. Brown Rice and Raisin Pudding

Preparation Time: 5 min
Cooking Time: 15 min
Servings: 2–3
Ingredients:

- 1 cup short-grain brown rice
- 1 ½ cup water
- 1 tbsp. vanilla extract
- 1 cinnamon stick
- 1 tbsp. butter
- 1 cup raisins
- 3 tbsp. honey
- ½ cup heavy cream

Directions:

1. Add the water, rice, cinnamon stick, vanilla, and butter into the Instant Pot.
2. Secure the lid of the cooker and press the Manual function key.
3. Adjust the time to 20 min and cook at high pressure.
4. After the beep, release the pressure naturally and remove the lid.
5. Stir in honey, raisins, and cream.
6. Cook on the Sauté function for 5 minutes.
7. Serve hot.

Nutrition: Calories: 438 kcal; **Fat:** 11.4 g; **Protein:** 5.0 g; **Carbs:** 83.5 g; **Net Carbs:** 80.6 g; **Fiber:** 2.9 g

58. Puréed Kale Curry

Preparation Time: 3 min
Cooking Time: 15 min
Servings: 2–3
Ingredients:

- 2 cups kale leaves, chopped
- 2 cups chicken broth
- 1 tsp. garlic paste
- 2-inch ginger sliced, shredded
- ¼ tsp. turmeric powder
- ¼ tsp. salt
- 1 green chili
- 1 tbsp. coconut oil
- ½ cup water

Directions:

1. Add kale with water and green chili in a blender, and blend till purée.
2. Now heat oil in a pan and add ginger with garlic, sauté for 1 minute.
3. Add kale and fry for 5 minutes, or its color is slightly changed.
4. Pour chicken broth and salt; leave to cook on low heat for 15–20 min.
5. Serve and enjoy.

Nutrition: Calories: 269.5 kcal; **Total Fat:** 6.3 g; **Total Carbohydrate:** 48.5 g; **Protein:** 7.9 g

59. Puréed General Tso's Chicken Thigh

Preparation Time: 15 min
Cooking Time: 15 min
Servings: 2–3
Ingredients:

- 10 oz. chicken thigh, boneless, skinless, cubed
- ½ tbsp. soy sauce
- ¼ tsp. salt
- ⅓ cup cornstarch
- 1 tbsp. oil
- 3 slices ginger, minced
- 1 garlic clove, diced
- 5 red chilies, seeds removed
- 2 stalks scallion, white parts

Sauce:

- 3 tbsp. Chinese rice vinegar
- 2 ½ tbsp. soy sauce
- ½ tbsp. dark soy sauce
- 1 tsp. hoisin sauce
- ¼ cup water
- 1 tbsp. cornstarch

Directions:

1. Cover meat in a container with salt and soy sauce; let it marinate for 15 min. Mix the ingredients for the sauce and put aside till needed.
2. Heat oil and put cornstarch on the chicken. Cook chicken until browned.
3. Remove from pot with a slotted spoon and place on paper towels to absorb excess oil.
4. Using another pan or wok, heat 1 ½ tablespoon of oil, then add ginger, chilies, and garlic.
5. Cook until chilies are fragrant. Put the sauce into a wok/pan and cook till it gets thick, then add chicken. Stir to combine and add scallions.

6. Add to a food processor and purée until smooth.
7. Serve hot.

Nutrition: Calories: 310 kcal; **Total Fat:** 5 g; **Total Carbohydrate:** 57 g; **Protein:** 7 g

60. Rustic Beef Ragu Purée

Preparation Time: 5 min
Cooking Time: 1 hour
Servings: 2–3
Ingredients:

- 4 lbs. beef
- Salt
- Pepper
- 2 tbsp. olive oil
- 2 large onions, finely minced
- ¼ cup tomato paste
- 4 garlic cloves, minced
- 1 cup lemon water, dry
- 2 (796 ml) cans of plum tomatoes, Italian, crushed
- 2-star anise pods
- 1 bay leaf
- Polenta, cooked
- Parmesan cheese, shredded

Directions:

1. Trim and discard the excess fat from the top of the roast. Remove the excess liquid from it by patting it dry, then proceed to season it with salt and pepper.
2. On a medium setting, heat the oil in a large pan. Now, for 3 to 4 min per side, char the beef, or char it until browned on every side before transferring it off to a platter.
3. Set your oven to preheat at 250°F and as it does, add in your seasoning of onions and tomato paste, occasionally stirring for 10 min or until the onion gets very soft. After this, garlic can be added while continuing cooking for a minute or 2.
4. Add lemon water while stirring. Immediately after, add the crushed tomatoes and tomato juice. Now, put the roast back into the pot and bring the mixture to a boil by setting the heat to high.
5. The bay leaf and star anise should be wrapped in a cheesecloth pouch, dipped into the sauce, and the pot covered. Move the pot now to your preheated oven for cooking for 3 hours. By this time, your meat should be tender, falling away from its bone, at which time you may discard the bay leaf and star anise.
6. Remove your meat for cooling for about 5 min.
7. Add the Beef into a food processor and blend until completely puréed. Return the puréed beef to the pot, and you may throw out any bone.
8. Serve and enjoy.

Nutrition: Calories: 310 kcal; **Total Fat:** 5 g; **Total Carbohydrate:** 57 g; **Protein:** 7 g

61.Cheesy Grits

Preparation Time: 10 min
Cooking Time: 10 min
Servings: 2–3
Ingredients:

- 1 cup grits, uncooked
- 3 eggs, lightly beaten
- 1 cup Cheddar cheese, shredded
- ¼ cup half-and-half

Directions:

1. Prepare the grits according to the package directions
2. Meanwhile, in a small bowl, combine the beaten eggs with the cheese.
3. When the grits are almost done, stir 3 tablespoons of the hot grits into the egg mixture.
4. Add the egg mixture to the cooking time grits; whisk the egg mixture into the grits until the grits are smooth.
5. Add half-and-half; continue whisking until the grits are of desired consistency.

Nutrition: Calories: 304.5 kcal; **Total Fat:** 9.6 g; **Carbohydrate:** 36.4 g; **Protein:** 16.9 g

62. High-Protein: Porridge

Preparation Time: 5 min
Cooking Time: 15 min; **Servings:** 2–3
Ingredients:

- ¾ cup water
- ¼ raw steel cut oats
- 1 tbsp. raisins, no sugar added
- 1 tbsp. walnuts, chopped
- 1 tbsp. creamy almond butter
- 1 tbsp. sugar-free strawberry jam

Directions:

1. Bring the water to a boil in a small saucepan over high heat.
2. Stir in the oats and raisins. Reduce the heat to low and simmer, uncovered, for 20 min, stirring regularly, until the oats have thickened and absorbed the water. Remove from the heat.
3. Stir in the walnuts. Let the mixture rest for 1 minute.
4. Top with the almond butter and strawberry jam. Enjoy warm.
5. **Post-Op Tip:** I suggest waiting until you are at least six months post-op before adding it to your weekly breakfast rotation. Eat slowly, chew well, and stop when you feel full.

Nutrition: (5½ oz.) **Protein:** 10 g; **Calories:** 338 kcal; **Fat:** 16 g; **Carbohydrate:** 43 g; **Fiber:** 7 g; **Total Sugar:** 7 g; **Added Sugar:** 0 g; **Sodium:** 6 g

63. Mushroom and Wild Rice Soup

Preparation Time: 10 min
Cooking Time: 2 hours; **Servings:** 2–3
Ingredients:

- ½ piece onion, white, chopped
- ½ cup white wine, or ½ cup chicken broth, fat-free, low sodium
- ¼ tsp. thyme, dried
- ¼ cup carrots, chopped
- 1 cup milk, half and half, fat-free
- 1 cup wild rice, cooked
- 1 tbsp. extra-virgin olive oil
- ¼ cup celery, chopped
- 1 ½ cup white mushrooms, fresh, sliced
- 2 ½ cups chicken broth, fat-free, low sodium
- 2 tbsp. flour
- ½ tsp. black pepper, freshly ground

Directions:

1. Heat a stockpot on medium, then add the olive oil.
2. Stir in the chopped onion as well as carrots and celery. Cook for 2 to 3 min or until tender and fragrant.
3. Pour in the chicken broth and white wine. Add the mushrooms as well, then stir to combine. Cover and allow the mixture to get heated through.
4. Meanwhile, place the flour in a large bowl. Add the milk, pepper, and thyme; stir to combine. Add the cooked rice and toss until well-combined.
5. Transfer the rice mixture into the vegetable pot. Stir well before cooking time on medium until bubbly and thickened.

Nutrition: Calories: 270 kcal; **Carbohydrate:** 18.5 g; **Protein:** 34.8 g; **Fat:** 7.1 g; **Saturated Fat:** 0.7 g; **Polyunsaturated Fat:** 6.4 g; **Cholesterol:** 75 mg; **Sodium:** 994 mg; **Fiber:** 1 g

64. Black Bean and Pumpkin Soup

Preparation Time: 5 min
Cooking Time: 15 min; **Servings:** 2–3
Ingredients:

- 1 piece onion, medium, chopped
- ½ tsp. black pepper, freshly ground
- 16 oz. pumpkin purée, canned
- 1 tbsp. cumin, ground
- 1 cup tomatoes, canned, diced
- 2 tbsp. olive oil, extra virgin
- 4 pieces garlic cloves, minced
- 1 tsp. chili powder
- 30 oz. black beans, canned, rinsed, drained
- 2 cups beef broth, low sodium

Directions:

1. Heat a soup kettle on medium after filling with the oil.
2. Add the garlic, onions, pepper, chili powder, and cumin. Stir and cook for about 2 to 3 min or until soft and fragrant.
3. Add the broth as well as pumpkin, tomatoes, and black beans. Stir to combine.
4. Allow the mixture to simmer for 20-5 min or until thickened to your desired consistency.
5. Remove from heat and process the black bean and pumpkin soup with an immersion blender.
6. **Servings:** and enjoy.

Nutrition: Calories: 266 kcal; **Carbohydrate:** 13 g; **Protein:** 4 g; **Fat:** 24 g; **Saturated Fat:** 21 g; **Sodium:** 879 mg; **Potassium:** 641 mg; **Fiber:** 3 g; **Sugar:** 4 g; **Vitamin A:** 17726 IU; **Vitamin C:** 23 mg; **Calcium:** 71 mg; **Iron:** 6 mg

65. Guava Smoothie

Preparation Time: 5–7 min
Cooking Time: 2 min; **Servings:** 2–3
Ingredients:

- 1 cup guava, seeds removed, chopped
- 1 cup baby spinach, finely chopped
- 1 banana, peeled and sliced
- 1 tsp. fresh ginger, grated
- ½ medium-sized mango, peeled and chopped
- 2 cups water

Directions:

1. Peel the guava and cut it in half. Scoop out the seeds and wash. Cut into small pieces and set aside.
2. Rinse the baby spinach thoroughly under cold running water. Drain well and tear into small pieces. Set aside.
3. Peel the banana and chop it into small chunks. Set aside.
4. Peel the mango and cut it into small pieces. Set aside.
5. Now, combine guava, baby spinach, banana, ginger, and mango in a juicer and process until well combined. Gradually add water and blend until all combined and creamy.
6. Transfer to a serving glass and refrigerate for 20 min before serving. Enjoy!

Nutrition: Net Carbs: 39.1 g; **Fiber:** 7.8 g; **Fat:** 1.4 g; **Sugar:** 2 g; **Calories:** 166 kcal

66. Watermelon, Cantaloupe, and Mango Smoothie

Preparation Time: 5 min
Cooking Time: 0 min; **Servings:** 2
Ingredients:

- ½ large mango, peeled
- ½ burro banana, peeled
- ½ cup cantaloupe, peeled
- ½ cup amaranth greens
- ½ cup watermelon chunks

Extra:

- 1 cup soft jelly coconut water

Directions:

1. Plug in a high-speed food processor or blender and add all the ingredients into its jar.
2. Cover the blender jar with its lid and then pulse for 40 to 60 seconds until smooth.
3. Divide the drink between 2 glasses and then serve.

Nutrition: Calories: 132 kcal; **Fat:** 1 g; **Protein:** 3.5 g; **Carbohydrate:** 30.1 g; **Fiber:** 3.2 g

67. BlackBerry and Banana Smoothie

Preparation Time: 5 min
Cooking Time: 0 min; **Servings:** 2
Ingredients:

- 1 burro banana, peeled
- ½ cup blackberries
- 2 pitted dates
- 1 cup mango chunks
- ¼ cup walnut milk, unsweetened

Extra:

- ¾ cup coconut water

Directions:

1. Plug in a high-speed food processor or blender and add all the ingredients into its jar.
2. Cover the blender jar with its lid and then pulse for 40 to 60 seconds until smooth.
3. Divide the drink between 2 glasses and then serve.

Nutrition: Calories: 147.7 kcal; **Fat:** 0.7 g; **Protein:** 5 g; **Carbohydrate:** 34 g; **Fiber:** 4.1 g

68. Green Smoothie with Raspberries

Preparation Time: 5 min
Cooking Time: 5 min; **Servings:** 2
Ingredients:

- 1 cup raspberries
- 1 cup kale leaves
- 1 tbsp. sea moss
- 2 tbsp. key lime juice
- 1 cup soft-jelly coconut milk

Directions:

1. Plug in a high-speed food processor or blender and add all the ingredients into its jar.
2. Cover the blender jar with its lid and then pulse for 40 to 60 seconds until smooth.
3. Divide the drink between 2 glasses and then serve.

Nutrition: Calories: 151 kcal; **Fat:** 1.2 g; **Protein:** 3 g; **Carbohydrate:** 37 g; **Fiber:** 8 g

69. Veggie-Ful Smoothie

Preparation Time: 5 min
Cooking Time: 0 min; **Servings:** 2
Ingredients:

- 1 pear, cored, deseeded
- ½ cup watercress
- ¼ avocado, peeled
- ½ cup Romaine lettuce
- ½ of cucumber, peeled, deseeded

Extra:

- 1 tbsp. date
- ½ cup spring water

Directions:

1. Plug in a high-speed food processor or blender and add all the ingredients into its jar.
2. Cover the blender jar with its lid and then pulse for 40 to 60 seconds until smooth.
3. Divide the drink between 2 glasses and then serve.

Nutrition: Calories: 145 kcal; **Fat:** 6 g; **Protein:** 1 g; **Carbohydrate:** 25 g; **Fiber:** 6 g;

70. Apple Pie Smoothie

Preparation Time: 5 min;
Cooking Time: 0 min; **Servings:** 2
Ingredients:

- ½ a large apple, deseeded
- ¼ cup walnuts
- 2 figs
- 1 tsp. Bromide Plus powder

Extra:

- 1 tbsp. date

Directions:

1. Plug in a high-speed food processor or blender and add all the ingredients into its jar.
2. Cover the blender jar with its lid and then pulse for 40 to 60 seconds until smooth.
3. Divide the drink between 2 glasses and then serve.

Nutrition: Calories: 170 kcal; **Fat:** 8 g; **Protein:** 2 g; **Carbohydrate:** 26 g; **Fiber:** 8 g

71. Banana Almond Smoothie

Preparation Time: 5 min
Cooking Time: 2 min; **Servings:** 2–3
Ingredients:

- 15 almonds
- 1 cup unsweetened almond milk

- 1 apple, peeled
- 1 banana, frozen

Directions:

1. Add all ingredients into the blender and blend until smooth and creamy.
2. Serve and enjoy.

Nutrition: Calories: 190 kcal; **Fat:** 5 g; **Carbohydrate:** 61 g; **Sugar:** 41 g; **Protein:** 14 g; **Cholesterol:** 18 mg

72. Protein: Spinach Shake

Preparation Time: 10 min
Cooking Time: 2 min; **Servings:** 2–3
Ingredients:

- ⅔ cup water
- ½ cup ice
- 5 drops liquid stevia
- ¼ cup vanilla protein powder
- ½ cup fat-free plain yogurt
- ½ tsp. vanilla extract
- 2 cups fresh spinach

Directions:

1. Add all ingredients into the blender and blend until smooth.
2. Serve and enjoy.

Nutrition: Calories: 54 kcal; **Fat:** 0.9 g; **Carbohydrate:** 5.5 g; **Sugar:** 4.6 g; **Protein:** 4.4 g; **Cholesterol:** 4 mg

73. Fresh Lemon Cream Shake

Preparation Time: 5 min
Cooking Time: 2 min; **Servings:** 2–3
Ingredients:

- ½ cup ice cubes
- 2 tsp. lemon zest, grated
- ½ cup fat-free plain yogurt
- 1 scoop vanilla protein powder
- 5 oz. water
- 5 drops liquid stevia

Directions:

1. Add all ingredients into the blender and blend until smooth and creamy.
2. Serve and enjoy.

Nutrition: Calories: 175 kcal; **Fat:** 0.1 g; **Carbohydrate:** 9.8 g; **Sugar:** 9 g; **Protein:** 33.1 g; **Cholesterol:** 4 mg

74. Avocado Banana Smoothie

Preparation Time: 10 min
Cooking Time: 2 min; **Servings:** 2–3
Ingredients:

- ½ tsp. vanilla
- 1 tbsp. honey
- 2 cups coconut milk, unsweetened
- 1 cup ice cubes
- 1 cup baby spinach
- ½ avocado
- 3 bananas

Directions:

1. Add all ingredients into the blender and blend until smooth and creamy.
2. Serve and enjoy.

Nutrition: Calories: 425 kcal; **Fat:** 33 g; **Carbohydrate:** 33 g; **Sugar:** 19 g; **Protein:** 4 g; **Cholesterol:** 0 mg

75. Banana Cherry Smoothie

Preparation Time: 5 min
Cooking Time: 2 min; **Servings:** 2–3
Ingredients:

- ½ tsp. vanilla
- 2 tbsp. unsweetened cocoa powder
- 2 ½ tbsp. chia
- 1 cup unsweetened almond milk
- 1 cup ice cubes
- 1 cup fresh spinach
- 1 banana
- 1 cup cherry

Directions:

1. Add all ingredients into the blender and blend until smooth and creamy.
2. Serve and enjoy.

Nutrition: Calories: 135 kcal; **Fat:** 5 g; **Carbohydrate:** 20 g; **Sugar:** 7 g; **Protein:** 4.6 g; **Cholesterol:** 0 mg

76. Squash Soup

Preparation Time: 5 min
Cooking Time: 15 min; **Servings:** 2–3
Ingredients:

- 3 cups butternut squash, chopped
- 4 cups vegetable stock
- 3 garlic cloves, chopped
- 1 tbsp. olive oil
- 1 ½ cup coconut milk
- ¾ tbsp. curry powder
- ½ tsp. onion flakes, dried
- 1 tsp. Kosher salt

Directions:

1. Add butternut squash, oil, onion flakes, curry powder, stock, garlic, and salt into a saucepan and boil over medium-high heat.
2. Turn heat to medium and simmer for 20 min.
3. Purée the soup using an immersion blender until smooth.

4. Return soup to the saucepan, stir in coconut milk, and cook for 2–3 minutes.
5. Serve and enjoy.

Nutrition: Calories: 144 kcal; **Fat:** 11 g; **Carbohydrate:** 10 g; **Sugar:** 2.5 g; **Protein:** 2 g; **Cholesterol:** 0 mg

77. Creamy Avocado Soup

Preparation Time: 20 min
Cooking Time: 2 min; **Servings:** 2–3
Ingredients:

- 2 avocados, peeled and pitted
- 2 cups vegetable stock
- 1 tbsp. fresh lemon juice
- ¾ cup heavy cream
- 2 tbsp. dry sherry
- Pepper
- Salt

Directions:

1. Add avocado, lemon juice, sherry, and stock to the blender and blend until smooth.
2. Pour the blended mixture into a bowl.
3. Add cream and stir well. Season with pepper and salt.
4. Serve and enjoy.

Nutrition: Calories: 102 kcal; **Fat:** 9.5 g; **Carbohydrate:** 1.9 g; **Sugar:** 0.3 g; **Protein:** 2.4 g; **Cholesterol:** 27 mg

78. Celery Soup

Preparation Time: 18 minutes
Cooking Time: 5 minutes; **Servings:** 2–3
Ingredients:

- 5 celery stalks, chopped
- 3 cups vegetable stock
- 3 tbsp. almonds, chopped
- Pepper
- Salt

Directions:

1. Add stock to a saucepan and bring to boil over high heat for 2 minutes.
2. Add celery and cook for 8 minutes.
3. Remove from heat and use an immersion blender to purée until smooth.
4. Add almonds and stir well.
5. Season with pepper and salt.
6. Serve and enjoy.

Nutrition: Calories: 80 kcal; **Fat:** 6 g; **Carbohydrate:** 5 g; **Sugar:** 2 g; **Protein:** 3 g; **Cholesterol:** 0 mg

79. Cauliflower Soup

Preparation Time: 35 minutes
Cooking Time: 10 minutes; **Servings:** 2–3
Ingredients:

- ½ head cauliflower, chopped
- 2 garlic cloves, minced
- 15 oz. vegetable stock
- ¼ tsp. garlic powder
- 1 onion, diced
- 1 tbsp. olive oil
- ¼ tsp. pepper
- ½ tsp. salt

Directions:

1. Heat oil in a saucepan over medium heat.
2. Add onion and garlic and sauté for 4–5 minutes.
3. Add cauliflower and stock and stir well. Bring to boil.
4. Cover and simmer for 15 minutes. Season with garlic powder, pepper, and salt.
5. Purée the soup using a blender until smooth.
6. Serve and enjoy.

Nutrition: Calories: 40 kcal; **Fat:** 2 g; **Carbohydrate:** 4 g; **Sugar:** 2 g; **Protein:** 3 g; **Cholesterol:** 0 mg

80. Avocado Milk Whip

Preparation Time: 10 minutes
Cooking Time: 0 minutes; **Servings:** 2
Ingredients:

- 1 avocado, peeled, pitted, diced
- 1 cup skimmed milk
- ½ cup non-fat cottage cheese
- ¼ cup fresh cilantro leaves, stems removed
- ½ tsp. lime juice
- ¼ tsp. garlic powder
- Chili powder, for garnish

Directions:

1. Put all ingredients in a blender and blend until smooth.
2. Divide the whip between 2 bowls and sprinkle with a dash of chili powder to serve.

Nutrition: Calories: 317 kcal; **Total Carbs:** 26.6 g; **Protein:** 11.5 g; **Total Fat:** 20.0 g; **Sugar:** 17.7 g; **Fiber:** 6.8 g; **Sodium:** 241 mg

81. Banana and Kale Smoothie

Preparation Time: 5 minutes
Cooking Time: 0 minutes; **Servings:** 2–3
Ingredients:

- 2 cups unsweetened almond milk
- 2 cups kale, stemmed, leaves chopped
- 2 bananas, peeled
- 1 to 2 packets stevia, or to taste
- 1 tsp. cinnamon, ground
- 1 cup ice, crushed

Directions:

1. Combine the almond milk, kale, bananas, stevia, cinnamon, and ice in a blender. Blend until smooth.
2. Serve immediately.

Nutrition: Calories: 181 kcal; **Total Carbs:** 37.0 g; **Protein:** 4.0 g; **Total Fat:** 4.0 g; **Sugar:** 15.0 g; **Fiber:** 6.0 g; **Sodium:** 210 mg

82. Beef Purée

Preparation Time: 30 minutes
Cooking Time: 2–5 hours; **Servings:** 2–3
Ingredients:

- 1 lb. (454 g) beef tenderloin steak
- 1 tsp. olive oil
- 1 tsp. soy sauce
- ½ tsp. salt, plus more to taste
- ½ tsp. garlic powder
- ½ tsp. onion powder
- ½ tsp. rosemary, dried and crushed
- ½ tsp. parsley, dried
- ¼ tsp. black pepper, freshly ground, plus more to taste
- Beef stock, as needed

Directions:

1. Pat the steak dry with paper towels and brush with olive oil and soy sauce. Mix salt, garlic powder, onion powder, rosemary, parsley, and pepper and rub over steak. Cook the steak in a slow cooker until cooked through and the internal temperature reaches 145°F (63°C), 8 to 10 hours at the low or 4 to 5 hours at the high setting.
2. Remove the steak from the slow cooker, reserving the cooking juices. Put the steak in a covered container and refrigerate it until chilled for about 2 hours.
3. Cut the chilled steak into 1-inch cubes. Put about 1 cup of steak cubes in a food processor and blend until fine and powdery. Add about ¼ cup reserved cooking juices plus stock as needed and process until smooth. Repeat with remaining steak cubes.
4. Season the puréed steak with salt and pepper and stir until thoroughly combined.
5. Serve immediately.

Nutrition: Calories: 168 kcal; **Total Carbs:** 1 g; **Protein:** 23.3 g; **Total Fat:** 7.9 g; **Sugar:** 0.3 g; **Fiber:** 0.2 g; **Sodium:** 410 mg

83. Blueberry and Spinach Smoothie

Preparation Time: 5 minutes
Cooking Time: 2 minutes; **Servings:** 2–3
Ingredients:

- 2 cups blueberries
- 3 cups fresh spinach, chopped
- ½ cup fresh coriander, chopped
- Juice of 1 lemon
- 1-inch fresh ginger, grated
- 2 cups water

Directions:

1. Put all the ingredients in the blender, and mix for 2 minutes or until smooth.
2. Serve immediately.

Nutrition: Calories: 121 kcal; **Total Carbs:** 30.0 g; **Protein:** 1.6 g; **Total Fat:** 0.6 g; **Sugar:** 26.6 g; **Fiber:** 2.6 g; **Sodium:** 25 mg

84. Broccoli Purée

Preparation Time: 30 minutes
Cooking Time: 5 minutes; **Servings:** 2–3
Ingredients:

- 1 lb. (454 g) fresh broccoli, cut into florets
- ½ cup water
- ½ tsp. salt, plus more to taste
- 1 tsp. butter
- 1 tsp. lemon juice
- ½ tsp. onion powder
- Black pepper, freshly ground to taste

Directions:

1. Mix the broccoli florets, water, and ½ teaspoon of salt in a medium saucepan and bring to a simmer. Reduce heat, cover the pan and simmer until the broccoli is tender, 5 to 10 minutes.
2. Drain the broccoli, reserving the cooking water. Add the butter, lemon juice, and onion powder, season with salt and pepper, and let cool.
3. Put about 1 cup broccoli florets and ¼ cup cooking water in a food processor and mix until smooth. Repeat with remaining broccoli.
4. Serve immediately.

Nutrition: Calories: 28 kcal; **Total Carbs:** 4.3 g; **Protein:** 2.4 g; **Total Fat:** 0.9 g; **Sugar:** 1 g; **Fiber:** 2.3 g; **Sodium:** 212 mg

85. Easy Chocolate and Orange Pudding

Preparation Time: 5 minutes
Cooking Time: 5 minutes; **Servings:** 2–3
Ingredients:

- 1 package sugar-free instant chocolate pudding mix
- ¼ cup chocolate protein powder
- 2 cups low-fat milk
- 1 tbsp. cocoa powder
- 1 tsp. orange extract

Directions:

1. In a small bowl, whisk the pudding and protein powders together with the milk for 2 minutes.

2. Add the cocoa powder and orange extract, and mix for 3 more minutes before serving.

Nutrition: Calories: 111 kcal; **Total Carbs:** 15.0 g; **Protein:** 10.0 g; **Total Fat:** 2.0 g; **Sugar:** 6.0 g; **Fiber:** 1.0 g; **Sodium:** 380 mg

86. Herbed Chicken Purée

Preparation Time: 30 minutes
Cooking Time: 15 minutes; **Servings:** 2–3
Ingredients:

- 2 (8-oz./227-g) chicken breasts, boneless, skinless
- 2 bay leaves
- ¾ tsp. salt, divided
- ¾ tsp. sage, ground
- ½ tsp. thyme, ground
- ¼ tsp. marjoram, ground
- ¼ tsp. rosemary, ground
- ¼ tsp. black pepper, freshly ground
- Dash nutmeg

Directions:

1. Put the chicken breasts, bay leaves, and ½ teaspoon. in a medium saucepan, add enough cold water to cover and bring to a boil. Reduce the heat, cover, and simmer gently until the chicken is cooked and the internal temperature reaches at least 165°F (74°C), 20 to 25 minutes.
2. Remove the chicken breasts from the broth. Strain and reserve the broth. Put chicken in a covered container and refrigerate until chilled for about 2 hours.
3. Cut the chilled chicken breasts into 1-inch cubes. Put about 1 cup of chicken cubes in a food processor and pulse until fine and powdery. Add about ¼ cup reserved broth and process until smooth. Repeat with remaining chicken cubes.
4. Mix the sage, thyme, marjoram, rosemary, pepper, and nutmeg with the remaining salt, sprinkle over the puréed chicken and stir until thoroughly combined.
5. Serve immediately.

Nutrition: Calories: 92 kcal; **Total Carbs:** 0.2 g; **Protein:** 17.1 g; **Total Fat:** 2 g; **Sugar:** 0 g; **Fiber:** 0.1 g; **Sodium:** 325 mg

87. Matcha Mango Smoothie

Preparation Time: 5 minutes
Cooking Time: 0 minutes; **Servings:** 2–3
Ingredients:

- 2 cups mango, cubed
- 2 tbsp. matcha powder
- 2 tsp. turmeric powder
- 2 cups almond milk
- 2 tbsp. honey
- 1 cup crushed ice

Directions:

1. Combine the mango, matcha, turmeric, almond milk, honey, and ice in a blender. Blend until smooth.
2. Serve immediately.

Nutrition: Calories: 285 kcal; **Total Carbs:** 68.0 g; **Protein:** 4.0 g; **Total Fat:** 3.0 g; **Sugar:** 63.0 g; **Fiber:** 6.0 g **Sodium:** 94 mg

88. Ricotta Peach Fluff

Preparation Time: 10 minutes
Cooking Time: 0 minutes; **Servings:** 2–3
Ingredients:

- ¼ cup ricotta cheese
- 1 ripe peach, diced
- 2 tbsp. skim milk

Directions:

1. Purée ricotta, diced peach, and milk in a blender until smooth.
2. Serve immediately

Nutrition: Calories: 355 kcal; **Total Carbs:** 54.0 g; **Protein:** 17.9 g; **Total Fat:** 8.7 g; **Sugar:** 50.0 g; **Fiber:** 2.0 g; **Sodium:** 183 mg

89. Simple Applesauce

Preparation Time: 10 minutes
Cooking Time: 8 minutes
Servings: 2–3
Ingredients:

- 2 medium apples, peeled, cored, and sliced
- ¼ cup water, plus more if needed
- Dash cinnamon
- Dash nutmeg

Directions:

1. Put all ingredients in a small saucepan and heat to simmer. Cook, frequently stirring, until apples are very soft, and put apart for about 15 minutes.
2. Purée applesauce with an immersion blender until very smooth, adding more water if necessary.
3. Serve immediately or refrigerate applesauce until chilled through, about 1 hour, before serving.

Nutrition: Cal: 63 kcal; **Total Carbs:** 16.8 g; **Prot:** 0.3 g; **Total Fat:** 0.2 g; **Sugar:** 12.6 g; **Fiber:** 2.9 g; **Sodium:** 0 mg

90. Split Pea and Carrot Soup

Preparation Time: 10 minutes
Cooking Time: 1 hour 10 minutes; **Servings:** 2–3
Ingredients:

- 1 tbsp. extra-virgin olive oil
- 2 large carrots, chopped
- 1 medium onion, diced

- 2 garlic cloves, minced
- 4 cups chicken broth
- 2 cups water
- Salt, to taste
- Black pepper, freshly ground to taste
- 2 bay leave, dried
- 1 (16-oz./454-g) bag green split peas

Directions:

1. In a large stockpot over medium heat, heat the oil.
2. Add the carrot, onion, and garlic. Sauté until soft, 5 to 7 minutes.
3. Add the broth, water, salt and pepper, bay leaves, and split peas. Stir well, and bring to a boil.
4. Reduce the heat to a simmer, cover, and cook for 1 hour, or until the peas are soft.
5. Remove the bay leaves, and serve immediately.

Nutrition: Calories: 92 kcal; **Total Carbs:** 20.0 g; **Protein:** 8.0 g; **Total Fat:** 1.0 g; **Sugar:** 2.0 g; **Fiber:** 8.0 g; **Sodium:** 264 mg

91. Herb and Melon Kefir Smoothie

Preparation Time: 10 minutes
Cooking Time: 15 minutes; **Servings:** 1
Ingredients:

- 4 oz. nonfat plain kefir
- ¼ cup nonfat plain Greek yogurt
- ¾ cup honeydew melon, chopped
- 4 fresh mint leaves
- 2 fresh basil leaves
- 1 tsp. honey
- ¼ tsp. vanilla extract

Directions:

1. Combine the kefir, yogurt, melon, mint, basil, honey, and vanilla in a blender.
2. Blend until smooth or until your desired consistency is reached. Pour into a glass and enjoy.

Nutrition: Protein: 11 g; **Calories:** 159 kcal; **Fat:** 2 g; **Carbohydrate:** 26 g; **Fiber:** 1 g; **Total Sugar:** 25 g; **Added Sugar:** 6 g; **Sodium:** 94 mg

92. Kefir and Yogurt Banana Flaxseed Shake

Preparation Time: 10 minutes
Cooking Time: 8 minutes to chill; **Servings:** 1
Ingredients:

- ⅓ cup nonfat plain kefir
- 6 oz. nonfat plain Greek yogurt
- ½ banana, fresh or frozen
- 1 tbsp. flaxseed, ground
- 1 tbsp. sunflower seed butter
- 1 tsp. sugar-free vanilla syrup or honey (optional)

Directions:

1. In a blender, combine the kefir, yogurt, banana, flaxseed, sunflower seed butter, and syrup (if using).
2. Blend until smooth. Pour into a glass and enjoy.
3. Alternatively, refrigerate for 10 to 15 minutes to chill before sipping.

Nutrition: Protein: 26 g; **Calories:** 329 kcal; **Fat:** 14 g; **Carbohydrate:** 28 g; **Fiber:** 5 g; **Total Sugar:** 17 g; **Added Sugar:** 0 g; **Sodium:** 157 mg

93. Peach Sunrise Smoothie

Preparation time: 6 minutes
Cooking Time: 0 minute
Serving: 2
Ingredients:

- 1 large unpeeled peach, pitted and sliced (about 1/2 cup)
- 6 ounces' vanilla or peach low-fat Greek yogurt
- 2 tablespoons low-fat milk
- 6 to 8 ice cubes

Direction:

1. Incorporate all ingredients in a blender and blend until thick and creamy. Serve immediately.

Nutrition: 98 calories; 16g fats; 3g protein

Review this Book

Thank you for reading this far!
We worked hard for almost a year to complete this 500-recipes cookbook, even comparing ourselves with different doctors. Rachel put in all the effort she could, thanks in part to her experience with daddy troubles. We are very pleased with this book, but now **what matters most is your feedback!**

If you enjoyed this book, please take a few moments **to leave a review on Amazon** about this work, or rating (it takes less than 5 seconds) hoose your amazon marketplace below).

We appreciate your time!

Scan this QR code to review on Amazon.com

Scan this QR code to review on Amazon.co.uk

Scan this QR code to review on Amazon.co.au

Scan this QR code to review on Amazon.ca

94. Best Chocolate Porridge

Preparation Time: 1 minute
Cooking Time: 3 minutes
Servings: 2–3
Ingredients:

- Small square dark unsweetened chocolate
- 1 tbsp. low-calorie sweetener
- 1 tbsp. chocolate protein powder
- 3 tbsp. porridge oats
- 1 cup skimmed milk

Directions:

1. Add chocolate, protein powder, milk, and oats to a jug. Mix well and transfer to microwave container, cook for 2 minutes. Stir and cook for 20–30 seconds more. Mix in your desired sweetener and spoon the mixture into a serving bowl.
2. Top with a couple of blackberries and a bit of chopped chocolate. Enjoy!

Nutrition: Calories: 324 kcal; **Fat:** 5 g; **Carbs:** 12 g; **Protein:** 8 g; **Sodium:** 177 g

95. Chocolate Chia Pudding

Preparation Time: 10 minutes
Cooking Time: 0 minutes
Servings: 4
Ingredients:

- 2 cups soy milk, unsweetened
- 10 drops liquid stevia
- ¼ cup cocoa powder, unsweetened
- ¼ tsp. cinnamon, ground
- ¼ tsp. vanilla extract
- ½ cup chia
- ½ cup fresh raspberries, for garnish

Directions:

1. Take a small-sized bowl and whisk in soy milk, stevia, cocoa powder, cinnamon, and vanilla and mix well until combined.
2. Stir in chia
3. Divide the mixture between 4 small dishes.
4. Cover and let it chill for 1 hour.
5. Once done, garnish with raspberries, and enjoy!

Nutrition: Calories: 312 kcal; **Fat:** 4 g; **Carbs:** 17 g; **Protein:** 8 g; **Sodium:** 221 g

96. Lemon-Blackberry Frozen Yogurt

Preparation Time: 10 minutes
Cooking Time: 0 minutes
Servings: 2–3
Ingredients:

- 4 cups blackberries, frozen
- ½ cup low-fat plain Greek yogurt
- 1 lemon, juiced
- 2 tsp. liquid stevia
- Fresh mint leaves, for garnish

Directions:

1. Take your food processor and add blackberries, yogurt, lemon juice, and stevia, blending well until smooth.
2. Serve immediately and enjoy with a garnish of fresh mint leaves.

Nutrition: Calories: 68 kcal; **Total Fat:** 0 g; **Saturated Fat:** 0 g; **Protein:** 3 g; **Carbs:** 15 g; **Fiber:** 5 g

97. Creamy Cauliflower Dish

Preparation Time: 10 minutes
Cooking Time: 5 minutes
Servings: 2–3
Ingredients:

- ½ tsp. pepper
- 4 tsp. extra virgin olive oil
- ½ tsp. garlic salt
- 1 tsp. butter, salted
- ⅓ cup low-fat buttermilk
- 3 garlic cloves
- Large head of cauliflower

Directions:

1. Break your cauliflower into small florets and transfer to a large microwave-proof bowl; add garlic and a quarter of water.
2. Microwave for 5 minutes until cauliflower is tender.
3. Use a garlic press and crush garlic cloves, add to the food processor and add to cauliflower.
4. Add pepper, garlic salt, butter, 2 teaspoons of olive oil, buttermilk.
5. Process well until creamy and smooth.
6. Drizzle remaining olive oil on top and enjoy!

Nutrition: Calories: 113 kcal; **Total Fat:** 6 g; **Saturated Fat:** 2 g; **Protein:** 5 g; **Carbs:** 13 g; **Fiber:** 3 g

98. Beetroot and Butterbean Hummus

Preparation Time: 5 minutes
Cooking Time: 0 minutes
Servings: 2–3
Ingredients:

- Salt and pepper, as needed
- 1 tbsp. extra-virgin olive oil
- 2 tbsp. fat-free Greek yogurt
- A bunch chives, chopped
- 1–2 garlic cloves, crushed
- 14 oz. butterbeans, drained and rinsed
- 8 oz. beetroot, cooked

Directions:

1. Dice beetroot and cut into small cubes.
2. Add butterbeans into a food processor and season with salt, pepper, yogurt, oil, chives, and garlic.
3. Blitz until the mixture is a nice purée.
4. Fold in diced beetroot and blitz gently.
5. Serve and enjoy!

Nutrition: Calories: 80 kcal; **Total Fat:** 2 g; **Saturated Fat:** 0 g; **Protein:** 4.2 g; **Carbs:** 10 g; **Fiber:** 0 g

99. Raisin and Oats Mug Cakes

Preparation Time: 10 minutes
Cooking Time: 1 minute; **Servings:** 2–3
Ingredients:

- 1 and ½ tbsp. flour
- 1 and ½ tbsp. almond milk
- ½ tbsp. raisins
- ¼ tsp. baking powder
- $^1/_{16}$ tsp. salt
- ½ tbsp. canola oil
- ⅛ tsp. baking soda
- ⅛ tsp. vanilla extract
- ⅛ tsp. hazelnut extract
- ¾ tbsp. oats
- 1 tsp. lemon juice
- ¼ tsp. baking powder

Directions:

1. Whisk in all ingredients in a microwave-proof mug and cook on high for 1 ute.
2. Let it cool, serve and enjoy!

Nutrition: Calories: 185 kcal; **Total Fat:** 1.7 g; **Saturated Fat:** 1 g; **Protein:** 8 g; **Carbs:** 39 g; **Fiber:** 10 g

100. No-Bake Peanut Butter Protein: Bites and Dark Chocolate

Preparation Time: 20 minutes + chill time
Cooking Time: 0 minutes; **Servings:** 2–3
Ingredients:

- 1 cup old-fashioned rolled oats
- 1 cup vanilla protein powder
- ¾ cup smooth, natural peanut butter
- 2 tbsp. flaxseed, ground
- 1 tbsp. flaxseed, ground
- 1 tbsp. chia
- 1 tsp. vanilla extract
- ¼ cup dark chocolate chips
- ¾ tsp. stevia baking blend
- 1 tbsp. water

Directions:

1. Mix in oats, protein powder, peanut butter, flaxseed, chia seeds, vanilla, chocolate chips, stevia, and water.
2. Let it chill for 30 minutes.
3. Roll the mixture into balls, eat and enjoy!

Nutrition: Calories: 181 kcal; **Total Fat:** 10 g; **Saturated Fat:** 0 g; **Protein:** 11 g; **Carbs:** 11 g; **Fiber:** 3 g

101. Egg White Scramble

Preparation Time: 5 minutes
Cooking Time: 5 minutes; **Servings:** 2–3
Ingredients:

- ¼ cup non-fat cottage cheese
- 2 egg whites, lightly beaten
- Non-stick cooking spray
- Pinch herbs, dried, such as oregano or basil
- Salt and black pepper, freshly ground, to taste

Directions:

1. In a medium bowl, mash cottage cheese with a fork to break up curds. Add egg whites and beat until smooth.
2. Spray a small nonstick skillet with cooking spray and heat over medium heat. Add egg mixture, sprinkle with herbs and stir gently until cooked through, 4 to 5 minutes.
3. Mash cooked egg mixture with a fork to desired consistency, season to taste with salt and pepper, and serve immediately. Enjoy!

Nutrition: Calories: 85 kcal; **Total Fat:** 1 g; **Saturated Fat:** 1 g; **Protein:** 15 g; **Carbs:** 2 g; **Fiber:** 0 g; **Sugar:** 0 g

102. Ham and Swiss Eggs

Preparation Time: 5 minutes
Cooking Time: 5 minutes

Servings: 2–3

Ingredients:

- 2 tsp. butter
- 4 eggs, lightly beaten
- 1 tbsp. skim milk
- Salt and black pepper, freshly ground, to taste
- ¼ cup Swiss cheese, shredded
- ¼ cup ham, finely minced, and cooked

Directions:

1. Whisk eggs and milk until thoroughly combined and season to taste with salt and pepper. Melt butter in a medium non-stick skillet over medium heat and add egg mixture. Cook and stir until eggs are completely set and cooked, 5 to 6 minutes.
2. Add cheese and ham to eggs and stir until combined and heated through. Season eggs to taste with salt and pepper and serve immediately. Enjoy!

Nutrition: Calories: 238 kcal; **Total Fat:** 16 g; **Saturated Fat:** 7 g; **Protein:** 20 g; **Carbs:** 2 g; **Fiber:** 0 g; **Sugar:** 0 g

103. Peanut Butter Cup Smoothies

Preparation Time: 10 minutes

Cooking Time: 0 minutes

Servings: 2

Ingredients:

- ½ cups skim milk
- ½ cup plain Greek yogurt
- 2 tbsp. creamy natural peanut butter
- 1 tbsp. unsweetened cocoa powder, sifted
- 8 to 10 ice cubes

Directions:

1. Place all ingredients in a blender container and pulse until thoroughly blended and smooth.
2. Pour into 2 large glasses to serve. Enjoy!

Nutrition: Calories: 175 kcal; **Total Fat:** 9 g; **Saturated Fat:** 2 g; **Prot:** 11 g; **Carbs:** 15 g; **Fiber:** 3 g; **Sugar:** 11 g

104. Berry Cheesecake Smoothies

Preparation Time: 10 minutes

Cooking Time: 0 minutes; **Servings:** 2

Ingredients:

- 8 to 10 ice cubes
- 1 cup mixed berries
- 2 tbsp. cream cheese
- 2 cups skim milk
- ¼ tsp. vanilla extract

Directions:

1. Place all ingredients in a blender container and pulse until thoroughly blended and smooth.
2. Pour into 2 large glasses to serve. Enjoy!

Nutrition: Calories: 182 kcal; **Total Fat:** 5 g; **Saturated Fat:** 3 g; **Protein:** 10 g; **Carbs:** 21 g; **Fiber:** 3 g; **Sugar:** 17 g

105. Tropical Porridge

Preparation Time: 5 minutes

Cooking Time: 5 minutes; **Servings:** 2–3

Ingredients:

- 1 cup coconut milk
- 2 tbsp. farina breakfast porridge mix (such as Cream of Wheat Malt-O-Meal)
- ½ cup ripe mango, diced
- 1 small banana, diced

Directions:

1. Heat coconut milk to a simmer in a small saucepan over medium heat. Whisk farina into milk and stir until smooth.
2. Reduce heat and simmer until porridge is thickened for about 2 minutes. Remove porridge from heat and stir in mango and banana to serve. Enjoy!

Nutrition: Calories: 172 kcal; **Total Fat:** 3 g; **Saturated Fat:** 3 g; **Protein:** 3 g; **Carbs:** 34 g; **Fiber:** 3 g; **Sugar:** 15 g

106. Delicious Mugastrone

Preparation Time: 1 minute

Cooking Time: 5 min; **Servings:** 2–3

Ingredients:

- Salt and pepper to taste
- ¼ oz. dry vermicelli
- 1 and ½ tbsp. mixed vegetables, frozen
- 1 tbsp. borlotti beans, cooked
- ⅔ cup tomato juice

Directions:

1. Add tomato sauce to a glass measuring cup, and add pepper, salt, noodles, veggies, and beans. Stir well.
2. Transfer to microwave and cook for 2–3 minutes.
3. Top with Parmesan, and enjoy!

Nutrition: Calories: 170 kcal; **Total Fat:** 4 g; **Saturated Fat:** 1 g; **Protein:** 5 g; **Carbs:** 16 g; **Fiber:** 4 g

107. Porridge with Berries

Preparation Time: 5 minutes

Cooking Time: 5 minutes

Servings: 2–3

Ingredients:

- 1 cup water
- 1 cup mixed berries, frozen
- 1 tbsp. lemon juice
- 1 tbsp. farina breakfast porridge mix (such as Cream of Wheat or Malt-O-Meal)

Directions:

1. Mix water, berries, and lemon juice in a small saucepan and heat to a boil over medium heat,

occasionally stirring, gently crushing berries to desired consistency.
2. Whisk farina into a saucepan and stir until smooth.
3. Reduce heat and simmer until porridge is thickened, about 2 minutes, stirring occasionally. Serve immediately and enjoy!

Nutrition: Calories: 95 kcal; **Total Fat:** 0 g; **Saturated Fat:** 0 g; **Protein:** 3 g; **Carbs:** 20 g; **Fiber:** 4 g; **Sugar:** 5 g

108. Strawberries with Whipped Yogurt

Preparation Time: 10 minutes
Cooking Time: 0 minutes
Servings: 2
Ingredients:

- 1 cup strawberries, sliced
- 1 cup (8 oz.) plain Greek yogurt
- 1 tbsp. heavy cream

Directions:

1. Pulse strawberries in a food processor or blender as necessary until mashed or puréed to desired consistency and set aside.
2. In a medium bowl with tall sides, beat yogurt and cream with an electric hand mixer until thickened and stiff peaks form, about 5 minutes.
3. Spoon strawberries into 2 bowls, top with whipped yogurt and serve immediately. Enjoy!

Nutrition: Calories: 210 kcal; **Total Fat:** 16 g; **Saturated Fat:** 10 g; **Prot:** 5 g; **Carbs:** 14 g; **Fiber:** 2 g; **Sugar:** 12 g

109. Gazpacho

Preparation Time: 15 minutes + 2 hours refrigerating
Cooking Time: 0 minutes
Servings: 2–3
Ingredients:

- 2 tbsp. vegetable oil
- 1 small red bell pepper, diced
- 1 small yellow onion, diced
- 2 garlic cloves, minced
- 2 large fresh ripe tomatoes, peeled, diced
- 1 small cucumber, peeled, diced
- 1 tbsp. lime juice
- 1 tbsp. balsamic vinegar
- 1 tbsp. fresh basil leaves, chopped
- 1 tsp. Kosher salt, plus more to taste
- ½ tsp. cumin, ground
- Black pepper, freshly ground, to taste

Directions:

1. In a medium saucepan, heat oil over medium heat and sauté bell pepper and onion until softened, about 5 minutes, stirring occasionally. Add garlic and sauté for about 1 minute more, stirring constantly.
2. Remove pan from heat and stir in tomatoes, cucumber, lime juice, vinegar, basil, salt, and cumin and season to taste with pepper.
3. If desired, pour the mixture into a blender container, pulse to desired consistency, or use an immersion blender.
4. Refrigerate soup until chilled through, about 2 hours. Serve and enjoy!

Nutrition: Calories: 124 kcal; **Total Fat:** 8 g; **Saturated Fat:** 5 g; **Protein:** 2 g; **Carbs:** 14 g; **Fiber:** 3 g; **Sugar:** 2 g

110. Chicken Cream Soup

Preparation Time: 30 minutes
Cooking Time: 25 minutes; **Servings:** 2–3
Ingredients:

- 2 chicken breasts, boneless, skinless (about 8 oz. each)
- 6 cups water
- 1 onion, quartered
- 2 bay leaves
- 1 tsp. garlic salt
- 2 cups mixed vegetables, chopped (such as onions, carrots, celery, green beans, or bell peppers)
- Salt and black pepper, freshly ground, to taste
- 3 tbsp. butter
- 2 tbsp. flour
- 2 cups skim milk

Directions:

1. Place chicken breasts, water, onion, bay leaves, and garlic salt in a large saucepan or stockpot and heat to a boil, skimming foam as necessary. Reduce heat, cover, and simmer until chicken is cooked for about 30 minutes.
2. Remove chicken breasts from the broth. Strain broth, discarding solids.
3. Add vegetables to the broth, season to taste with salt and pepper, and heat to a boil. Reduce heat, cover, and simmer until vegetables are tender about 20 minutes.
4. Meanwhile, cut or shred chicken into bite-size pieces and set aside. Melt butter in a small nonstick skillet. Sprinkle flour over butter and whisk until smooth. Add milk to skillet in a thin stream, whisking constantly. Heat milk mixture to a simmer, whisking occasionally. Simmer for 2 minutes, whisking constantly.
5. Add milk mixture to the broth and whisk to combine. Add chicken to soup and stir until heated through. Season soup to taste with salt and pepper and serve. Enjoy!

Nutrition: Calories: 167 kcal; **Total Fat:** 8 g; **Saturated Fat:** 4 g; **Protein:** 15 g; **Carbs:** 9 g; **Fiber:** 1 g; **Sugar:** 5 g

111. Mushroom Soup with Brie

Preparation Time: 15 minutes
Cooking Time: 15 minutes
Servings: 2–3
Ingredients:

- 2 tbsp. butter
- 2 packages (8 oz.) baby bella mushrooms, sliced
- 1 onion, julienned
- 2 garlic cloves, minced
- 1 tsp. thyme, dried
- ½ cup white wine
- 2 tbsp. flour
- 3 cups chicken stock
- 3 cups skim milk
- 2 oz. Brie, rind removed as necessary

Directions:

1. Melt butter in a large saucepan and sauté mushrooms and onion until softened and caramelized, 8 to 10 minutes, stirring frequently. Add garlic and thyme sauté for about 1 minute more, stirring constantly. Add wine and stir to deglaze the pan.
2. Sprinkle flour into the saucepan and stir to coat. Add broth and heat to a boil, stirring occasionally. Reduce heat and simmer the soup for about 10 minutes, stirring occasionally.
3. Add milk to soup and heat to a simmer. Stir Brie into the soup and stir until melted. Remove soup from heat and process with an immersion blender to desired consistency. Serve immediately and enjoy!

Nutrition: Calories: 229 kcal; **Total Fat:** 11 g; **Saturated Fat:** 6 g; **Prot:** 14 g; **Carbs:** 18 g; **Fiber:** 1 g; **Sugar:** 11 g

112. Carrot Pudding

Preparation Time: 10 minutes
Cooking Time: 8 minutes; **Servings:** 2–3
Ingredients:

- ⅔ cup carrot purée
- 1 tsp. vanilla paste
- 1 tsp. lemon zest
- 4 cups of coconut milk
- Cornstarch (a mixture of 2 tbsp. cornstarch and 4 tbsp. water)
- 1 whole egg

Directions:

1. Add carrot and milk to a saucepan and place it over low heat, cover and cook until tiny bubbles appear.
2. Whisk egg, cornstarch slurry, and lemon zest in a bowl and add into the pan in a steady stream.
3. Cover and cook for 15 minutes more.
4. Divide between dessert bowls and enjoy!

Nutrition: Calories: 159 kcal; **Total Fat:** 10 g; **Saturated Fat:** 2 g; **Protein:** 4 g; **Carbs:** 18 g; **Fiber:** 3 g

113. Fancy Scrambled Eggs

Preparation Time: 5 minutes
Cooking Time: 5 minutes
Servings: 2–3
Ingredients:

- 4 whole eggs
- ⅛ tsp. salt
- ⅛ tsp. pepper
- 2 tbsp. olive oil
- 2 tbsp. red bell pepper, chopped
- 1 garlic clove, chopped
- 1 and ½ tsp. chives, chopped

Directions:

1. Take a bowl and beat eggs, pepper, and salt.
2. Take a large skillet and place it over medium heat; add oil, red bell pepper, and garlic for 5 minutes.
3. Add egg mixture and chives to skillet.
4. Cook and stir over low heat until eggs are cooked.

Nutrition: Calories: 199 kcal; **Total Fat:** 15 g; **Saturated Fat:** 2 g; **Protein:** 13 g; **Carbs:** 2 g; **Fiber:** 0 g

114. Yogurt Crème Brulee Custard

Preparation Time: 10 minutes
Cooking Time: 0 minutes; **Servings:** 2–3
Ingredients:

- 2 cups thick Greek yogurt
- 1 cup strawberries purée

Directions:

1. Take a bowl and add strawberries purée and yogurt.
2. Divide the mixture between four ramekins.
3. Serve and enjoy!

Nutrition: Calories: 357 kcal; **Total Fat:** 27 g; **Saturated Fat:** 4 g; **Protein:** 6 g; **Carbs:** 22 g; **Fiber:** 4 g

115. BBQ'd Baked Beans

Preparation Time: 10 minutes
Cooking Time: 30 minutes; **Servings:** 2–3
Ingredients:

- 1 yellow onion, chopped
- 5 garlic cloves, minced
- ¼ lb. potatoes, peeled and diced
- 6 cups water
- 1 cup BBQ sauce
- 2 tbsp. spicy brown mustard
- 2 tbsp. adobo sauce
- Splash Guinness
- 2 tsp. salt
- 1 tsp. pepper

Directions:

1. Wash beans thoroughly and soak overnight.

2. Set your oven to pre-heat and add potatoes to the oven; let them brown.
3. When brown, in a pan, add onions and Sauté until tender.
4. Keep Sautéing and add garlic; cook for 1 minute.
5. Pour beans, water, and cover; cook on low for 60 minutes until beans are tender.
6. Add BBQ sauce, adobo sauce, mustard salt, pepper, and stir.
7. Remove cover and let it simmer until sauce thickens and beans are cooked thoroughly.

Nutrition: Calories: 70 kcal; **Total Fat:** 1 g; **Saturated Fat:** 0 g; **Protein:** 3 g; **Carbs:** 14 g; **Fiber:** 3 g

116. Pumpkin Pancakes

Preparation Time: 5 minutes
Cooking Time: 10 minutes; **Servings:** 2–3
Ingredients:

- 1 large egg, beaten
- ¼ cup vanilla yogurt
- ¾ cup milk
- ¾ cup pumpkin, canned
- 2 tbsp. butter, melted
- 1 cup whole flour
- ¼ tsp. salt
- 2 tbsp. stevia
- 2 tsp. baking powder
- ½ tsp. baking soda
- ½ tsp. cinnamon
- ¼ tsp. nutmeg
- ½ tsp. powdered ginger

Directions:

1. Mix well in a bowl; combine egg, milk, pumpkin, yogurt, and melted butter.
2. Add flour, salt, stevia, baking powder, baking soda, and spices; stir or whisk until dry ingredients are moistened, and a few lumps remain.
3. Pour or spoon the butter into the buttered skillet to make pancakes; when bubbles begin to form, and the underside is browned, turn over to brown the other side.
4. Remove cooked pancakes and repeat the process with the remaining batter.

Nutrition: Calories: 221.7 kcal; **Fat:** 3.6 g; **Carbs:** 37.2 g; **Protein:** 12 g

117. Vegan Porridge

Preparation Time: 5 minutes
Cooking Time: 8 minutes
Servings: 2–3
Ingredients:

- 2 tbsp. coconut flour
- 3 tbsp. flaxseed meal
- 2 tbsp. protein powder
- 1 ½ cup unsweetened almond milk
- Powdered erythritol

Directions:

1. Mix the golden flaxseed, coconut flour, and protein powder in a bowl.
2. Add to a saucepan, along with almond milk, and cook over medium heat. When the mixture starts to thicken, stir in the preferred sweetener portion. Serve with your favorite toppings.

Nutrition: Calories: 112 kcal; **Fat:** 5.7 g; **Carbs:** 11 g; **Protein:** 3.7 g

118. Chicken Sausage and Egg "Pizza"

Preparation Time: 10 minutes
Cooking Time: 25 minutes
Servings: 2–3
Ingredients:

- 1 lb. bulk chicken sausages
- 8 oz. crescent rolls, refrigerated
- 1 cup hash brown potatoes, frozen
- 1 cup Cheddar cheese, shredded
- 3 eggs
- ¼ cup milk
- ½ tsp. salt
- ¼ tsp. black pepper
- ¼ cup Parmesan cheese, grated

Directions:

1. Heat oven to 375°F.
2. Add chicken sausages to a medium skillet and allow it to cook on medium heat; stir until chicken sausages are browned and crumbly. Drain the fat.
3. Remove crescent rolls from the package and place evenly around a 9-inch pizza pan; pinch seams together to form the pizza crust.
4. Remove starch from potatoes by slicing them and soaking them in lukewarm water, then strain 4 times.
5. Spoon the chicken sausage over the top of the pizza dough; top with potatoes and Cheddar cheese.
6. In a bowl, whisk pepper, salt, milk, and eggs; gently pour over the top of the chicken sausage mixture. Sprinkle with Parmesan cheese if desired.
7. Set oven to 375°F and bake for 25 minutes.

Nutrition: Calories: 281.4, **Fat:** 16.2 g, **Carbs:** 18.3 g, **Protein:** 15.3 g

119. Cheesy Tomato Omelet

Preparation Time: 2 minutes
Cooking Time: 8 minutes
Servings: 2–3
Ingredients:

- ½ tsp. butter

- 1 large egg
- 1 tbsp. milk or water
- Salt
- Black pepper
- Garlic powder
- 1 slice Cheddar cheese
- 1 tbsp. tomato, chopped

Directions:

1. In a 6-inch nonstick skillet, melt butter over medium heat; turn the skillet to coat evenly.
2. In a small bowl, whisk egg and milk or water; pour into skillet. Sprinkle garlic powder, pepper, and salt over the top of the egg.
3. When edges of the egg mixture begin to cook, lift edges with a spatula and tip the skillet so uncooked egg flows underneath to cook.
4. Repeat step 3 until the top is almost dry. Place cheese slice on top, then the tomatoes over half of the omelet.
5. When cheese begins to melt, fold in half and serve.

Nutrition: Calories: 272.4 kcal; **Fat:** 19.1 g; **Carbs:** 6.4 g; **Protein:** 18.4 g

120. Colorful Scrambled Eggs

Preparation Time: 10 minutes
Cooking Time: 5 minutes; **Servings:** 2–3
Ingredients:

- 4 eggs
- ⅛ tsp. salt
- ⅛ tsp. pepper
- 2 tbsp. olive oil
- 2 tbsp. red bell pepper, chopped
- 1 garlic clove, chopped
- 1 ½ tsp. chives, chopped

Directions:

1. Mix eggs, pepper, and salt; set aside.
2. In a large skillet, heat oil; add red bell pepper and garlic. Over medium heat, cook for 5 minutes, stirring constantly.
3. Add egg mixture and chives to skillet; cook and stir over low heat until eggs are cooked.

Nutrition: Calories: 199 kcal; **Fat:** 15.21 g; **Carbs:** 1.96 g; **Protein:** 13.01 g

121. Corn Meal Mush with Polish Sausage

Preparation Time: 10 minutes
Cooking Time: 10 minutes
Servings: 2–3
Ingredients:

- 16 oz. cornmeal mush, refrigerated
- 16 oz. Polish sausage, skinless
- ½ tsp. butter
- Stevia

Directions:

1. Cut both mush and sausage into 1-inch slices; set aside.
2. In a skillet, melt butter. Add mush as you lay the slices side by side. Cook until softened and lightly browned on one side, about 10 minutes; turn over to brown the other side.
3. After turning mush over to brown both sides, add sausage to skillet; place around edges of the skillet and between mush slices to warm throughout (you may also use a separate skillet to heat sausage).
4. Serve with maple syrup drizzled on top.

Nutrition: Calories: 110.4 kcal; **Fat:** 1.1 g; **Carbs:** 23.4 g; **Protein:** 2.5 g

122. Chunky Mediterranean Tomato Soup

Preparation Time: 10 minutes
Cooking Time: 8 minutes
Servings: 2–3
Ingredients:

- 400 g vegetable mix, grilled and frozen
- 2 tbsp. garlic, chopped
- Basil leaves, fresh
- 400 g can tomato, chopped
- 1 reduced-salt vegetable stock cube
- 50 g Ricotta

Directions:

1. Heat the pan to medium, put in vegetable mix and garlic, then cook until vegetables start to soften.
2. Add the basil, tomatoes, stock cube, and 2 cans of water, then chop with a blender.

Nutrition: Calories: 212 kcal; **Fat:** 7 g; **Carbs:** 24 g; **Protein:** 11 g

123. Fried Deli Turkey Mushroom Sandwich

Preparation Time: 5 minutes
Cooking Time: 8 minutes
Servings: 2–3
Ingredients:

- 1 slice deli turkey
- 1 Portobello mushroom, grilled
- Ketchup
- Mustard

Directions:

1. Cut deli turkey from center of the slice to outside edge so that it will lay flat in skillet.

2. Place a skillet on medium heat; place deli turkey in the pan and cook until it begins to brown; turn over and cook the other side until lightly browned.
3. Place fried deli turkey into grilled mushroom; top with ketchup and mustard if desired.

Nutrition: Calories: 259 kcal; **Fat:** 5.2 g; **Carbs:** 11 g; **Protein:** 8.2 g

124. Denver Sandwich

Preparation Time: 3 minutes
Cooking Time: 7 minutes; **Servings:** 1
Ingredients:

- ½ tsp. butter
- 1 tbsp. onion, chopped
- 1 tbsp. green pepper, chopped
- 1 egg, beaten
- 5 oz. ham, shaved and chopped
- Salt
- Pepper
- 1 Portobello mushroom, grilled

Directions:

1. Melt butter in a skillet. Add green pepper and onion, and cook over low heat until softened, about 5 minutes.
2. Whisk the egg in a bowl; add ham.
3. Pour egg mixture into the pan over onion and green pepper; sprinkle salt and pepper to taste.
4. Cook over low heat until nearly set, then flip over, cooking for another 30 seconds to set.
5. Serve between 2 slices of mushrooms.

Nutrition: Calories: 293.8 kcal; **Fat:** 12.9 g; **Carbs:** 28.2 g; **Protein:** 15.9 g

125. Curried Chicken Salad Sandwich

Preparation Time: 15 minutes
Cooking Time: 0 minutes
Servings: 2–3
Ingredients:

- ⅓ cup mayonnaise
- ⅓ cup vanilla yogurt
- 1 tsp. lemon juice
- ½ tsp. sweet curry powder
- ¼ tsp. onion powder
- ¼ tsp. celery seeds
- 2 cup chicken breast, chopped
- ¼ cup green grapes, chopped
- 2 Portobello mushrooms

Directions:

1. Mix mayonnaise, lemon juice, celery seeds, yogurt, onion powder, and curry powder; stir until well blended.
2. Add chicken and grapes; mix gently.
3. Cover; refrigerate to chill.
4. Spoon chilled chicken salad into Portobello mushrooms to serve.

Nutrition: Calories: 332.5 kcal; **Fat:** 9.4 g; **Carbs:** 14.3 g; **Protein:** 20 g

126. Ham and Swiss Sandwich

Preparation Time: 30 minutes
Cooking Time: 0 minutes; **Servings:** 2–3
Ingredients:

- ⅓ cup mayonnaise
- 1 tsp. parsley flakes
- ½ tsp. prepared mustard
- ¼ tsp. onion powder
- 5 oz. ham, ground, smoked
- ½ cup Swiss cheese, shredded
- 2 Portobello mushrooms
- 2 tomato slices

Directions:

1. Mix mayonnaise, parsley, mustard, and onion powder; stir until well blended.
2. Add ham and cheese; mix just until combined. Refrigerate to chill.
3. Spoon ham and cheese mixture into Portobello mushrooms; top with tomato slices, if desired.

Nutrition: Calories: 390 kcal; **Fat:** 11 g; **Carbs:** 36 g; **Protein:** 24 g

127. Egg Salad Sandwich

Preparation Time: 1 hour
Cooking Time: 0 minutes; **Servings:** 2–3
Ingredients:

- ½ cup mayonnaise
- 2 tbsp. pickle relish
- 1 tsp. prepared mustard
- ¼ tsp. salt
- ¼ tsp. black pepper
- 4 hard-cooked eggs, chopped
- 1 sliced
- 2 Portobello mushrooms

Directions:

1. Mix mayonnaise, relish, mustard, salt, and pepper in a medium bowl.
2. Add chopped eggs; mix gently. Refrigerate to chill.
3. Spoon chilled egg salad into Portobello mushrooms; top with tomato slices if desired.

Nutrition: Calories: 259 kcal; **Fat:** 9.5 g; **Carbs:** 10 g; **Protein:** 12.8 g

128. Easy Baked Tomatoes

Preparation Time: 10 minutes

Cooking Time: 25 minutes; **Servings:** 2–3

Ingredients:

- ¼ cup pine nuts
- Greek seasoning as needed
- ¼ cup low-fat Parmesan
- Olive oil spray as needed
- 5–6 whole tomatoes

Directions:

1. Preheat your oven to 350°F.
2. Slice tomatoes in half lengthwise and transfer to a pan with the cut side up.
3. Spray tops of tomato with olive oil spray.
4. Season with pine nuts, cheese, and Greek seasoning.
5. Bake for 50 minutes and serve, enjoy!

Nutrition: Calories: 73 kcal; **Total Fat:** 5 g; **Saturated Fat:** 1 g; **Protein:** 3 g; **Carbs:** 6 g; **Fiber:** 1 g

129. Black Bean Chipotle Hummus

Preparation Time: 10 minutes
Cooking Time: 0 minutes
Servings: 2–3

Ingredients:

- 1 (15 oz.) can, black beans, drained and rinsed
- 1 lime, juiced
- 1 chipotle pepper in adobo sauce
- 1 tsp. adobo sauce
- 1 tsp. garlic, minced
- 2 tsp. cumin, ground
- 2 tbsp. extra-virgin olive oil
- ¼ cup fresh cilantro, chopped

Directions:

1. Take your food processor and add black beans, lime juice, chipotle pepper, adobo sauce, garlic, cumin, olive oil, and cilantro; blend on high for 2–3 minutes until smooth.

Nutrition: Calories: 143 kcal; **Fat:** 2 g; **Carbs:** 18 g; **Protein:** 5 g; **Sodium:** 125 g

130. Finely Crispy Wok Veggies

Preparation Time: 10 minutes
Cooking Time: 10 minutes; **Servings:** 2–3

Ingredients:

- 1 medium red bell pepper, cut into strips
- 1 medium green bell pepper, cut into strips
- 7-8 pieces baby corn
- ½ cup button mushrooms, canned
- 1 cup cauliflower, chopped into bite-sized pieces
- 1 medium carrot, peeled and cut into strips
- 1 tsp. oyster sauce
- 1 tbsp. olive oil
- 1 tsp. salt

Directions:

1. Wash bell peppers and cut them in half.
2. Remove seeds and cut them into strips.
3. Take a large wok pan and heat olive oil over medium heat; add carrots and cauliflower and cook for 8-10 minutes.
4. Add red and green pepper strips, baby corn, button mushrooms, and oyster sauce, and cook for 5–7 minutes.

Nutrition: Calories: 234 kcal; **Fat:** 1 g; **Carbs:** 21 g; **Protein:** 12 g; **Sodium:** 322 g

131. Tomato Omelet

Preparation Time: 5 minutes
Cooking Time: 5 minutes; **Servings:** 2–3

Ingredients:

- ½ tsp. butter
- 1 large whole egg
- 1 tbsp. milk
- Salt and pepper to taste
- Garlic powder
- 1 slice Cheddar cheese
- 1 tbsp. tomato, chopped

Directions:

1. Take a 6-inch non-stick skillet and melt butter over medium heat; coat well.
2. Take a small bowl, whisk in egg and milk, and pour into a skillet.
3. Season with garlic, pepper, and salt.
4. Once the edges of the egg mix begin to cook, lift with a spatula and tip the skillet so uncooked egg flows underneath.
5. Repeat step 3 until the top is almost dry. Place a cheese slice on top, then tomato over half the omelet.

Nutrition: Calories: 218 kcal; **Fat:** 2 g; **Carbs:** 12 g; **Protein:** 6 g; **Sodium:** 143 g

132. Stuffed Avocado

Preparation Time: 15 minutes
Cooking Time: 10 minutes
Servings: 2–3

Ingredients:

- 2 medium-sized ripe avocados, cut in half
- 6 large eggs
- 1 medium tomato, finely chopped
- 3 tbsp. olive oil
- 2 tbsp. fresh parsley, chopped
- 4 tbsp. Greek yogurt
- 1 tbsp. fresh rosemary, chopped
- ½ tsp. salt
- ¼ tsp. pepper, ground

Directions:

1. Preheat your oven to 350°F. Take a small baking dish and grease it with oil; keep it on the side.
2. Cut avocado in half and scrape out flesh from the center. Take a medium bowl and whisk in eggs, tomatoes, parsley, rosemary, salt, and pepper. Stir until thoroughly incorporated, and spoon mixture into avocado shells.
3. Spread stuffed avocado on a baking sheet and bake for 15–20 minutes.
4. Remove and top with yogurt; enjoy!

Nutrition: Calories: 158 kcal; **Fat:** 6 g; **Carbs:** 18 g; **Protein:** 16 g; **Sodium:** 213 g

133. Cheese-Filled Acorn Squash

Preparation Time: 10 minutes
Cooking Time: 50 minutes;
Servings: 2–3
Ingredients:

- 1 lb. tofu, firm
- 1 tsp. basil
- 1 pinch black pepper, freshly ground
- 1 tsp. onion, chopped finely
- 1 tsp. garlic powder
- 1 cup Cheddar cheese, reduced-fat, shredded
- 2 pieces acorn squash, halved, seeded
- 1 cup celery, diced
- 1 cup mushrooms, fresh, sliced
- 1 tsp. oregano
- ⅛ tsp. salt
- 8 oz. tomato sauce

Directions:

1. Set the oven at 350°F to preheat.
2. Arrange the acorn squash pieces at the bottom of a glass dish with their cut sides facing down.
3. Place in the microwave oven and cook for about 20 minutes or until softened. Set aside.
4. Heat a saucepan (nonstick) on medium, then add the tofu (sliced into cubes). Cook until browned before stirring in the onion and celery. Cook for 2 minutes or until the onion is translucent.
5. Add the mushrooms. Stir to combine and cook for an additional 2 to 3 minutes. Pour in the tomato sauce as well as the dry seasonings.
6. Give everything a good stir, then spoon equal portions of the mixture inside the acorn squash pieces.
7. Cover and place in the oven to cook for about 15 minutes. Uncover and top with the cheese before returning to the oven. Cook for 5 more minutes or until the cheese is melted and bubbling.

Nutrition: Calories: 328 kcal; **Carbohydrate:** 47.5 g; **Protein:** 16.9 g; **Fat:** 10.8 g; **Saturated Fat:** 5.8 g; **Polyunsaturated Fat:** 5 g; **Cholesterol:** 42 mg; **Sodium:** 557 mg; **Fiber:** 7.7 g; **Sugar:** 5.9 g

134. Cheesy Spinach Bake

Preparation Time: 5 minutes
Cooking Time: 35 minutes; **Servings:** 2–3
Ingredients:

- 2 eggs
- ½ cup Parmesan cheese
- 2 cups cottage cheese, fat-free/low-fat
- 10 oz. spinach, frozen, thawed, drained

Directions:

1. Set the oven to 350°F to preheat. Meanwhile, line a baking pan (8x8) with parchment paper.
2. Place all ingredients in a large bowl; stir to combine. Pour the cheesy spinach mixture into the baking pan. Place in the oven to bake for 20 to 30 minutes or until the cheese on top is bubbling.
3. Remove from the oven and allow to cool for 5 minutes.
4. Serve sprinkled with garlic, salt, and pepper. Enjoy.

Nutrition: Calories: 292 kcal; **Carbohydrate:** 4.5 g; **Protein:** 26 g; **Fat:** 19.1 g; **Saturated Fat:** 7.2 g; **Monounsaturated Fat:** 11.9 g; **Cholesterol:** 545 mg; **Sodium:** 73.5 mg; **Fiber:** 2 g

135. Greek Yogurt, Granola, and Berry Parfait

Prep Time: 10 minutes
Cooking Time: 15 minutes or Less
Servings: 2–3
Ingredients:

- ½ cup nonfat plain Greek yogurt
- 1 tbsp. rolled oats
- ¼ cup fresh blueberries
- ¼ cup fresh raspberries
- 1 tbsp. walnuts, chopped
- 1 tbsp. pecans, chopped
- 1 tsp. honey

Directions:

1. Place the yogurt in a 6-oz. glass.
2. Top with oats, blueberries, raspberries, walnuts, and pecans. Drizzle the honey on top. Enjoy immediately.

Storage Tip: You can prepare your own granola with rolled oats and your favorite nuts, as well as additional goodies such as coconut flakes, dried fruit, or fruit chips. Store it in an airtight container in a dry, dark place for up to 3 months. Use it in this parfait, a smoothie, or as a snack on its own.

Nutrition: (8 oz.): Protein: 16 g; **Calories:** 245 kcal; **Fat:** 11 g; **Carbohydrate:** 25 g; **Fiber:** 5 g; **Total Sugar:** 21 g; **Added Sugar:** 6 g; **Sodium:** 46 g

136. Florentine Eggs

Preparation Time: 10 minutes
Cooking Time: 10 minutes; **Servings:** 2–3
Ingredients:

- 2 large eggs
- 1 tbsp. extra-virgin olive oil, unfiltered
- 5 tbsp. egg fast alfredo sauce
- 1 tbsp. organic parmigiana Reggiano wedge, divided
- 3 g organic baby spinach
- 1 pinch red pepper flakes

Directions:

1. Set oven rack in the top groove nearest to the broiler. Set broiler to preheat.
2. Place olive oil in a non-stick skillet and heat over medium-high heat.
3. Gently fry eggs over medium flame until egg whites are opaque, but the yolk is still runny. It takes roughly 4 minutes. Do not turn over eggs.
4. Prepare casserole in the meantime. Dribble olive oil in each casserole container or spray with cooking time spray (olive oil).
5. In the bottom of the casserole, spread half of the Alfredo sauce. Slide the half-done egg gently atop the sauce.
6. Spread leftover Alfredo sauce and half of the Parmesan cheese over eggs.
7. Set casserole under the broiler and broil for 2–3 minutes or until the eggs have formed and the top has bubbly golden spots.
8. Remove from broiler and top with thinly sliced (julienne) baby spinach leaves, unused Parmesan cheese, and a dash of red pepper flakes. Serve instantly.

Nutrition: Calories: 529 kcal; **Total Fat:** 3 g; **Total Carbohydrate:** 3 g; **Protein:** 29 g;

137. Mexican Scrambled Eggs

Preparation Time: 10 minutes
Cooking Time: 5 minutes; **Servings:** 2–3
Ingredients:

- 6 eggs lightly beaten
- 1 tomato, diced
- 3 oz. cheese, shredded
- 1 tbsp. butter, for frying

Directions:

1. Set a large skillet with butter over medium heat and allow it to melt.
2. Add tomatoes and green onions, then cook, while stirring, until fragrant (about 3 minutes).
3. Add eggs, and continue to cook, while stirring, until almost set (about 2 minutes)
4. Add cheese, and season to taste. Continue cooking time until the cheese melts (about another minute).

Nutrition: Calories: 239 kcal; **Total Fat:** 3.7 g; **Total Carbohydrate:** 0 g

138. Spinach Omelet

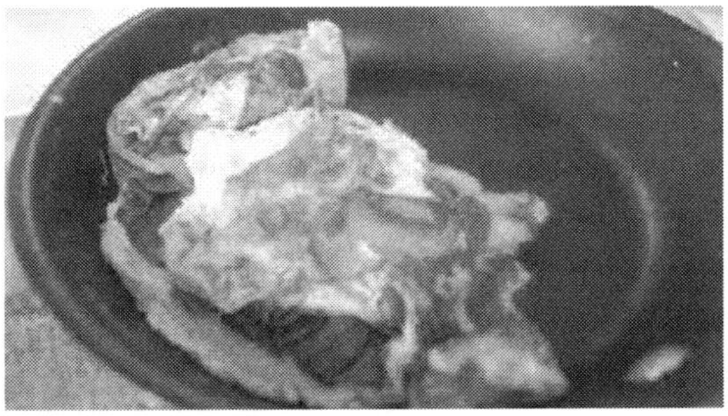

Preparation Time: 10 minutes
Cooking Time: 10 minutes; **Servings:** 2–3
Ingredients:

- 2 tbsp. olive oil
- 1 cup spinach, chopped
- 1 cup Swiss chard, chopped
- 3 eggs
- 1 tsp. garlic powder
- ½ tsp. sea salt
- ¼ tsp. red pepper flakes

Directions:

1. Grease the pressure cooker's bottom with 2 tablespoons of olive oil.
2. Press the beans/lentils button and add greens. Stir-fry for 5 minutes. Remove from the cooker and set aside.
3. Whisk together eggs, garlic powder, salt, and red pepper flakes. Pour the mixture into the stainless-steel insert.
4. Spread the eggs evenly with a wooden spatula and cook for about 2–3 minutes.
5. Using a spatula, ease around the edges and slide to a serving plate. Add greens and fold it over in half.

Nutrition: Calories: 227 kcal; **Total Fat:** 3 g; **Total Carbohydrate:** 2.3 g; **Protein:** 20 g

139. Open-Face Feta and Basil Omelet

Preparation Time: 10 minutes
Cooking Time: 5 minutes; **Servings:** 1
Ingredients:

- 1 large egg
- 2 tbsp. nonfat milk
- 1 tbsp. fresh basil leaves or ½ tsp. basil, dried
- 1 tbsp. scallion, chopped
- black pepper, freshly ground
- 1 tsp. olive oil
- ½ oz. feta cheese, crumbled
- 1 small tomato, cut into wedges

Directions:

1. In a small bowl, whisk the egg with a fork. Add the milk and beat lightly to combine.
2. Add the basil and scallion and season with pepper to taste. Mix well.
3. In a small pan over medium-low heat, heat the oil. Pour the egg mixture into the pan and sprinkle the feta and tomato on top. Cook for 3 to 4 minutes until the egg is set with no remaining liquid.
4. Do not stir. Transfer to a plate and enjoy it warm.

Storage Tip: Make extra omelets, cool them, and refrigerate them in an airtight container for up to 3 days.
Nutrition: (2½ oz.): Protein: 10 g; **Calories:** 174 kcal; **Fat:** 13 g; **Carbohydrate:** 6 g; **Fiber:** 1 g; **Total Sugar:** 5 g; **Added Sugar:** 0 g; **Sodium:** 234 mg

140. Lox, Egg White, and Avocado Scramble

Preparation Time: 10 minutes
Cooking Time: 5 minutes
Servings: 2–3
Ingredients:

- 1 tsp. olive oil
- 2 large egg whites
- Black pepper, freshly ground
- 2 oz. lox
- 1 ½ tsp. capers, drained and rinsed
- 1 ½ tsp. red onion, chopped
- ⅛ avocado, peeled, pitted, and cut into slices

Directions:

1. In a small skillet over low heat, heat the oil. Add the egg whites and cook for 2 to 3 minutes, stirring occasionally, or until no liquid remains. Season with pepper to taste. Spoon the cooked eggs onto a plate.
2. Top with the lox, capers, red onion, and avocado. Enjoy immediately.

Nutrition: (4 oz.): Protein: 17 g; **Calories:** 167 kcal; **Fat:** 10 g; **Carbohydrate:** 2 g; **Fiber:** 1 g; **Total Sugar:** 1 g; **Added Sugar:** 0 g; **Sodium:** 1334 mg

141. Ricotta and Spinach Frittata

Preparation Time: 10 minutes
Cooking Time: 15 minutes
Servings: 2–3
Ingredients:

- 1 ½ tsp. olive oil
- 1 tbsp. onion, diced
- 1 tbsp. mushroom, diced
- ¼ cup fresh spinach
- 1 large egg
- 2 tbsp. part-skim ricotta
- Salt
- Black pepper, freshly ground

Directions:

1. In a small skillet over medium-low heat, heat the oil. Add the onion and sauté for 5 to 7 minutes until golden brown.
2. Add the mushroom and spinach to the skillet. Cook for about 5 minutes until the mushroom is soft and the spinach wilts.
3. In a small bowl, whisk the egg with a fork until smooth.
4. Add the ricotta to the skillet and pour the egg over the top. Season with salt and pepper to taste.
5. Cook for 3 to 4 minutes, without stirring, or until the egg is firm. Serve warm and enjoy.

Storage Tip: Let the frittata cool completely; then refrigerate in an airtight container for up to 3 days.
Nutrition: (4½ oz.): Protein: 10 g; **Calories:** 177 kcal; **Fat:** 14 g; **Carbohydrate:** 3 g; **Fiber:** <1 g; **Total Sugar:** 1 g; **Added Sugar:** 0 g; **Sodium:** 92 mg

142. Hearty Whole-Grain Breakfast Burrito

Preparation Time: 10 minutes
Cooking Time: 10 minutes
Servings: 1
Ingredients:

- ½ tsp. olive oil or olive oil spray
- 1 large egg
- ¼ cup Fat-free beans, refried
- 1 tbsp. low-fat Cheddar cheese, shredded
- 1 medium (8-inch) whole-grain tortilla
- ⅛ avocado, peeled, pitted, and diced
- ¼ cup fresh spinach
- Salsa, for serving (optional)

Directions:

1. In a small skillet over medium-low heat, heat the oil.
2. Crack the egg into the skillet and cook, scrambling it with a spatula, for 1 to 2 minutes, or until the egg is almost cooked.
3. Add the beans and cook for 2 to 3 minutes to warm.
4. Add the Cheddar cheese, mix well, and cook for 1 to 2 minutes until the cheese melts.
5. Warm the tortilla on a plate in the microwave on high power for about 1 minute.
6. Spoon the eggs, beans, and cheese onto the warm tortilla. Top with avocado, spinach, and salsa (if using). Fold into a burrito and enjoy.

Storage Tip: Double or triple the burrito filling and, once cool, refrigerate in an airtight container for up to 3 days. When ready to eat, warm a tortilla as you reheat the filling; then spoon the filling into the tortilla and top with spinach, avocado, and salsa.
Nutrition: (5½ oz.): Protein: 14 g; **Calories:** 256 kcal; **Fat:** 12 g; **Carbohydrate:** 23 g; **Fiber:** 14 g; Total **Sugar:** 1 g; **Added Sugar:** 0 g; **Sodium:** 525 mg

143. Turkey, Cheese, and Hash Brown Mini-Bake

Preparation Time: 10 minutes
Cooking Time: 20 minutes; **Servings:** 2–3
Ingredients:

- Olive oil spray
- 4 oz. lean ground turkey
- Salt
- black pepper, freshly ground
- Onion powder, for seasoning
- Garlic powder, for seasoning
- 1 tbsp. green chiles, canned, diced
- ½ cup hash browns, frozen
- 2 tbsp. low-fat Cheddar cheese, shredded

Directions:

1. Preheat the oven to 425°F.
2. Coat 2 (6-oz.) ramekins with olive oil spray.
3. Evenly divide the ground turkey between the prepared ramekins. Season with salt, pepper, onion powder, and garlic powder to taste. Top each with 1 ½ teaspoon of green chiles and ¼ cup of hash browns.
4. Bake for 10 to 15 minutes or until the turkey is fully cooked with no pink remaining.
5. Top each with 1 tablespoon of Cheddar cheese and bake for 3 to 5 minutes more until the cheese melts. Enjoy warm.

Cooking Tip: Double or triple this recipe and cook it in a casserole dish or muffin tin for extra portions you can reheat and eat throughout the week.
Nutrition: (1 ramekin; 4 oz.): Protein: 18 g; **Calories:** 179 kcal; **Fat:** 7 g; **Carbohydrate:** 10 g; **Fiber:** 1 g; **Total Sugar:** 1 g; **Added Sugar:** 0 g; **Sodium:** 154 g

144. Smoothie Bowl with Greek Yogurt and Fresh Berries

Preparation Time: 5 minutes
Cooking Time: 5 minutes
Servings: 2–3
Ingredients:

- ¾ cup vanilla almond milk, unsweetened or low-fat milk
- ¼ cup low-fat plain Greek yogurt
- ⅓ cup (1 handful) fresh spinach
- ½ scoop (⅛ cup) plain or vanilla protein powder
- ¼ cup mixed berries, frozen
- ¼ cup fresh raspberries
- ¼ cup fresh blueberries
- 1 tbsp. almonds, sliced, slivered
- 1 tsp. chia seeds

Post-Op Servings:

- 1 bowl

Directions:

1. In a blender, combine the milk, yogurt, spinach, protein powder, and frozen berries. Blend on high speed for 3 to 4 minutes until the powder is well dissolved and no longer visible.
2. Pour the smoothie into a small bowl.
3. Decorate the smoothie with fresh raspberries, blueberries, almonds, and chia seeds.
4. Serve with a spoon, and enjoy!

Serving tip: You can make this smoothie bowl with various other fruits and toppings to change it up. Try a mango-pineapple version. Top with unsweetened, flaked coconut, and use coconut milk in the smoothie base for a more tropical vibe.
Nutrition: (1 bowl): Calories: 255 kcal; **Total Fat:** 10 g; **Protein:** 20 g; **Carbs:** 21 g; **Fiber:** 8 g; **Sugar:** 10 g; **Sodium:** 262 mg

145. High-Protein: Pancakes

Preparation Time: 5 minutes
Cooking Time: 5 minutes
Servings: 2–3
Ingredients:

- 3 eggs
- 1 cup low-fat cottage cheese
- ⅓ cup whole-wheat pastry flour
- 1 ½ tbsp. coconut oil, melted
- Nonstick cooking spray

Post-Op Servings:

- 1 to 2 ½ pancakes

Directions:

1. In a large bowl, lightly whisk the eggs.
2. Whisk in the cottage cheese, flour, and coconut oil until combined.
3. Heat a large skillet or griddle over medium heat, and lightly coat with the cooking spray.
4. Using a measuring cup, pour ⅓ cup of batter into the skillet for each pancake. Cook for 2 to 3 minutes, or until bubbles appear across the surface of each pancake. Flip over the pancakes and cook for 1 to 2 minutes on the other side, or until golden brown.
5. Serve immediately.

Serving tip: Top these pancakes with fresh berries, plain yogurt, unsweetened applesauce, or sugar-free syrup. You can even try them with natural peanut butter and bananas on a general diet.
Nutrition: (1 pancake): Calories: 182 kcal; **Total Fat:** 10 g; **Protein:** 12 g; **Carbs:** 10 g; **Fiber:** 3 g; **Sugar:** 1 g; **Sodium:** 68 mg

146. Baked Egg, Parm, and Spinach Cup

Preparation Time: 10 minutes
Cooking Time: 10 minutes
Servings: 2–3
Ingredients:

- Nonstick cooking spray
- ¼ cup fresh spinach, chopped
- 1 large egg
- 1 tbsp. nonfat milk
- ½ tomato, diced
- 1 tbsp. Parmesan cheese, grated
- black pepper, freshly ground

Directions:

1. Preheat the oven to 400°F. Coat a 6-oz. ramekin with cooking spray.
2. Place the spinach in the ramekin; then crack the egg over the top.
3. Add the milk, tomato, and Parmesan cheese. Season with pepper to taste.
4. Bake for 10 minutes or until set. Enjoy warm.

Storage Tip: Double or triple the recipe and make several egg cups at once. Let the egg cups cool; then tightly cover with plastic wrap and refrigerate for 3 days. You can cook several at once in a muffin tin (for 10 to 15 minutes until set), cool, and then refrigerate each in a sealed plastic zip-top bag for up to 3 days.
Nutrition: (1 ramekin; 3 oz.): Protein: 9 g; **Calories:** 112 kcal; **Fat:** 7 g; **Carbohydrate:** 5 g; **Fiber:** 1 g; **Total Sugar:** 3 g; **Added Sugar:** 0 g; **Sodium:** 183 g

147. Pumpkin Muffins with Walnuts and Zucchini

Preparation Time: 10 minutes
Cooking Time: 25 minutes
Servings: 2–3
Ingredients:

- Nonstick cooking spray or baking liners
- 2 cups old-fashioned oats
- 1¾ cup whole-wheat pastry flour
- ¼ cup flaxseed, ground
- 2 tbsp. baking powder
- 1 tsp. baking soda
- 1 tsp. cinnamon, ground
- ¼ tsp. nutmeg, ground
- ¼ tsp. ginger, ground
- ¼ tsp. allspice, ground
- 2 cups zucchini, shredded
- 1 cup pumpkin, canned, or fresh pumpkin purée
- 1 cup low-fat milk
- 4 eggs, lightly beaten
- ¼ cup applesauce, unsweetened
- 1 tsp. liquid stevia
- ½ cup walnuts, chopped

Post-Op Servings:

- 1 muffin

Directions:

1. Preheat the oven to 375°F. Prepare 2 muffin tins by coating the cups with the cooking spray, or use baking liners.
2. Mix the oats, flour, flaxseed, baking powder, baking soda, cinnamon, nutmeg, ginger, and allspice in a large bowl.
3. Mix the zucchini, pumpkin, milk, eggs, applesauce, and stevia in a separate medium bowl.
4. Add the wet ingredients to the dry and stir to combine. Gently stir in the walnuts.
5. Fill the cups of the muffin tins about half full with the batter.
6. Bake until the muffins are done, when a toothpick inserted in the center comes out clean, about 25 minutes.
7. Let the muffins cool for 5 minutes before removing them from the tins. Place on a baking rack to finish cooling.
8. Wrap leftover muffins in plastic wrap and freeze. Reheat frozen muffins in the microwave for about 20 seconds.

Nutrition: (1 muffin): Calories: 128 kcal; **Total Fat:** 5 g; **Protein:** 5 g; **Carbs:** 18 g; **Fiber:** 3 g; **Sugar:** 1 g; **Sodium:** 86 mg

148. Wisconsin Scrambler with Aged Cheddar Cheese

Preparation Time: 10 minutes
Cooking Time: 10 minutes
Servings: 2–3
Ingredients:

- Nonstick cooking spray
- 8 oz. extra-lean turkey sausage (nitrate-free)
- 6 large eggs, beaten
- ¼ cup fat-free milk
- ½ tsp. onion powder
- ½ tsp. garlic powder
- 3 oz. extra-sharp Wisconsin Cheddar cheese, shredded

Post-Op Servings:

- ½ cup
- ½ to 1 cup

Directions:

1. Coat a large skillet with the cooking spray and place it over medium-high heat. Add the turkey sausage and brown it, using a wooden spoon to break it into small pieces, until cooked through and no longer pink, about 7 minutes.
2. In a medium bowl, whisk together the eggs and milk. Mix in the onion and garlic powders.
3. Add the eggs to the skillet. Reduce the heat to medium-low and stir gently and constantly with a rubber spatula for 5 minutes, until the eggs are fluffy and cooked through.

Top with the cheese and serve.

Serving tip: One of the best tips a colleague has ever given me is to "only eat cheese if you can taste the flavor." Limit cheese intake to recipes where you can savor the flavor, such as crumbling blue cheese on a salad, jazzing up vegetables with Parmigiano-Reggiano, or including a high-protein snack of sliced Gouda with fruit.

Nutrition: (½ cup): Calories: 169 kcal; **Total Fat:** 11 g; **Protein:** 15 g; **Carbs:** 2 g; **Fiber:** 0 g; **Sugar:** 1 g; **Sodium:** 413 mg

149. Andrea's Hangry Eggs with Cauliflower

Preparation Time: 5 minutes
Cooking Time: 5 minutes
Servings: 2–3
Ingredients:

- ½ (10-oz.) bag cauliflower florets, frozen
- 4 thin slices (nitrate-free) deli ham
- Nonstick cooking spray
- 2 large eggs

Post-Op Servings:

- ½ recipe

Directions:

1. Place the cauliflower with 2 tbsp. water in a microwave-safe bowl or steamer. Cover and cook on high for 4 minutes, or until tender. During the last 30 seconds, add the ham to heat it thoroughly. Drain off any water after cooking.
2. Coat a small skillet with the cooking spray and place it over medium-high heat. Crack 2 eggs into a small dish and set aside.

3. When the skillet is hot, carefully add the eggs. Reduce the heat to medium-low. Jiggle the pan slightly and then allow eggs to cook for 2 to 3 minutes, or until the whites turn opaque and the yolk starts to cook but is still soft in the center. If necessary, use a rubber spatula to adjust the egg slightly to prevent it from sticking. Place the cauliflower on a plate and the ham on top of the cauliflower. Add the eggs, allowing the yolk to spill over the entire dish. Eat immediately.

Serving tip: If tolerated, this is also excellent served over steamed asparagus tips instead of cauliflower.

Nutrition: (½ recipe): Calories: 109 kcal; **Total Fat:** 6 g; **Protein:** 11 g; **Carbs:** 4 g; **Fiber:** 2 g; **Sugar:** 1 g; **Sodium:** 378 mg

150. Southwestern Scrambled Egg Burritos

Preparation Time: 10 minutes
Cooking Time: 10 minutes
Servings: 8
Ingredients:

- 12 eggs
- ¼ cup low-fat milk
- 1 tsp. extra-virgin olive oil
- ½ onion, chopped
- 1 red bell pepper, diced
- 1 green bell pepper, diced
- 1 (15-oz.) can black beans, drained and rinsed
- 8 (7- to 8-inch) whole-wheat tortillas, such as La Tortilla Factory low-carb tortillas
- 1 cup salsa, for serving

Post-Op Servings:

- Burrito filling (no tortilla)
- ½ to 1 burrito

Directions:

1. In a large bowl, whisk together the eggs and milk. Set aside.
2. Heat the olive oil in a large skillet over medium-high heat and add the onion and bell peppers. Sauté for 2 to 3 minutes, or until tender. Add the beans and stir to combine.
3. Add the egg mixture. Reduce the heat to medium-low and stir gently and constantly with a rubber spatula for 5 minutes, until the eggs are fluffy and cooked through.
4. Divide the scrambled egg mixture among the tortillas. Fold over the bottom end of the tortilla, fold in the sides, and roll tightly to close.
5. Serve immediately with the salsa, or place each burrito in a zip-top bag and refrigerate for up to 1 week. To eat, reheat each burrito in the microwave for 60 to 90 seconds. These will also keep well in the freezer for up to 1 month.

Serving Tip: To get more vegetables into your breakfast, buy a bag of frozen California-blend mixed vegetables. Heat some in a skillet with extra-virgin olive oil, add eggs, and—voilà!—a quick veggie-packed egg burrito.

Nutrition: (1 burrito): Calories: 250 kcal; **Total Fat:** 10 g; **Protein:** 19 g; **Carbs:** 28 g; **Fiber:** 13 g; **Sugar:** 1 g; **Sodium:** 546 mg

151. Farmer's Egg Casserole with Broccoli, Mushroom, and Onions

Preparation Time: 10 Minutes
Cooking Time: 40 Minutes
Servings: 2–3
Ingredients:

- Nonstick cooking spray
- 2 tsp. extra-virgin olive oil
- 1 onion, diced
- ½ cup mushrooms, chopped
- 2 cups broccoli florets, roughly chopped
- 12 eggs
- 2 tbsp. low-fat milk
- ½ tsp. oregano, dried
- ½ tsp. basil, dried
- ¼ tsp. thyme, dried
- 1 cup poultry breast, chopped or shredded, cooked, such as leftover turkey or chicken, chicken breast, canned; or turkey lunch meat (nitrate-free)
- 1 cup Swiss cheese, shredded
- ¼ cup Parmigiano-Reggiano cheese, shredded

Post-Op Servings:

- 1 (3-x-4-inch) piece

Directions:

1. Preheat the oven to 350°F. Spray a 9-x-13-inch baking dish with the cooking spray.
2. In a large skillet over medium heat, add the olive oil. When the oil is hot, add the onion and sauté for 1 to 2 minutes or until tender. Add the mushrooms and cook for an additional 2 to 3 minutes, or until tender.
3. Place the broccoli florets in a steamer or microwave-safe bowl and 2 tbsp. water. Cover and microwave/steam for about 4 minutes or just until tender. Drain off any liquid and set it aside.
4. Whisk together the eggs, milk, oregano, basil, and thyme in a large bowl.
5. Add the cooked vegetables, poultry, and Swiss cheese to the egg mixture and stir to combine.
6. Pour the mixture into the baking dish and sprinkle the Parmigiano-Reggiano cheese over the top.
7. Bake for 35 to 40 minutes, or until lightly browned. Let the casserole rest for 5 minutes before serving.
8. Store leftovers in the refrigerator for up to 1 week. Reheat before eating.

Serving tip: Customize this egg casserole with whatever is in your pantry. Try to use vegetables that are in season. Try a Southwest version with chopped bell peppers and topped with fresh salsa. Make a spinach-artichoke bake with canned artichoke hearts. Egg casseroles can be a great way to get plenty of vegetables and a variety of proteins, so shake it up to keep it interesting.
Nutrition: (1 [3-x-4-inch] piece): Calories: 147 kcal; **Total Fat:** 10 g; **Protein:** 12 g; **Carbs:** 2 g; **Fiber:** 1 g; **Sugar:** 0 g; **Sodium:** 193 mg

152. Blueberry Greek Yogurt Pancakes

Preparation Time: 10 minutes
Cooking Time: 8 minutes
Servings: 2–3
Ingredients:

- 2 large eggs
- ¾ cup plain 2-percent-fat Greek yogurt
- ½ tbsp. honey, divided
- ½ tsp. vanilla extract
- ½ cup whole wheat flour
- 1 tsp. baking powder
- 1 pinch salt
- ¼ tsp. cinnamon
- 1 cup fresh blueberries, frozen or thawed
- 2 tbsp. natural peanut butter, divided

Directions:

1. In a bowl, beat eggs. Blend in yogurt, 2 tbsp. nectar, and vanilla. Mix flour, heating powder, salt, and cinnamon in another bowl. Blend in ½ cup of blueberries.
2. In an enormous nonstick skillet covered with a cooking splash over medium-low heat, drop a stacking ¼ cup hitter for every flapjack. Cook until the underside is dark-colored and air pockets structure on top, around 3 minutes. Flip and cook for around 3 minutes more.
3. Top each presentation with ½ tablespoon nectar, 1 tablespoon nutty spread, and ¼ cup blueberries.

Nutrition: Calories: 6 kcal; **Carbs:** 54 g; **Sugar:** 25 g; **Protein:** 23 g

153. Egg White Porridge with Strawberries and Peanut Butter

Preparation Time: 2 minutes
Cooking Time: 5 minutes
Servings: 2–3
Ingredients:

- ½ cup porridge
- ½ cup unsweetened almond milk
- 6 large fresh (or frozen, thawed) strawberries, cored and chopped
- 2 tsp. honey
- ½ tsp. vanilla extract
- 1 pinch salt
- ⅓ cup liquid egg whites
- 1 tbsp. peanut butter

Directions:

1. In a little pot, heat porridge, 2 cups almond milk, ⅓ cup water, strawberries, nectar, vanilla, and salt. Heat to the point of boiling; at that point, decrease to stew and cook, blending once in a while, until the blend is thick, 5 to 7 minutes. Expel from warm.
2. In a bowl, whisk egg whites until somewhat bubbly. Add cooked cereal to egg whites a spoonful at once, rushing between every option, until oats are completely joined.
3. Pour blend into the pot and cook over low heat, always mixing, until oats are thick, 2 minutes. Be mindful not to turn the warmth excessively high so eggs don't scramble.
4. Top cereal with nutty spread.

Nutrition: Calories: 412 kcal; **Carbs:** 54 g; **Sugar:** 17 g; **Protein:** 20 g

154. Hearty Shakshuka

Preparation Time: 5 minutes
Cooking Time: 25 minutes
Servings: 2–3
Ingredients:

- 2 garlic cloves
- ½ green onion
- Olive oil cooking spray
- 14.5 oz. whole tomatoes, peeled and canned
- A pinch paprika, smoked
- ½ tsp. cumin, ground
- ½ tsp. oregano, dried
- ¼ tsp. cayenne pepper
- 2 tbsp. soy protein powder
- A pinch salt and pepper to taste
- 6 oz. can mixed beans
- 3 large eggs
- A handful fresh parsley, chopped

Directions:

1. Mince the garlic and finely chop the onion.
2. Cook in a large deep skillet with olive oil cooking spray over medium heat until soft and transparent (about 5 minutes).
3. Add the canned tomatoes and their juices.
4. Crush the tomatoes as you add them to the skillet.
5. Add the smoked paprika, cumin, oregano, cayenne, protein powder, salt, and pepper.
6. Stir to combine.

7. Allow the sauce to reach a simmer, occasionally stirring, for 5–7 minutes.
8. The sauce should be thickened at this point.
9. Drain the beans and add them to the skillet.
10. Stir to combine.
11. Return to a simmer.
12. Simmer for 2–3 minutes more.
13. Crack eggs into the skillet.
14. Place a lid on top.
15. Simmer for 5 minutes or until the whites are set (the yolks should be soft).
16. Top the skillet with the chopped parsley to serve.

Nutrition: Calories: 337 kcal; **Protein:** 27 g; **Carbs:** 47 g; **Fiber:** 12 g; **Sugar:** 11 g; **Fat:** 5 g

155. Protein-Packed Breakfast Bars

Preparation Time: 10 minutes
Cooking Time: 15 minutes
Servings: 2–3
Ingredients:

- 2 cup porridge oats
- 1 tbsp. smooth nut butter
- 1 tbsp. coconut oil, melted
- 1 tbsp. agave/maple syrup
- 1 tbsp. whey/soy vanilla protein powder
- 1 tsp. cinnamon, ground

Directions:

1. Heat the oven to 160°F.
2. Grease and line the base of an 18 x 25 cm tin with a little cooking spray.
3. Mix the oats and nut butter in the tin.
4. Place in the oven for 5–10 minutes to toast.
5. Meanwhile, warm the coconut oil in a pan over low heat.
6. Add the oat mix, syrup, protein powder, and cinnamon to the pan.
7. Mix everything until all the oats are well-coated.
8. Tip into the tin, press down lightly, then bake for 30 minutes.
9. Cool in the tin and cut it into bars.

Nutrition: Calories: 121 kcal; **Protein:** 6 g; **Carbs:** 16 g; **Fiber:** 2 g; **Sugar:** 6 g; **Fat:** 4 g

156. Very Berry Muesli

Preparation Time: 2 hours
Cooking Time: 2 hours
Servings: 2–3
Ingredients:

- 1 cup oats
- 1 cup fruit-flavored yogurt
- ½ cup milk
- ⅛ tsp. salt
- ½ cup raisins, dried
- ½ cup apple, chopped
- ½ cup blueberries, frozen
- ¼ cup walnuts, chopped

Directions:

1. Combine yogurt, salt, and oats in a medium bowl, mix well, then cover the mixture tightly.
2. Place in the refrigerator to cool for 6 hours.
3. Add raisins and apples the gently fold.
4. Top with walnuts and servings. Enjoy!

Nutrition: Calories: 198 kcal; **Carbs:** 31.2 g; **Fat:** 4.3 g; **Protein:** 6 g

157. Strawberry and Mushroom Breakfast Sandwich

Preparation Time: 5 minutes
Cooking Time: 5 minutes
Servings: 2–3
Ingredients:

- 8 oz. cream cheese
- 1 tbsp. honey
- 1 tbsp. lemon zest, grated
- 4 Portobello mushrooms, sliced
- 2 cup strawberries, sliced

Directions:

1. Add honey, lemon zest, and cheese to a food processor and process until fully incorporated.
2. Use cheese mixture to spread on mushrooms as you would butter.
3. Top with strawberries. Enjoy!

Nutrition: Calories: 180 kcal; **Fat:** 16 g; **Carbs:** 6 g; **Protein:** 2 g

158. Shakshuka Egg Bake

Preparation Time: 10 minutes
Cooking Time: 15 minutes
Servings: 2–3
Ingredients:

- 1 tsp. extra-virgin olive oil
- ½ onion, minced
- 1 garlic clove, minced
- ½ tsp. paprika, smoked
- ½ tsp. cumin, ground
- 1 (15-oz.) can tomatoes, diced
- 2 oz. feta cheese, crumbled
- 4 large eggs

Directions:

1. Preheat the oven to 350°F.
2. In a medium skillet over medium heat, heat the oil. Add the onions and garlic, and sauté until

translucent, about 5 minutes. Add the paprika and cumin, and cook a minute longer.
3. Stir in the tomatoes until well combined. Simmer until some of their liquid has evaporated and the mixture begins to thicken to form a sauce, 5 to 10 minutes.
4. Divide the sauce evenly among 4 ramekins, and repeat with the cheese, sprinkling evenly.
5. Using a spoon, create wells in the tomato sauce and crack an egg over each, being careful to keep the yolk intact.
6. Bake in the ramekins for 15 minutes, until the yolk, is done to your liking, longer if you like a hard-cooked yolk, and servings. (If you do not have ramekins, crack the eggs into spoon-made wells in the pan and let cook for 5 to 10 minutes, or per your preference.)

Ingredient tip: for a variation on flavor, add diced bell pepper, chopped spinach, or chili powder.

Nutrition: Calories: 144 kcal; **Total Fat:** 9 g; **Protein:** 9 g; **Carbohydrate:** 7 g; **Fiber:** 1 g; **Sugar:** 4 g; **Sodium:** 455 mg

159. Ricotta Baked in the Oven

Preparation Time: 10 minutes
Cooking Time: 15 minutes
Servings: 4–5
Ingredients:

- ¼th cup Parmesan cheese, grated
- ½ cup ricotta cheese (low-fat)
- 1 tsp. Dijon mustard
- 1 tsp. thyme, ground
- ¼th cup Cheddar cheese, shredded
- 1 egg

Directions:

1. Heat the oven to a temperature of 400°F.
2. Put all the ingredients in one bowl. Stir and mix them well. The mixture will appear to be gritty and slightly brown. But it must be smooth.
3. Use one cookie scoop and divide the mixture into 4 muffin pan wells. You can use muffin pans made of silicone to clean them quickly and easily.
4. Bake it for about 20 minutes. Then remove it from the oven and let it cool a bit. It is ready to be servings.

Nutrition:
Note: This recipe is for making 4 ricotta muffins. Every muffin provides approximately: **Fat:** 4 g; **Carbohydrate:** 4 g; **Protein:** 8 g

160. Poached Eggs Italian Style

Preparation Time: 10 minutes
Cooking Time: 10 minutes
Servings: 2
Ingredients:

- 3 to 4 pieces jarred red pepper, roasted and sliced
- 16 oz. marinara sauce, with the lowest level of sugar
- 4 eggs
- 4 leaves fresh basil
- 1 pinch salt
- 1 pinch pepper

Directions:

1. Heat a big, rimmed skillet on medium heat. Put the marinara sauce. Then add the red peppers. Crack the eggs one by one, making a "well" with the back of one spoon. Sprinkle pepper and salt.
2. Allow it to cook till the eggs become firm, or for around 12 minutes. If you'd like, you can put the lid on for 2 minutes at the end.
3. Remove from the heat. Sprinkle basil and serve in a bowl or plate.

Nutrition: Fat: 6 g; **Protein:** 8 g; **Carbohydrate:** 7 g

161. Denver Egg Muffins with Ham Crust

Preparation Time: 15 minutes
Cooking Time: 15 minutes; **Servings:** 2–3
Ingredients:

- Nonstick cooking time spray
- 12 slices deli ham
- ½ cup Cheddar cheese
- 1 tsp. extra-virgin olive oil
- ½ onion, diced
- ½ green pepper, minced
- 10 large eggs
- ¼ cup low-fat milk

Directions:

1. Preheat the oven to 350°F.
2. Grease a 12-compartment muffin tin with cooking time spray.
3. Line each cup with a ham slice, pushing it down to fit tightly against the edge of the well.
4. In a small skillet over medium heat, heat the oil. Add the onion and green pepper, and sauté for 3 minutes, or until soft. Remove from the heat, and drain any liquid from the pan.
5. In a large bowl, whisk the eggs and milk. Add the cheese and cooked vegetables, and whisk again.
6. Ladle ¼ cup of the egg mixture into each cup. If there is any leftover, divide evenly among the cups.
7. Bake for 20 to 25 minutes or until the eggs are firm and no longer runny and serve. Post-op Serving's suggestions

Ingredient tip: switch things up, and be creative with your vegetables, meat, and cheese. Try broccoli and Cheddar, sundried tomato and feta, or sausage with pepper jack cheese. Garnish with hot sauce, salsa, avocado, herbs, or light sour cream.

Nutrition: Calories: 99 kcal; **Total Fat:** 6 g; **Protein:** 8 g; **Carbohydrate:** 1 g; **Fiber:** 0 g; **Sugar:** 1 g; **Sodium:** 206 mg

162. Cheesy Slow Cooker Egg Casserole

Preparation Time: 15 minutes
Cooking Time: 2 hours
Servings: 2–3
Ingredients:

- 1 lb fresh Italian chicken sausage
- Nonstick cooking time spray
- 1 (30-oz.) bag hash browns, frozen
- 1 medium red bell pepper, seeded and diced
- ½ medium onion, diced
- 1 (4-oz.) can mild green chiles, diced
- 1 ½ cup low-fat Cheddar cheese, shredded, divided into 3 ½-cups servings
- 12 large eggs 1 cup low-fat milk
- ½ tsp. salt
- ½ tsp. black pepper, freshly ground

Directions:

1. Remove the casings from the sausage, and discard.
2. In a large skillet over medium heat, brown the meat, breaking it into smaller pieces as it cooks, about 7 minutes, or until no longer pink.
3. Spray a 5-quart slow cooker with nonstick cooking time spray, and layer half of the frozen hash browns, cooked sausage, pepper, onion, and chiles, plus ½ cup of cheese. Repeat with the remaining hash browns, sausage, pepper, onion, chilies, and another ½ cup of cheese.
4. Whisk the eggs, milk, salt, and pepper in a large bowl.
5. Pour the egg mixture over the potato-sausage layers, and top with the remaining ½ cup of cheese.
6. Cook on high for 4 hours or low for 8 hours, and serve.

Post-op serving suggestions:
Ingredient tip: if you cannot find fresh Italian chicken sausage, look for pre-cooked sausage in the refrigerator sector of your grocery store. Dice into small pieces and brown in a skillet before adding to the slow cooker.
Nutrition: Calories: 348 kcal; **Total Fat:** 17 g; **Protein:** 27 g; **Carbohydrate:** 24 g; **Fiber:** 3 g; **Sugar:** 3 g; **Sodium:** 783 mg

163. Make-Ahead Breakfast Burritos

Preparation Time: 15 minutes
Cooking Time: 20 minutes
Servings: 8
Ingredients:

- 12 large eggs
- ¼ cup low-fat milk
- 1 tsp. extra-virgin olive oil
- ½ medium yellow onion, diced
- 1 medium green bell pepper, seeded and diced
- 1 cup black beans, canned, drained, and rinsed
- 8 (7- to 8-inch) whole wheat tortillas
- ½ cup Cheddar cheese, shredded
- 8 oz. salsa

Directions:

1. In a large bowl, whisk together the eggs and milk.
2. In a large skillet over medium heat, heat the oil. Add the onion, bell pepper, and black beans. Sauté until the onion is translucent, about 5 minutes, and transfer to a plate.
3. Pour the egg mixture into the skillet and gently stir until the eggs are fluffy and firm. Remove from the heat.
4. Divide the eggs and onion mixture evenly among the tortillas, and top with the cheese and salsa.
5. With both sides of the first tortilla tucked in, roll tightly. Repeat with the remaining tortillas.
6. Serve immediately, or freeze for up to 3 months. If freezing, wrap the burritos in paper towels and cover them tightly with aluminum foil for storage.

Post-op Servings suggestions:
Ingredient tip: if you cannot tolerate doughy textures after surgery, skip the tortilla and spoon the filling into a bowl.
Nutrition: Calories: 264 kcal; **Total Fat:** 12 g; **Protein:** 21 g; **Carbohydrate:** 24 g; **Fiber:** 11 g; **Sugar:** 3 g; **Sodium:** 593 mg

164. Magic Hot Cereal

Preparation Time: 5 minutes
Cooking Time: 5 minutes
Servings: 2–3
Ingredients:

- 3/4 cup water
- ¼ cup Bob's Red Mill 7 Grain Hot Cereal
- ¼ tsp. orange rind, finely grated
- 1 dash Kosher salt
- 1 dash cinnamon, ground
- 1 pinch fresh nutmeg, ground
- 4–5 tbsp. vanilla soy milk
- 2 drops vanilla extract
- 1 tsp. butter
- 2 tbsp. maple syrup

Directions:

1. In a small pot, add the orange rind to water and bring to a boil.
2. Add cereal, salt, cinnamon, and nutmeg, and reduce heat. Stir while cooking and add the soy milk a

tablespoon at a time when the liquid has been fully absorbed by the cereal.

3. When the cereal is done, about 6 minutes, add vanilla extract, butter, and maple syrup. Stir to mix and serve hot.

Nutrition: Calories: 265 kcal; **Fat:** 8.5 g; **Fiber:** 7.1 g; **Carbs:** 39.7 g; **Protein:** 12.5 g

165. Baked Broccoli and Eggs

Preparation Time: 10 minutes
Cooking Time: 15 minutes
Servings: 2–3
Ingredients:

- 4 oz. margarine, light
- 10 oz. broccoli, frozen, thawed, chopped
- 4 oz. pimiento, jarred, chopped
- 6 tbsp. flour
- 1 dash black pepper, freshly ground
- ½ cup mushrooms, sliced, fresh
- 6 pieces eggs, large
- ½ lb. Cheddar cheese, low-fat
- 2 lb. cottage cheese, nonfat
- 1 tsp. salt
- 1 dash paprika

Directions:

1. Set the oven to 350°F to preheat.
2. Meanwhile, place the eggs, broccoli, and all other ingredients in a large bowl. Stir to combine.
3. Use cooking time spray to coat the sides and bottom of a casserole dish (2-quart).
4. Fill the preparation time dish with the broccoli-egg mixture and spread it evenly.
5. Bake in the oven for one hour and 30 minutes.

Nutrition: Calories: 129 kcal; **Carbohydrate:** 2 g; **Protein:** 10 g; **Fat:** 9 g; **Saturated Fat:** 4 g; **Cholesterol:** 179 mg; **Sodium:** 218 mg; **Potassium:** 113 mg; **Fiber:** 1 g; **Sugar:** 2 g; **Vitamin A:** 363 IU; **Vitamin C:** 1 mg; **Calcium:** 142 mg; **Iron:** 1 mg

166. Broccoli and Tofu Quiche

Preparation Time: 10 minutes
Cooking Time: 15 minutes
Servings: 2–3
Ingredients:

- ¼ tsp. salt
- ¼ lb. mushrooms, chopped
- 1 tbsp. pickled plum/white miso paste
- 1-piece yellow onion, chopped
- 2 tbsp. sesame tahini
- ½ cup bulgur wheat, uncooked
- 1 tbsp. sesame oil
- ½ lb. broccoli, chopped
- 1 ½ lb. tofu
- 1 tbsp. tamari

Directions:

1. Set the oven at 350°F to preheat.
2. Fill a small pot with water (1 cup) and heat on medium.
3. Bring to a boil before adding the bulgur and salt. Stir to combine and allow the mixture to boil again. Reduce heat to low and cover to cook for about 15 minutes. Meanwhile, grease a pie pan (9-inch) with a little oil.
4. Pour the cooked bulgur into the pie pan, pressing lightly to spread it evenly at the bottom.
5. Place in the oven to bake for about 12 minutes or until crusty on top. Let stand to cool.
6. Heat a large skillet (nonstick) on medium-high before adding the onions.
7. Stir in the mushrooms and broccoli and cook for 2 minutes.
8. Cover and immediately remove from heat. Meanwhile, fill the food processor with the tofu.
9. Add the tamari, tahini, and umeboshi paste.
10. Process until well-combined and smooth, then pour into a large bowl.
11. Add the cooked veggies and gently toss until evenly coated.
12. Transfer the veggie mixture onto the crusted bulgur.
13. Bake in the oven for about half an hour. Once done, let stand on a wire rack. After 10 minutes, slice into 6 portions and serve immediately.

Nutrition: Calories: 248 kcal; **Carbohydrate:** 27.2 g; **Protein:** 30.6 g; **Fat:** 3.6 g; **Saturated Fat:** 0.4 g; **Cholesterol:** 50 mg; **Sodium:** 718 mg; **Fiber:** 6.1 g

167. Sunday Morning Special

Preparation Time: 20 minutes
Cooking Time: 10 minutes
Servings: 1
Ingredients:

- 125 ml cottage cheese, low fat
- 1 egg, large
- 75 ml onion, diced
- ¼ tsp. garlic, minced
- 1 generous tbsp. whole wheat flour
- Pepper and salt, for taste
- Cooking time spray for the pan

Directions:

1. Spray the pan and pre-heat for a minute.
2. Sauté the garlic and onions while stirring the egg, cottage cheese, flour, pepper, and salt together.
3. Add the cooked ingredients to the bowl mixture, stirring until well combined.

4. Spray the pan again and spoon the mixture into the pan. Create 4 pancakes.
5. Cook on each side for 4 minutes.

Nutrition: Protein: 36 g; **Fat:** 96 g; **Carbohydrate:** 10 g

168. Simple Sunshine Scramble

Preparation Time: 5 minutes
Cooking Time: 10 minutes
Servings: 1
Ingredients:

- 1 egg
- 1 garlic clove, small minced
- 1 tsp. pesto
- 2 cherry tomatoes, quartered
- 1-piece bacon turkey, crumbled
- 1 tsp. Parmesan cheese, grated fine
- Cooking time spray for the pan

Directions:

1. Lightly whisk the egg in a mixing bowl. Add a dash of water to the egg and the pesto. Whisk again lightly.
1. Spray the pan lightly with cooking time spray and heat to medium-high.
2. Sauté the garlic until the aroma is released. Stir in bacon to crisp.
3. Slide pan contents out onto a side dish. Add tomatoes to the pan, sauté until the liquid is almost gone, and add egg mixture to the pan; cook as you prefer your scrambled eggs, and stir in the bacon/garlic mixture and Parmesan cheese just before the eggs are cooked. Serve with a slice of orange for that complete sunshine feel.

Nutrition: Protein: 60 g; **Fat:** 144 g; **Carbohydrate:** 8 g

169. Black Beans Purée with Scrambled Eggs

Preparation Time: 20 minutes
Cooking Time: 30 minutes
Servings: 1
Ingredients:
For making the scrambled egg part of the recipe:

- ⅛ tsp. salt
- 1 egg
- ⅛ tsp. pepper

Black beans purée:

- 3 tbsp. enchilada sauce (green)
- ½ cup black beans, rinsed
- 2 tbsp. vegetable or chicken broth
- 1 tbsp. protein powder

Directions:
Black beans purée:

1. Put the beans in a small-sized saucepan on medium heat. Then put the enchilada sauce. Heat for 2 minutes. Keep stirring all the time. Then add the chicken broth.
2. Shift the mixture to one blender or use one hand to make a smooth mixture. Transfer it into one bowl.
3. Let it cool a bit, and then mix the protein powder. Stir well. Cover it to keep it warm till you cook the egg.
4. Keep the leftovers in the fridge so you can eat them later.

Scrambled egg:

1. Heat 1 non-stick pan on medium heat. In the meantime, put the egg in one small bowl and whisk it well to incorporate air into it.
2. Pour the egg into the heated pan. Sprinkle pepper and salt. Use 1 rubber spatula to move the egg in the pan while it gets cooked. When it is almost done and still has a slightly liquid texture, you should fold it and take it out on a plate.
3. Put 1 tablespoon of the black beans purée. Also, put 1 teaspoon of enchilada sauce (green).

Nutrition: Fat: 5 g; **Protein:** 11 g; **Carbohydrate:** 6 g

170. Veggie Quiche Muffins

Preparation Time: 20 minutes
Cooking Time: 30 minutes
Servings: 12
Ingredients:

- ¾ cup Cheddar cheese, shredded
- 1 cup green onion
- 1 cup broccoli, chopped
- 1 cup tomatoes, diced
- 2 cups milk
- 4 eggs
- 1 cup pancake mix
- 1 tsp. oregano
- ½ tsp. salt tsp. pepper

Directions:

1. Set oven to 375°F, and lightly grease a 12-cup muffin tin with oil.
2. Sprinkle tomatoes, broccoli, onions, and Cheddar into muffin cups.
3. Combine remaining ingredients in a medium bowl, whisk to combine, then pour evenly on top of veggies.
4. Set to bake in a preheated oven for about 40 minutes or until golden brown.
5. Allow to cool slightly (about 5 minutes), then serve. Enjoy!

Nutrition: Calories: 58.8 kcal; **Fat:** 3.2 g; **Carbs:** 2.9 g; **Protein:** 5.1 g

171. Steel Cut Oat Blueberry Pancakes

Preparation Time: 10 minutes
Cooking Time: 10 minutes
Servings: 4
Ingredients:

- 1 ½ cup water
- ½ cup oats
- ⅛ tsp. salt
- 1 cup flour
- ½ tsp. baking powder
- ½ tsp. baking soda
- 1 egg
- 1 cup milk
- ½ cup Greek yogurt
- 1 cup blueberries, frozen
- ¾ cup agave nectar

Directions:

1. Combine oats, salt, and water in a medium saucepan, and allow to come to a boil over high heat.
2. Set it to low and simmer for 10 minutes or until oats are tender. Set aside.
3. Combine all remaining ingredients, except agave nectar, in a medium bowl, then fold in oats.
4. Preheat the grill and lightly grease. Cook ¼ cup of batter for about 3 minutes per side. Garnish with agave.

Nutrition: Calories: 257 kcal; **Fat:** 7 g; **Carbs:** 46 g; **Protein:** 14 g

172. Simply Vanilla Frozen Greek Yogurt

Preparation Time: 5 minutes + 8 hours to freeze
Cooking Time: 0 minutes
Servings: 2–3
Ingredients:

- 4 cups nonfat plain Greek yogurt
- 4 tbsp. vanilla whey protein powder
- 4 tbsp. vanilla extract
- 4 tsp. stevia or no-calorie sweetener

Directions:

1. In a large bowl or loaf pan, combine the yogurt, protein powder, vanilla extract, and stevia.
2. Cover and freeze overnight or for at least 8 hours.
3. About an hour before serving, set in the refrigerator to thaw slightly. Serve and enjoy.

Nutrition: Per Serving (1 Cup): Calories: 183 kcal; **Protein:** 28 g; **Fat:** 1 g; **Carbohydrate:** 12 g; **Fiber:** 1 g; **Sugar:** 8 g; **Sodium:** 96 mg

173. Greek Chop-Chop Salad

Preparation Time: 15 minutes
Cooking Time: 0 minutes
Servings: 4–5
Ingredients:

- 1 medium English cucumber, chopped (2 cups)
- 1 cup cherry tomatoes, halved
- 1 red bell pepper, seeded and diced
- ½ red onion, diced
- ½ cup Kalamata olives, pitted, roughly chopped
- 1 cup feta cheese, crumbled
- ½ cup balsamic dressing

Directions:

1. In a large bowl, toss the cucumber, tomatoes, bell pepper, onion, olives, and cheese with the dressing, and serve.

Nutrition: Calories: 173 kcal; **Total Fat:** 13 g; **Protein:** 4 g; **Carbohydrate:** 10 g; **Fiber:** 1 g; **Sugar:** 4 g; **Sodium:** 883 mg

174. Roasted Garden Vegetables

Preparation Time: 5 minutes
Cooking Time: 15 minutes
Servings: 2–3
Ingredients:

- 1 medium bell pepper, cut into strips
- 1 small onion, halved then sliced
- 1 small zucchini, sliced into rounds
- 1 pint grape tomatoes
- 2 tbsp. extra-virgin olive oil
- Salt
- Black pepper, freshly ground

Directions:

1. Preheat the oven to 400°F.
2. Using 1 or 2 large baking sheets, arrange the vegetables to lie flat, lightly touching each other.
3. Evenly pour the olive oil over the vegetables and gently toss to coat, using either a spoon or your hands. Add salt and pepper to taste.
4. Roast for 20 to 30 minutes, or until soft and lightly charred, stirring halfway through, and serve.

Nutrition: Calories: 75 kcal; **Total Fat:** 5 g; **Protein:** 0 g; **Carbohydrate:** 8 g; **Fiber:** 1 g; **Sugar:** 4 g; **Sodium:** 2 mg

175. Asian Cabbage Salad

Preparation Time: 10 minutes
Cooking Time: 0 minutes
Servings: 2–3
Ingredients:

- 1 (14-oz.) package coleslaw
- 1 red bell pepper, thinly sliced
- 1 large carrot, grated
- ¼ cup scallions, diced
- ¼ cup fresh cilantro, chopped
- ¼ cup peanuts, chopped
- ⅓ cup Spicy Peanut Dressing, plus more if desired

Directions:

1. In a large bowl, combine coleslaw, bell pepper, carrot, scallions, cilantro, and peanuts.
2. Toss with the dressing, add more as desired, and serve.

Nutrition: Calories: 123 kcal; **Total Fat:** 6 g; **Protein:** 6 g; **Carbohydrate:** 16 g; **Fiber:** 6 g; **Sugar:** 6 g; **Sodium:** 198 mg

176. Southwest Deviled Eggs

Preparation Time: 10 minutes
Cooking Time: 0 minutes; **Servings:** 2–3
Ingredients:

- 6 large hard-boiled eggs
- 2 tbsp. low-fat, plain Greek yogurt
- ¼ tsp. spicy mustard
- ⅛ tsp. salt
- ½ tsp. Taco Seasoning

Directions:

1. Peel the eggs, and halve them lengthwise.
2. Remove the yolks, and transfer them to a small bowl, setting the whites aside.
3. Add the yogurt, spicy mustard, salt, and taco seasoning to the bowl with the yolks, and mash everything together.
4. Spoon the mixture into the egg white halves, and serve.

Nutrition: Calories: 83 kcal; **Total Fat:** 5 g; **Protein:** 7 g; **Carbohydrate:** 1 g; **Fiber:** 0 g; **Sugar:** 1 g; **Sodium:** 129 mg

177. Rajun' Cajun Roll-Ups

Preparation Time: 5 minutes
Cooking Time: 0 minutes; **Servings:** 2–3
Ingredients:

- 4 slices nitrate-free Cajun deli turkey
- 4 tsp. spicy mustard, divided
- 4 slices pepper Jack cheese
- ½ steak tomato, seeded and diced
- ¼ red onion, thinly sliced
- 2 cups lettuce, shredded
- ½ avocado, diced
- ¼ cup banana peppers, chopped

Directions:

1. On a cutting board, lay out 1 slice of deli turkey and spread with 1 teaspoon of mustard.
2. Top with 1 slice of cheese, ¼ of the diced tomato and red onion slices, ¼ cup shredded lettuce, and ¼ each of the diced avocado and banana peppers.
3. Wrap the deli turkey tightly but delicately around the filling, and pin it with a toothpick.
4. Repeat the process 3 times with the remaining ingredients, and serve.

Nutrition: Cal: 152 kcal; **Total Fat:** 9 g; **Protein:** 10 g; **Carbohydrate:** 6 g; **Fiber:** 2 g; **Sugar:** 1 g; **Sod:** 498 mg

178. Everything Parmesan Crisps

Preparation Time: 10 minutes
Cooking Time: 5 minutes; **Servings:** 2–3
Ingredients:

- 1 tsp. poppy seeds
- 1 tsp. sesame seeds
- 1 tsp. garlic flakes
- 1 tsp. onion flakes
- 12 tbsp. Parmesan cheese, grated

Directions:

1. Preheat the oven to 400°F.
2. Mix the poppy seeds, sesame seeds, garlic flakes, and onion flakes in a small bowl.
3. Line a sheet pan with a silicone baking mat or parchment paper. Pour 1 tablespoon of Parmesan onto the mat and gently pat down with your fingers to make a 2- to 2 ½-inch round.
4. Repeat 11 more times, keeping at least 1 inch between each round.
5. Bake for 3 minutes. Remove from the oven, and sprinkle ¼ teaspoon of the seasoning over each Parmesan round.
6. Bake for another 3 to 5 minutes, or until golden and crisp, and serve.

Nutrition: Calories: 23 kcal; **Total Fat:** 2 g; **Protein:** 2 g; **Carbohydrate:** 0 g; **Fiber:** 0 g; **Sugar:** 0 g; **Sodium:** 85 mg

179. Edamame Hummus

Preparation Time: 10 minutes
Cooking Time: 5 minutes; **Servings:** 2–3
Ingredients:

- 1 ½ cup edamame, frozen, thawed, rinsed, and drained
- ¼ cup tahini
- 2 tbsp. extra-virgin olive oil
- 2 garlic cloves, peeled
- ½ tsp. cumin, ground
- 3 to 4 tsp. lemon juice, freshly squeezed (juice of 1 lemon)
- Salt
- Black pepper, freshly ground
- 2 to 4 tbsp. water
- Raw veggies, for serving

Directions:

1. In a food processor, combine the edamame, tahini, olive oil, garlic, cumin, and lemon juice. Process until smooth, stopping to scrape down the sides as needed.
2. Add salt and pepper to taste. Process again until combined.
3. To thin, if desired, add 1 tablespoon of water and process. Repeat this step until you reach your desired consistency.
4. Transfer to a serving bowl, and serve with raw veggies.

Nutrition: Calories: 115 kcal; **Total Fat:** 9 g; **Protein:** 4 g; **Carbohydrate:** 6 g; **Fiber:** 2 g; **Sugar:** 1 g; **Sodium:** 20 mg

180. Chia Chocolate Pudding

Preparation Time: 5 minutes + 2–8 hours to chill
Cooking Time: 0 minutes; **Servings:** 2–3
Ingredients:

- ½ cup almond milk, unsweetened
- ½ cup nonfat plain Greek yogurt
- 2 tbsp. chia seeds
- 1 tbsp. vanilla whey protein
- 1 tsp. cocoa powder, unsweetened
- ½ tsp. stevia or no-calorie sweetener

Directions:

1. In a canning jar, combine the almond milk, yogurt, chia seeds, whey protein, cocoa powder, and stevia.
2. Seal with lid and let sit in the refrigerator overnight.
3. Enjoy straight from the jar or in a separate bowl if you consume a smaller serving.

Nutrition: Calories: 257 kcal; **Protein:** 25 g; **Fat:** 12 g; **Carbohydrate:** 21 g; **Fiber:** 11 g; **Sugar:** 5 g; **Sod:** 122 mg

181. Spicy Roasted Chickpeas

Preparation Time: 5 minutes
Cooking Time: 1 hour; **Servings:** 2–3
Ingredients:

- 2 (15-oz.) cans organic garbanzo beans (rinsed and drained)
- 1 ½ tbsp. chili powder
- 1 tbsp. cumin, ground
- 2 tsp. cayenne powder, ground
- 2 tsp. garlic powder
- 2 tsp. paprika
- 1 tsp. salt
- 1 tbsp. extra-virgin olive oil

Directions:

1. Preheat the oven to 300°F. Line a baking sheet with aluminum foil.
2. Mix the beans, chili powder, cumin, cayenne, garlic powder, paprika, salt, and olive oil in a large bowl, coating the beans well.
3. Spread evenly on a baking sheet.
4. Bake for 30 minutes, and stir gently.
5. Bake for another 20 to 30 minutes, until hard and crunchy, and serve.

Nutrition: Calories: 144 kcal; **Total Fat:** 4 g; **Protein:** 7 g; **Carb:** 22 g; **Fiber:** 6 g; **Sugar:** 4 g; **Sodium:** 311 mg

182. Mashed Cauliflower

Preparation Time: 10 minutes
Cooking Time: 5 minutes; **Servings:** 2–3
Ingredients:

- 1 large head cauliflower
- ¼ cup water
- ⅓ cup low-fat buttermilk
- 1 tbsp. garlic, minced
- 1 tbsp. extra-virgin olive oil

Directions:

1. Break the cauliflower into small florets. Place in a large microwave-safe bowl with the water. Cover

and microwave for about 5 minutes until the cauliflower is soft. Drain the water from the bowl.
2. In a blender or food processor, purée the buttermilk, cauliflower, garlic, and olive oil on medium speed until the cauliflower is smooth and creamy.
3. Serve immediately.

Nutrition: Calories: 62 kcal; **Total Fat:** 2 g; **Protein:** 3 g; **Carbs:** 8 g; **Fiber:** 3 g; **Sugar:** 3 g; **Sodium:** 54 mg

183. Pickle Roll-Ups

Preparation Time: 20 minutes
Cooking Time: 0 minutes
Servings: 2–3
Ingredients:

- ¼ lb. deli ham (nitrate-free), thinly sliced (about 8 slices)
- 8 oz. Neufchâtel cheese, at room temperature
- 1 tsp. dill, dried
- 1 tsp. onion powder
- 8 whole Kosher dill pickle spears

Directions:

1. Get a large cutting board or clean counter space to assemble your roll-ups.
2. Lay the ham slices on the work surface and carefully spread on the Neufchâtel cheese.
3. Season each lightly with the dill and onion powder.
4. Place an entire pickle on the end of the ham and carefully roll.
5. Slice each pickle roll-up into mini rounds about ½- to 1-inch wide.
6. Skew each with a toothpick for easier serving.

Nutrition: Calories: 86 kcal; **Total Fat:** 7 g; **Protein:** 4 g; **Carbs:** 4 g; **Fiber:** 0 g; **Sugar:** 2 g; **Sodium:** 540 mg

184. Italian Eggplant Pizzas

Preparation Time: 15 minutes
Cooking Time: 15 minutes
Servings: 2–3
Ingredients:

- 1 large eggplant, cut into ¼- to ½-inch rounds
- 1 tbsp. salt
- 1 tbsp. extra-virgin olive oil
- 2 tsp. garlic, minced
- ½ tsp. oregano, dried
- 1 cup Marinara Sauce with Italian Herbs
- 1 cup fresh basil leaves
- 1 cup part-skim mozzarella cheese, shredded
- ¼ cup Parmigiano-Reggiano cheese, shredded

Directions:

1. Preheat the oven to 425°F. Line a large rimmed baking sheet with aluminum foil.
2. Put the eggplant rounds on paper towels and sprinkle them with salt. Let them sit for 10 to 15 minutes to help release some of the water in the eggplant. Pat dries afterward. It's okay to wipe off some of the salt before baking.
3. Mix the olive oil, garlic, and oregano in a small bowl.
4. Place the eggplant rounds 1-inch apart on the baking sheet. Using a pastry brush, coat each side of the eggplant with the olive oil mixture. Bake the eggplant for 15 minutes.
5. Create pizzas by layering 1 to 2 tablespoons of marinara sauce, 2 basil leaves, about 1 tablespoon of mozzarella cheese, and about ½ tablespoon of Parmigiano-Reggiano cheese on each baked eggplant round.
6. Bake the pizzas for an additional 10 minutes or until the cheese is melted and starts to brown.
7. Serve immediately and enjoy!

Nutrition: Calories: 99 kcal; **Total Fat:** 6 g; **Protein:** 5 g; **Carbs:** 7 g; **Fiber:** 2 g; **Sugar:** 4 g; **Sodium:** 500 mg

185. Tomato, Basil, and Cucumber Salad

Preparation Time: 15 minutes
Cooking Time: 15 minutes
Servings: 2–3
Ingredients:

- 1 large cucumber, seeded and sliced
- 4 medium tomatoes, quartered
- 1 medium red onion, thinly sliced
- ½ cup fresh basil, chopped
- 3 tbsp. red wine vinegar
- 1 tbsp. extra-virgin olive oil
- ½ tsp. Dijon mustard
- ½ tsp. black pepper, freshly ground

Directions:

1. Mix the cucumber, tomatoes, red onion, and basil in a medium bowl.
2. Whisk together the vinegar, olive oil, mustard, and pepper in a small bowl.
3. Pour the dressing over the vegetables and gently stir until well combined.
4. Cover and chill for at least 30 minutes before serving.

Nutrition: Calories: 72 kcal; **Total Fat:** 4 g; **Protein:** 1 g; **Carbs:** 8 g; **Fiber:** 1 g; **Sugar:** 4 g; **Sodium:** 5 mg

186. Roasted Root Vegetables

Preparation Time: 15 minutes
Cooking Time: 45 minutes
Servings: 2–3
Ingredients:

- Nonstick cooking spray
- 2 medium red beets, peeled
- 2 large parsnips, peeled

- 2 large carrots, peeled
- 1 medium butternut squash (about 2 lb), peeled and seeded
- 1 medium red onion
- 2 tbsp. extra-virgin olive oil
- 4 tsp. garlic, minced
- 2 tsp. thyme, dried

Directions:

1. Preheat the oven to 425°F. Spray a large rimmed baking sheet with the cooking spray.
2. Roughly chop the beets, parsnips, carrots, and butternut squash into 1-inch pieces. Cut the onion into half and then each half into 4 large chunks.
3. Arrange the vegetables in a single, even layer on the baking sheet, and sprinkle them with olive oil, garlic, and thyme. Use a spoon to mix the vegetables to coat them with the oil and seasonings.
4. Roast for 45 minutes, stirring the vegetables every 15 minutes until all the vegetables are tender.
5. Serve immediately.

Nutrition: Calories: 68 kcal; **Total Fat:** 3 g; **Protein:** 1 g; **Carbs:** 11 g; **Fiber:** 1 g; **Sugar:** 5 g; **Sodium:** 30 mg

187. Tomato and Mozzarella Bites

Preparation Time: 30 minutes
Cooking Time: 15 minutes; **Servings:** 2–3
Ingredients:

- 20 grape tomatoes, halved
- 20 fresh basil leaves
- 20 small balls fresh mozzarella cheese
- Salt and pepper, as need
- ½ cup balsamic vinegar
- ¼ cup extra-virgin olive oil
- 20 toothpicks

Directions:

1. Use a toothpick to spear half a tomato, a basil leaf, a ball of mozzarella, and another half a tomato. With the ingredients, repeat.
2. Place and sprinkle with salt and pepper on a serving plate. Mix the vinegar and oil in a small bowl to act as a dipping sauce.

Nutrition: Calories: 225 kcal; **Carbohydrate:** 5.4 g; **Fat:** 17.9 g; **Cholesterol:** 39.3 mg; **Sodium:** 151.8 mg

188. Homemade Potato Chips

Preparation Time: 30 minutes
Cooking Time: 5 minutes/batch
Servings: 2–3
Ingredients:

- 7 medium potatoes, unpeeled (about 2 lb.)
- $^2/_4$ ice water
- 5 tsp. salt
- 2 tsp. garlic powder
- 1-½ tsp. celery salt
- 1-½ tsp. pepper
- Oil for deep-fat frying

Directions:

1. Slice the potatoes into thin slices using a vegetable peeler or a metal cheese slicer. Place it in a wide bowl; add salt and ice water. For 30 minutes, soak.
2. Place the potatoes on paper towels and pat them dry. Combine the garlic powder, celery salt, and pepper in a small bowl; set aside.
3. Heat 1-½ in. in a cast iron skillet up to 375°F crude. Fry the potatoes until golden brown in clusters, stirring for 3–4 minutes.
4. With a slotted spoon, remove; drain onto paper towels. Sprinkle with the seasoning mixture immediately. Store it in an air-tight jar.

Nutrition: ¾ cup of: Calories: 176 kcal; **Fat:** 8 g; **Cholesterol:** 0; **Sodium:** 703 mg; **Carbohydrate:** 24 g; **Protein:** 3 g

189. Brie with Apricot Topping

Preparation Time: 25 minutes
Cooking Time: 0 minutes; **Servings:** 2–3
Ingredients:

- ½ cup apricots, dried, chopped
- 2 tbsp. brown sugar
- 2 tbsp. water
- 1 tsp. balsamic vinegar
- Dash salt
- ½ to 1 tsp. fresh rosemary, minced, or ¼ tsp. rosemary, dried, crushed
- 1 round Brie cheese (8 oz.)
- Assorted crackers

Directions:

1. Heat the oven to 400°F. Mix the first five ingredients in a small saucepan; bring it to a boil. Cook, and when slightly thickened, stir with medium heat. Remove from heat; add rosemary and stir.
2. From the top of the cheese, cut the rind off. Put the cheese in an ovenproof, non-greased serving dish. Spoon the apricot mix with the cheese; bake until the cheese is softened, 10-12 minutes, uncovered. Serve soft, crackers included.

Nutrition: 1 Servings: Calories: 4–529 kcal; **Fat:** 8 g; **Cholesterol:** 28 mg; **Sodium:** 204 mg; **Carbohydrate:** 9 g; **Protein:** 6 g

190. Chocolate Peanut Butter Protein: Balls

Preparation Time: 10 minutes
Cooking Time: 5 minutes; **Servings:** 2–3

Ingredients:

- 1 ½ cup old-fashioned rolled oats
- 1 cup natural peanut butter
- ¼ cup honey
- 2 scoops (64 g) chocolate protein powder
- 2 tbsp. chocolate chips

Directions:

1. Place the oats, peanut butter, honey, chocolate chips and protein powder in a large bowl and stir to blend.
2. It takes a little arm muscle to get the mixture to blend, and it can seem too thick at first, but as you keep mixing, it will come together. I used my hands at the end to knead the dough, which seemed to help.
3. Use a cookie scoop and shape the dough into balls until mixed.
4. Store in the freezer.

Nutrition: Calories: 114 kcal; **Sugar:** 5 g; **Fat:** 6 g; **Carbohydrate:** 8 g; **Fiber:** 1 g; **Protein:** 6 g

191. Zucchini Pizza Boats

Preparation Time: 5 minutes
Cooking Time: 15 minutes; **Servings:** 2–3
Ingredients:

- 2 medium zucchinis
- ½ cup tomato sauce
- ½ cup mozzarella cheese, shredded
- 2 tbsp. Parmesan cheese

Directions:

1. Set oven to 350°F.
2. Slice zucchini in half lengthwise and spoon out the core and seeds to form boats.
3. Place zucchini halves skin side down in a small baking dish.
4. Add the remaining ingredients inside the hollow center, then set to bake until golden brown and fork-tender (about 30 minutes).
5. Serve and enjoy.

Nutrition: Net Carbs: 23.6 g; **Fiber:** 4 g; **Fat:** 7.9 g; **Sugar:** 1 g; **Calories:** 214 kcal

192. Hummus

Preparation Time: 2 hours, 20 minutes
Cooking Time: 0 minutes; **Servings:** 2–3
Ingredients:

- 1 can chickpeas, drained and rinsed
- 1 tbsp. peanut butter
- ½ lemon, juice only
- 1 tsp. lemon rind, minced
- 1 tsp. salt
- ¼ tsp. red pepper flakes, crushed
- 1 tbsp. olive oil
- 1 garlic clove
- Option, substitute pesto for peanut butter

Directions:

1. Place everything in the food processor. Start to purée while slowly drizzling in 2 tablespoons of water. Purée until exceptionally creamy.
2. Place in a bowl and keep cool in the fridge until ready to enjoy with any chopped, sliced, or whole vegetable of your choice. These could include sweet bell peppers, cherry tomatoes, radishes, fennel, jicama, and snap peas.

Nutrition: Protein: 19 g; **Fat:** 77 g; **Carbohydrate:** 80 g

193. Cheese Chips

Preparation Time: 20 minutes
Cooking Time: 30 minutes; **Servings:** 2–3
Ingredients:

- 10 tbsp. Parmesan cheese, shredded
- Garlic powder
- 2 tbsp. fresh basil, finely chopped

Directions:

1. Heat the oven to 350°F. Line a baking sheet with parchment paper.
2. Scoop 1 tablespoon of cheese and drop in a plop on the baking sheet.
3. With your fingers, gently spread the cheese into a thin circle and add a pinch of garlic powder and a pinch of basil.
4. Repeat until all of the cheese is gone.
5. Place sheet in oven until circle edges are golden brown. Give them a minute to cool.

Nutrition: Protein: 26 g; **Fat:** 239 g; **Carbohydrate:** 231 g

194. Caprese Salad Bites

Preparation Time: 10 minutes
Cooking Time: 15 minutes; **Servings:** 2–3
Ingredients:
For the bites:

- 24 cherry tomatoes
- 12 mozzarella balls
- 12 fresh basil leaves

For the balsamic glaze:

- ½ cup balsamic vinegar
- 2 tbsp. extra-virgin olive oil
- 1 garlic clove, minced
- 1 tsp. Italian seasoning

Directions:
To make the bites:

1. Using 12 toothpicks or short skewers, assemble each with 1 cherry tomato, 1 mozzarella ball, 1 basil leaf, and another tomato.
2. Place on a serving platter or in a large glass storage container that can be sealed.

To make the glaze:

1. In a small saucepan, bring the balsamic to a simmer. Simmer for 15 minutes or until syrupy. Set aside to cool and thicken.
2. Whisk olive oil, garlic, Italian seasoning, and cooled vinegar in a small bowl.
3. Drizzle the olive oil and balsamic glaze over the skewers. Serve immediately or keep in the refrigerator for a tasty snack.

Ingredient tip: If you do not have mozzarella balls, you can use string cheese—cut each piece into sixths.

Nutrition: Calories: 39 kcal; **Total Fat:** 3 g; **Protein:** 1 g; **Carbohydrate:** 3 g; **Fiber:** 0 g; **Sugar:** 0 g; **Sodium:** 11 mg

195. Kale, Butternut Squash, and Sausage Pasta

Preparation Time: 35 minutes
Cooking Time: 25 minutes; **Servings:** 2–3
Ingredients:

- 6 links Italian sausage, spicy or sweet
- 4 cups kale, roughly chopped
- 1 cup butternut squash, diced
- 3 garlic cloves, grated
- ¼ cup parsley, minced
- 1 lb whole wheat pasta (orecchiette)
- ½ cup Parmigiano-Reggiano, grated
- ¼ cup olive oil, divided
- Salt and pepper, to taste

Directions:

1. Preheat the oven to 400°F.
2. Line a baking sheet with foil. Coat butternut squash with olive oil, salt, and pepper. Arrange onto a single layer on the baking sheet. Roast until golden brown, about 25-30 minutes. Toss once, halfway through.
3. Preparation timer orecchiette pasta according to package directions. Set aside 1 cup of cooked pasta liquid. Set cooked pasta aside.
4. In a deep pan over medium-high heat, heat 1 tablespoon of olive oil. Remove sausage from casings and add to the pan. Begin browning the meat.
5. Add grated garlic when the sausage is halfway cooked. Continue cooking time until thoroughly cooked, about 7-9 minutes. Deglaze pan with cooked pasta liquid.
6. Stir kale, 2 tablespoons of olive oil, salt, and pepper into the sausage pan. Wait 2–3 minutes until kale is bright green.
7. Toss in cooked pasta, roasted butternut squash, parsley, and Parmigiano-Reggiano.
8. Topped with Parmigiano-Reggiano and parsley as preferred.

Nutrition: Calories: 384 kcal; **Carbohydrate:** 53.2 g; **Protein:** 24 g; **Fat:** 12.2 g; **Saturated Fat:** 3.9 g; **Cholesterol:** 54 mg; **Sodium:** 820 mg; **Fiber:** 7.9 g

196. Lemon Juice Salmon with Quinoa

Preparation Time: 10 minutes
Cooking Time: 15 minutes; **Servings:** 2–3
Ingredients: 1 lemon

- 2 8-oz. salmon fillets, boneless
- 14 cherry tomatoes, halved
- 10 white button mushrooms, thinly sliced
- 8-10 asparagus spears
- 2 tbsp. dill, roughly chopped
- 2 garlic cloves, minced
- 2 tsp. olive oil
- 2 tsp. capers (optional)

Directions:

1. Preheat the oven to 350°F.
2. On a large piece of parchment paper, layer minced garlic.
3. Place a layer of asparagus on top of garlic.
4. Arrange a salmon fillet on top of the asparagus.
5. Place the mushrooms and cherry tomatoes around the salmon.
6. Drizzle with lemon juice and olive oil. Season with salt, pepper, dill, and capers.
7. Fold paper up above the ingredients, careful to maintain the layered arrangement.
8. Tightly seal by folding the edges several times.
9. Bake for 20–25 minutes, or until salmon is flaky. Serve with rice, pasta, or quinoa.

Nutrition: Calories: 302 kcal; **Carbohydrate:** 2.2 g; **Protein:** 30.4 g; **Fat:** 18.9 g; **Saturated Fat:** 3 g; **Cholesterol:** 88 mg; **Sodium:** 634 mg

197. Asian Peanut Cabbage Slaw

Preparation Time: 10 minutes
Cooking Time: 10 minutes; **Servings:** 2–3
Ingredients:

- 1 (14-oz.) package coleslaw
- 1 red bell pepper, thinly sliced
- 1 large carrot, grated
- ¼ cup scallions, diced
- ¼ cup fresh cilantro, chopped
- ¼ cup peanuts, chopped
- ⅓ cup spicy peanut dressing, plus more if desired

Directions:

1. In a large bowl, combine coleslaw, bell pepper, carrot, scallions, cilantro, and peanuts. Toss with the dressing, add more as desired, and serve.

Ingredient tip: powdered peanut butter is made by dehydrating peanuts and grinding them into a powder. It reduces fat content but preserves protein and flavor. Use powdered peanut butter in any recipe that calls for traditional

peanut butter, and you'll achieve the same great flavor. You can find powdered peanut butter in your local grocery store with nut butter.
Nutrition: Cal: 123 kcal; **Total Fat:** 6 g; **Protein:** 6 g; **Carbohydrate:** 16 g; **Fiber:** 6 g; **Sugar:** 6 g; **Sod:** 198 mg

198. Cinnamon Fried Bananas

Preparation Time: 7 minutes
Cooking Time: 5 minutes; **Servings:** 2–3
Ingredients:

- 1 cup panko breadcrumbs
- 1 tbsp. cinnamon
- ½ cups almond flour
- 2 Egg whites
- 3 Ripe bananas
- 2 tbsp. coconut oil

Directions:

1. Heat coconut oil and add breadcrumbs, then mix around 3 minutes until golden and pour into a bowl.
2. Peel and cut bananas in half.
3. Roll half of each banana into flour, eggs, and crumb mixture.
4. Place into the Smart Air Fryer Oven. Cook 10 minutes at 280°F.

Nutrition: Calories: 221 kcal; **Fat:** 9 g; **Carbs:** 5 g; **Protein:** 4 g

199. Spinach and Artichoke Dip

Preparation Time: 10 minutes
Cooking Time: 5 minutes; **Servings:** 2–3
Ingredients:

- 10 oz. baby spinach
- 14 oz. artichokes, frozen
- 8 oz. light cream cheese
- ½ cup onion, finely chopped
- ½ cup Parmesan cheese

Ingredients from the kitchen store:

- 1 tbsp. lemon juice
- 3 garlic cloves, finely grated
- ½ tsp. red pepper flakes
- ½ tsp. oregano
- ½ tsp. pepper ground
- ¼ tsp. salt

Directions:

1. Wash, dry, and steam baby spinach.
2. In a medium-size nonstick saucepan, pour cooking oil and sauté onion and garlic for 5 minutes on low-medium heat for about 5 minutes.
3. In a food processor, put the spinach and chop.
4. Now add artichokes and blend them for a few moments.
5. Transfer the blended artichokes and spinach into a medium-size bowl.
6. Add oregano, lemon juice, red pepper, and cream cheese and stir well.
7. Cook it at low-medium temperature until it starts bubbling.
8. Now add salt, Parmesan cheese, and pepper.
9. Serve fresh

Nutrition: Calories: 122 kcal; **Fat:** 4 g; **Carbs:** 18 g; **Protein:** 12 g; **Sodium:** 280 g

200. Slow Cooker Boston Beans

Preparation Time: 5 minutes
Cooking Time: 15 minutes; **Servings:** 2–3
Ingredients:

- 1 lb. white northern beans, dry.
- 1 cup onion, finely chopped
- 2 slices turkey bacon, chopped
- 1 cup dark molasses
- 2 tbsp. ketchup
- ¼ cup brown sugar
- 1 tbsp. mustard
- ½ tsp. salt
- ½ tsp. black pepper
- 3 cups water

Directions:

1. In a medium bowl, soak the beans. Drain the beans and keep them aside.
2. Put all the ingredients in a slow cooker. Set the timer for 30 minutes and start cooking. Serve hot.

Nutrition: Calories: 134 kcal; **Fat:** 6; **Carbs:** 12 g; **Protein:** 8 g; **Sodium:** 234 g

201. Low Cholesterol: Scalloped Potatoes

Preparation Time: 10 minutes
Cooking Time: 35 minutes; **Servings:** 2–3
Ingredients:

- 4 cups potatoes
- ½ cup onion, coarsely chopped
- 1 tbsp. parsley chopped
- 1 ½ cup skim milk
- 3 tbsp. low cholesterol margarine
- ¼ tsp. pepper, ground
- ½ tsp. salt
- 3 tbsp. whole grain flour

Directions:

1. Wash, clean potatoes, and finely slice the potatoes.
2. Stack the potatoes and onion layer by layer in a casserole.

3. Drizzle flour between onion and potatoes.
4. Pour milk into a medium bowl, add parsley, pepper, and salt, and bring to low-medium heat. Once the milk becomes hot, pour it over the potato-onion layer.
5. Cover the casserole and bake it for 1 hour at 350°F. Remove the cover and bake it for another 3 minutes.

Nutrition: Calories: 184 kcal; **Fat:** 6 g; **Carbs:** 32 g; **Protein:** 6 g; **Sodium:** 324 g

202. Green Beans Greek Style

Preparation Time: 5 minutes
Cooking Time: 8 minutes; **Servings:** 2–3
Ingredients:

- 1 cup tomato bouillon soup
- 2 cups green beans
- 8 oz. water
- 1 tsp. onion powder
- 1 tsp. oregano
- 1 tsp. garlic powder
- A parsley dash

Directions:

1. In a large saucepan, pour water.
2. Add tomato soup into the water.
3. Now add all the ingredients into the saucepan.
4. Cover the pan and cook for about 15 minutes until the beans become tender.
5. Serve hot as a side dish.

Nutrition: Calories: 134 kcal; **Fat:** 2 g; **Carbs:** 32 g; **Protein:** 12 g; **Sodium:** 309 g

203. Marinated Mushrooms

Preparation Time: 10 minutes
Cooking Time: 15 minutes; **Servings:** 2–3
Ingredients:

- 1 cup beef soup
- 1 tsp. parsley flakes
- 1 lb. mushrooms

Ingredients from kitchen store:

- 1 tsp. onion powder
- 8 oz. water
- 1 tsp. garlic powder
- ¼ tsp. salt

Directions:

1. In a medium bowl, dissolve the beef soup in water
2. Put all the remaining ingredients in the soup and water mix. Cover it and boil in low-medium heat for at least 2 hours.

Nutrition: Calories: 186 kcal; **Fat:** 2 g; **Carbs:** 31 g; **Protein:** 8 g; **Sodium:** 155 g

204. Mock Mashed Potatoes

Preparation Time: 5 minutes
Cooking Time: 18 minutes; **Servings:** 2–3
Ingredients:

- 1 cup tomato chicken soup
- 4 oz. cauliflower, frozen
- ¼ tsp. salt
- 6 cup water

Directions:

1. Cook cauliflower for about 15 minutes in a small saucepan by adding the salt until it becomes soft.
2. Drain excess water after cooking.
3. Mash the cooked cauliflower. Add the chicken soup to the masked cauliflower and heat the mix for 2 minutes. Serve hot.

Nutrition: Calories: 165 kcal; **Fat:** 3 g; **Carbs:** 33 g; **Protein:** 12 g; **Sodium:** 318 g

205. No Dish Summer Medley

Preparation Time: 10 minutes
Cooking Time: 10 minutes; **Servings:** 2–3
Ingredients:

- 2 cup chicken soup
- ½ cup celery, sliced
- ½ cup yellow summer squash
- ½ cup mushrooms, chopped
- ¼ tsp. salt
- ¼ tsp. black pepper powder

Directions:

1. In a medium saucepan, mix all the ingredients except the chicken soup.
2. Now pour the chicken soup over it.
3. Add salt and pepper.
4. Cover and cook for 20 minutes until it starts to boil

Nutrition: Calories: 212 kcal; **Fat:** 4 g; **Carbs:** 18 g; **Protein:** 8 g; **Sodium:** 234 g

206. Puréed Classic Egg Salad

Preparation Time: 5 minutes
Cooking Time: 2 minutes; **Servings:** 2–3
Ingredients:

- 2 eggs, hard-boiled
- 1 tbsp. low-fat mayonnaise
- 1 tbsp. Greek yogurt, plain

Directions:

1. Cut the boiled eggs into even portions.
2. Put the slices of eggs into a food mixer and chop.
3. Add salt, mayonnaise, and Greek yogurt as the seasonings to the eggs.
4. Mix finely as far as the egg salad becomes smooth.

Nutrition: Calories: 134 kcal; **Fat:** 2 g; **Carbs:** 12 g; **Protein:** 6 g; **Sodium:** 320 g

207. Maple-Mashed Sweet Potatoes

Preparation Time: 5 minutes
Cooking Time: 5 minutes; **Servings:** 2–3
Ingredients:

- 1 lb. sweet potatoes
- 1 cup carrots, thinly sliced
- 2 tbsp. maple syrup
- ¼ tsp. nutmeg
- ¼ tsp. pepper, fresh ground
- 4 cup water

Directions:

1. Wash and clean sweet potatoes.
2. Peel and cut into small chunks.
3. In a large bowl, pour water and bring to boil.
4. Put carrots and sweet potatoes into it.
5. Reduce heat and continue cooking for about 10 minutes until the carrots and sweet potatoes become soft.
6. Drain the vegetables using a colander and put them into a bowl.
7. Mas the vegetables until it becomes smooth.
8. Sprinkle ground pepper and nutmeg into it and stir.
9. Drizzle maple syrup over it, and stir.

Nutrition: Calories: 212 kcal; **Fat:** 4 g; **Carbs:** 18 g; **Protein:** 6 g; **Sodium:** 176 g

208. Garlic-Parmesan Cheesy Chips

Preparation Time: 2 minutes + 20 minutes to cool
Cooking Time: 7 minutes; **Servings:** 2–3
Ingredients:

- ¼ cup Parmesan cheese, shredded
- ¼ cup sharp Cheddar cheese, shredded
- ¼ tsp. garlic powder
- Dash salt

Directions:

1. Preheat the oven to 400°F. Line a large baking sheet with parchment paper.
2. In a medium mixing bowl, combine the Parmesan cheese, Cheddar cheese, garlic powder, and salt. Mix well.
3. Place 2 teaspoons of the cheese mixture about an inch or 2 on the baking sheet, making about 12 chips.
4. Bake for 5 to 7 minutes, or until the chips are golden brown around the edges.
5. Remove from the oven and let sit for 15 to 20 minutes, or until the chips start to crisp. Enjoy.

Nutrition: Per Serving (6 Chips): Calories: 98 kcal; **Protein:** 8 g; **Fat:** 7 g; **Carbohydrate:** 1 g; **Fiber:** 0 g; **Sugar:** 0 g; **Sodium:** 333 mg

209. Cheesy Baked Radish Chips

Preparation Time: 5 minutes
Cooking Time: 35 minutes; **Servings:** 2–3
Ingredients:

- 1 cup radishes, thinly sliced (2 bunches radishes)
- 1 tbsp. extra-virgin olive oil
- 3 tbsp. nutritional yeast flakes
- ¼ tsp. salt
- Dash black pepper, freshly ground (optional)

Directions:

1. Preheat the oven to 375°F. Line a baking sheet with parchment paper.
2. Place the radishes into a small bowl and toss in the oil.
3. In a small cup, mix the nutritional yeast, salt, and pepper (if using).
4. Place the oil-coated radish slices onto the prepared baking sheet in a single layer and lightly sprinkle the nutritional yeast mixture onto each slice.
5. Bake for about 15 minutes, flip the chips and bake for another 15 minutes. Remove crispy chips, then continue to bake any remaining chips for a few more minutes until crispy and golden brown.
6. Serve and enjoy alone or with your favorite low-carbohydrate dip.

Nutrition: Per Serving (½ Cup Chips): Calories: 99 kcal; **Protein:** 5 g; **Fat:** 7 g; **Carbohydrate:** 4 g; **Fiber:** 2 g; **Sugar:** 0 g; **Sodium:** 313 mg

210. Savory Cheese Biscuits

Preparation Time: 5 minutes
Cooking Time: 8 minutes; **Servings:** 2–3
Ingredients:

- 1 cup almond flour
- ¼ cup Parmesan cheese, shredded
- ¼ cup Cheddar cheese, shredded
- 2 tsp. baking powder
- 2 tsp. garlic powder
- ½ tsp. salt
- 2 large eggs

Directions:

1. Preheat the oven to 350°F. Line a large baking sheet with parchment paper and set aside.
2. Add the almond flour, Parmesan cheese, Cheddar cheese, baking powder, garlic powder, and salt to a large bowl. Mix well. Add the eggs and combine.
3. Scoop a heaping tablespoon of the mixture onto the baking sheet. Using a spatula, flatten the batter

slightly into about 2-inch circles. Repeat, placing biscuits about an inch apart. It should yield 8 small biscuits.

4. Bake for 15 minutes or until the top of the biscuits is slightly golden brown. Serve warm.

Nutrition: Per Serving (2 Biscuits): Calories: 275 kcal; **Protein:** 15 g; **Fat:** 23 g; **Carbohydrate:** 8 g; **Fiber:** 3 g; **Sugar:** 1 g; **Sodium:** 447 mg

211. Italian Herb Muffins

Preparation Time: 5 minutes
Cooking Time: 12 minutes ; **Servings:** 2–3
Ingredients:

- Nonstick cooking spray
- 8 tbsp. almond flour
- ¼ cup Parmesan cheese, shredded
- 1 large egg
- 1 tsp. garlic powder
- 1 tsp. Italian seasoning
- 1 tsp. baking powder
- ¼ tsp. salt

Directions:

1. Preheat the oven to 350°F. Line a muffin pan with 4 cupcake liners and spray the liners with nonstick cooking spray.
2. In a large mixing bowl, combine the almond flour, Parmesan cheese, egg, garlic powder, Italian seasoning, baking powder, and salt. Mix well until fully incorporated.
3. Scoop a heaping tablespoon of the mixture into the lined cups until all the batter is used.
4. Bake for 12 minutes or until golden brown on the tops. Enjoy warm.

Nutrition: Per Serving (1 Muffin): Calories: 128 kcal; **Protein:** 7 g; **Fat:** 10 g; **Carbohydrate:** 5 g; **Fiber:** 2 g; **Sugar:** 1 g; **Sodium:** 217 mg

212. Cheesy Cauliflower Tots

Preparation Time: 5 minutes
Cooking Time: 8 minutes
Servings: 2–3
Ingredients:

- 1 cup cauliflower rice
- ½ cup almond flour
- ½ cup mozzarella cheese, shredded
- 1 large egg
- 1 tbsp. cornstarch
- ¼ tsp. salt

Directions:

1. Preheat the oven to 400°F. Line a large baking sheet with parchment paper and set aside.
2. In a large mixing bowl, combine the cauliflower rice, almond flour, mozzarella cheese, egg, cornstarch, and salt. Mix well until fully incorporated.
3. Scoop a heaping tablespoon of the mixture onto the baking sheet about an inch apart until all the batter is used.
4. Bake for 13 to 15 minutes, until crispy and golden brown. Serve and enjoy.

Nutrition: Per Serving (4 Tots): Calories: 152 kcal; **Protein:** 9 g; **Fat:** 11 g; **Carbohydrate:** 6 g; **Fiber:** 2 g; **Sugar:** 1 g; **Sodium:** 253 mg

213. Mozzarella Mushroom Caps

Preparation Time: 5 minutes
Cooking Time: 10 minutes; **Servings:** 4
Ingredients:

- 12 white mushroom caps
- 4 oz. fresh mozzarella pearls
- 2 tbsp. almond flour
- 1 tbsp. butter, whipped
- ½ tsp. garlic powder
- Dash salt

Directions:

1. Preheat the oven to 350°F. Line a baking sheet with parchment paper.
2. Wash the mushrooms and carefully remove the cap from each one. Place the mushrooms onto the lined baking sheet.
3. Place 3 mozzarella pearls (about 1 tbsp.) in each mushroom cap.
4. Mix the almond flour, whipped butter, garlic powder, and salt in a small bowl. Sprinkle the mixture on top of each mushroom cap.
5. Bake for about 20 minutes or until the cheese has melted. Enjoy warm.

Nutrition: Per Serving (3 Mushroom Caps): Calories: 117 kcal; **Protein:** 8 g; **Fat:** 9 g; **Carbohydrate:** 4 g; **Fiber:** 1 g; **Sugar:** 0.25 g; **Sodium:** 141 mg

214. Almond-Crusted Mozzarella Sticks

Preparation Time: 10 minutes + 2 hours to freeze
Cooking Time: 6 minutes
Servings: 2–3
Ingredients:

- 1 tbsp. cornstarch
- 8 tbsp. almond flour
- ½ tsp. Italian seasoning
- ¼ tsp. salt
- 2 large eggs
- 6 (1-oz.) light mozzarella sticks

- 1 tbsp. extra-virgin olive oil

Directions:

1. Place the cornstarch on a small plate. Mix the almond flour, Italian seasoning, and salt on a separate small plate. Beat the eggs in a small bowl and place them between the 2 plates.
2. Cut the mozzarella sticks in half. Lightly coat each mozzarella stick in cornstarch, dip, coat in the egg, and coat well in the almond flour mixture. Coat each mozzarella piece well with the batter to enclose the cheese in the mixture, so it doesn't spread onto the baking sheet while baking. Place each coated mozzarella piece on a large plate. Repeat until all the mozzarella pieces are coated.
3. Cover the plate with plastic wrap and place the mozzarella sticks in the freezer for about 2 hours.
4. Preheat the oven to 400°F. Line a baking sheet with parchment paper.
5. Place the mozzarella pieces about 1-inch apart on the baking sheet. Using a basting brush, coat each side of each mozzarella piece lightly with the oil.
6. Bake for 4 to 6 minutes until the cheese starts to bubble, and the crust turns slightly golden. Watch closely to make sure the cheese does not start to spread. Enjoy warm.

Nutrition: Calories: 182 kcal; **Protein:** 11 g; **Fat:** 15 g; **Carb:** 4 g; **Fiber:** 1 g; **Sugar:** 1 g; **Sodium:** 311 mg

215. Almond Light-as-Air Cookies

Preparation Time: 5 minutes
Cooking Time: 5 minutes; **Servings:** 2–3
Ingredients:

- 8 tbsp. almond flour
- 1 tbsp. low-sugar vanilla whey protein powder
- 1 tbsp. butter, whipped
- 2 tsp. vanilla extract
- 1 tsp. baking powder
- 1 tsp. pure cane sugar, finely granulated
- ½ tsp. stevia or no-calorie sweetener
- ¼ tsp. salt

Directions:

1. Preheat the oven to 350°F. Line a large baking sheet with parchment paper.
2. In a large bowl, combine the almond flour, protein powder, whipped butter, vanilla extract, baking powder, sugar, stevia, and salt and mix well until fully incorporated.
3. Scoop a heaping tablespoon of the mixture onto the baking sheet about an inch apart. Using a spatula, flatten the batter slightly into about 2-inch circles. It should yield 8 cookies.
4. Bake for 7 to 9 minutes, or until the edges of cookies are slightly golden brown. Keep a close eye on the cookies since as soon as this happens, and you will want to remove the cookies from the oven to prevent overcooking.
5. Allow the cookies to cool slightly before serving.

Nutrition: Per Serving (2 Cookies): Calories: 117 kcal; **Protein:** 6 g; **Fat:** 9 g; **Carbohydrate:** 5 g; **Fiber:** 2 g; **Sugar:** 2 g; **Sodium:** 288 mg

216. Strawberry Gelatin Tea

Preparation Time: 5 minutes
Cooking Time: 5 minutes
Servings: 1
Ingredients:

- ½ cup strawberries, frozen and sliced
- ¼ tsp. stevia or no-calorie sweetener
- ½ cup hot water
- 2 tbsp. plain gelatin powder

Directions:

1. In a small saucepan, cook the strawberries over medium heat for 3 minutes, stirring, until softened.
2. Stir in the stevia. Remove the pan from the heat and set it aside.
3. Pour the hot water into a mug. Mix in the gelatin powder a bit while continuously stirring with a fork. Keep stirring as you add in the cooked strawberries.
4. Blend the mixture in a blender for about 30 seconds until frothy.
5. Pour into a mug. Sip once cooled and enjoy as a tea within about 15 minutes or so before it starts to set.

Nutrition per serving (¾ cup or 12 tbsp.): Calories: 89 kcal; **Protein:** 12 g; **Fat:** 0 g; **Carbohydrate:** 10 g; **Fiber:** 2 g; **Sugar:** 5 g; **Sodium:** 47 mg

217. Subtly Sweet Coconut Milk "Flan"

Preparation Time: 5 minutes + 1 hour to chill
Cooking Time: 5 minutes
Servings: 1
Ingredients:

- ½ cup light coconut milk, unsweetened
- 2 tsp. vanilla extract
- 1 tsp. stevia or no-calorie sweetener
- 1 tbsp. (1 packet) plain gelatin powder

Directions:

1. In a small saucepan, heat the coconut milk for 1 to 2 minutes, then sprinkle in the vanilla extract and stevia and stir to dissolve.
2. Sprinkle in the gelatin while constantly stirring to dissolve the gelatin completely. Remove from the heat.
3. Transfer the mixture to a blender and blend for about 30 seconds or so until frothy. Pour into a small jar or mug.

4. Allow the dessert to set in the refrigerator for about an hour.
5. Serve and enjoy.

Nutrition: Calories: 130 kcal; **Protein:** 6 g; **Fat:** 7 g; **Carbohydrate:** 5 g; **Fiber:** 0 g; **Sugar:** 3 g; **Sodium:** 51 mg

218. Avocado Hummus

Preparation Time: 10 minutes
Cooking Time: 5 minutes
Servings: 2–3
Ingredients:

- ½ avocado, chopped
- 2 tbsp. olive oil
- ½ tsp. onion powder
- 1 tsp. tahini
- ½ tsp. garlic, minced
- 1 tbsp. lemon juice
- 1 cup edamame, frozen and thawed
- Pepper
- Salt

Directions:

1. Add all ingredients into the blender and blend until smooth.

Nutrition: Calories: 215 kcal; **Fat:** 17 g; **Carbohydrate:** 10 g; **Sugar:** 0.3 g; **Protein:** 9.1 g; **Cholesterol:** 0 mg

219. Beef Chop Salad

Preparation Time: 15 minutes
Cooking Time: 0 minutes
Servings: 2–3
Ingredients:

- 1 medium English cucumber, chopped (2 cups)
- 1 cup cherry tomatoes, halved
- 1 red bell pepper, seeded and diced
- ½ red onion, diced
- ½ cup pitted kalamata olives, roughly chopped
- 1 cup feta cheese, crumbled
- ½ cup balsamic dressing

Directions:

1. In a large bowl, toss the cucumber, tomatoes, bell pepper, onion, olives, and cheese with the dressing and servings.

Ingredient tip: Looking for a protein boost? Add diced chicken breast or chickpeas.

Nutrition: Calories: 173 kcal; **Total Fat:** 13 g; **Protein:** 4 g; **Carbohydrate:** 10 g; **Fiber:** 1 g; **Sugar:** 4 g; **Sodium:** 883 mg

220. Lush Roasted Vegetable Salad

Preparation Time: 15 minutes
Cooking Time: 30 minutes; **Servings:** 2–3
Ingredients:

- 1 small eggplant, diced
- 1 small zucchini, diced
- 1 small yellow summer squash, diced
- ½ cup grape tomatoes, halved
- 1 (15-oz./425-g) can chickpeas, drained and rinsed
- 3 tbsp. extra-virgin olive oil, divided
- ⅓ cup packaged quinoa
- 1 cup low-sodium vegetable or chicken broth
- 2 tbsp. lemon juice, freshly squeezed
- 1 tsp. fresh garlic, minced; or 1 garlic clove, minced
- 1 tbsp. basil, dried
- 1 tsp. oregano, dried

Directions:

1. Preheat the oven to 425°F (220°C). Line a baking sheet with parchment paper.
2. Spread the eggplant, zucchini, yellow squash, tomatoes, and chickpeas across the baking sheet and toss them with 1 tablespoon of olive oil.
3. Bake in the oven for 30 minutes, stirring once halfway through. The finished vegetables should be tender, and the tomatoes should be juicy. The chickpeas will be firm and crispy.
4. While the vegetables and chickpeas are roasting, place the quinoa and broth in a small saucepan over medium-high heat. Cover and bring to a boil. Reduce the heat to low and cook for about 15 minutes until all liquid has been absorbed. Remove the pan from the heat and fluff the quinoa with a fork.
5. Whisk together the lemon juice, garlic, and the remaining 2 tablespoons of olive oil in a small dish. Mix in the basil and oregano.
6. Combine the quinoa and roasted vegetables with chickpeas, and dress in a large bowl. Gently stir to combine. Serve and enjoy!

Nutrition: Calories: 200 kcal; **Total Carbs:** 27.0 g; **Protein:** 7.0 g; **Total Fat:** 9.0 g; **Sugar:** 4.0 g; **Fiber:** 8.0 g; **Sodium:** 160 mg

221. Seitan Bites

Prep Time: 15 minutes
Cooking Time: 15 minutes
Servings: 2–3
Ingredients:

- Nonstick cooking spray
- 1 large egg
- ½ cup flaxseed meal
- 1 ½ tbsp. garlic powder
- 1 ½ tbsp. onion powder
- 1 (8-oz./227 g) package seitan, cut into strips or small, 2-inch pieces
- ½ cup buffalo wing sauce

Directions:

1. Preheat the oven to 350°F (180°C). Coat a baking sheet with cooking spray.
2. In a medium bowl, whisk the egg.
3. Mix the flaxseed meal, garlic powder, and onion powder in another medium bowl.
4. Coat each seitan piece in egg, allowing the excess egg to drip off, then lightly coat with the dry mixture.
5. Gently transfer coated pieces to the prepared baking sheet. Bake for 12 to 15 minutes, or until crispy, flipping halfway through.
6. Transfer to a large bowl and coat with the buffalo wing sauce.
7. Serve immediately.

Nutrition: Calories: 87 kcal; **Total Carbs:** 5.0 g; **Protein:** 8.0 g; **Total Fat:** 4.0 g; **Sugar:** 0 g; **Fiber:** 2.0 g; **Sodium:** 517 mg

222. Sloppy Joes in Lettuce

Preparation Time: 5 minutes
Cooking Time: 35 minutes
Servings: 2–3
Ingredients:

- 2 cups vegetable broth
- 1 cup green lentils, well rinsed
- 1 tbsp. extra-virgin olive oil
- ½ medium yellow onion, minced
- ½ green bell pepper, minced
- 2 garlic cloves, minced
- 1 (15-oz./425-g) can tomato sauce
- 1 to 2 tbsp. sugar substitute
- 1 tbsp. Worcestershire sauce
- 2 tsp. chili powder
- 1 tsp. cumin, ground
- 1 tsp. paprika
- Lettuce leaves and sliced jalapeños, and red onion, for serving

Directions:

1. In a small saucepan over medium-high heat, combine the broth and lentils. Bring to a boil, then reduce to a simmer and cook uncovered for about 18 minutes, or until tender. Drain any excess liquid.
2. In a large skillet over medium heat, heat the oil. Add the onion, bell pepper, and garlic, and cook for 4 to 5 minutes, until tender and the onions are slightly brown.
3. Add the tomato sauce, sugar substitute, Worcestershire, chili powder, cumin, paprika, and lentils. Stir to combine.
4. Continue cooking for 5 to 10 minutes over medium heat, until warmed through and thickened.
5. Refrigerate leftovers in an airtight container. Reheat in the microwave or stovetop, adding extra water or broth if needed to soften.
6. Serve in lettuce leaves with sliced jalapeños and red onion.

Nutrition: Calories: 163 kcal; **Total Carbs:** 26.0 g; **Protein:** 10.0 g; **Total Fat:** 3.0 g; **Sugar:** 6.0 g; **Fiber:** 11.0 g; **Sodium:** 525 mg

223. Spaghetti Squash Noodles

Preparation Time: 10 minutes
Cooking Time: 25 minutes
Servings: 2–3
Ingredients:

- 1 small (3- to 4-lb./1.4- to 1.8-kg) spaghetti squash
- ¼ cup low-sodium soy sauce
- 3 garlic cloves, minced
- 1 tbsp. oyster sauce
- 1-inch ginger root, peeled and minced
- 2 tbsp. extra-virgin olive oil
- 1 small white onion, diced
- 3 celery stalks, thinly sliced
- 2 cups cabbage, shredded
- Nonstick cooking spray

Directions:

1. Preheat the oven to 350°F (180°C). Coat a baking sheet with cooking spray.
2. Halve the spaghetti squash, remove and discard the seeds, and place the halves cut-side down on the prepared baking sheet. Bake for 30 to 45 minutes or until the flesh is tender and can be scraped with a fork.
3. Remove from the oven, and let cool. Scrape out the flesh with a fork, creating small noodles. Set aside.
4. Whisk together the soy sauce, garlic, oyster sauce, and ginger in a small bowl.
5. In a large skillet over medium heat, heat the oil. Add the onion and celery and cook, stirring, until tender, 3 to 4 minutes.
6. Add the cabbage and cook, stirring, until heated through, 1 to 2 minutes.
7. Add the spaghetti squash and sauce mixture. Continue cooking for another 2 minutes.

Nutrition: Calories: 252 kcal; **Total Carbs:** 39.0 g; **Protein:** 6.0 g; **Total Fat:** 11.0 g; **Sugar:** 15.0 g; **Fiber:** 9.0 g; **Sodium:** 950 mg

224. Super Veg Chili

Preparation Time: 10 minutes
Cooking Time: 40 minutes
Servings: 3–4
Ingredients:

- 1 tbsp. extra-virgin olive oil
- 1 cup yellow onion, chopped
- 1 cup tomatoes, canned and diced
- ½ cup edamame, shelled
- 1 tsp. cilantro, dried
- 1 tsp. chili powder
- 1 tsp. cumin, ground
- ¼ tsp. salt
- 1 cup soy protein crumbles, meatless
- 1 cup water
- 8 tbsp. Cheddar cheese, shredded

Directions:

1. In a medium saucepan, heat the oil over medium heat. Cook the onion for 5 to 7 minutes, frequently stirring, until it is translucent.
2. Add the tomatoes and their juices, edamame, cilantro, chili powder, cumin, and salt. Cook for about 10 min.
3. Add the soy protein crumbles and water to the pan and cook for another 10 minutes.
4. Simmer the chili for at least 5 to 10 minutes until the chili thickens.
5. Remove from the heat and top the chili with Cheddar cheese to serve.

Nutrition: Calories: 134 kcal; **Total Carbs:** 9.0 g; **Protein:** 10.0 g; **Total Fat:** 7.0 g; **Sugar:** 3.0 g; **Fiber:** 3.0 g; **Sodium:** 351 mg

225. Tempeh and Avocado Lettuce Wraps

Preparation Time: 10 minutes
Cooking Time: 30 minutes
Servings: 2–3
Ingredients:

- 1 (8-oz./227-g) package bacon-flavored tempeh
- ¼ cup low-sodium soy sauce
- ¼ cup apple cider vinegar
- 1 tsp. sugar substitute
- ¼ tsp. cumin, ground
- 1 ½ tsp. liquid smoke
- 4 Romaine lettuce leaves
- 2 tsp. mayonnaise
- 4 tomato slices
- ½ avocado, quartered

Directions:

1. Preheat the oven to 350°F (180°C). Line a baking sheet with parchment paper.
2. Slice the tempeh lengthwise into quarter-inch slices. You will get about 12 slices per package. It is easiest to cut the tempeh loaf in half lengthwise. Then cut each half into thirds, and then each third in half to make 12 slices.
3. To make the marinade, combine the soy sauce, vinegar, sugar substitute, cumin, and liquid smoke in a medium bowl. Whisk well.
4. Put the tempeh in a dish, and cover with marinade. Cover and chill overnight, or at least for one hour.
5. Put the marinated tempeh strips on the prepared baking sheet.
6. Bake for 15 minutes, or until lightly brown and crispy. Flip and bake for another 15 minutes.
7. Serve 2 strips of tempeh in each lettuce leaf with mayo, a tomato slice, and an avocado quarter.

Nutrition: Calories: 129 kcal; **Total Carbs:** 10.0 g; **Protein:** 7.0 g; **Total Fat:** 7.0 g; **Sugar:** 2.0 g; **Fiber:** 4.0 g; **Sodium:** 888 mg

226. Seven-Layer Mexican Salad

Preparation Time: 20 minutes
Cooking Time: 30 minutes; **Servings:** 2–3
Ingredients:
Dressing:

- ¼ tsp. garlic salt
- ½ tsp. cumin
- 1 tbsp. olive oil
- 2 limes lime juice
- ½ Jalapeño
- ¼ cup cilantro
- Avocado

Salad:

- 2 green onions, chopped
- 1 cup low-fat Cheddar cheese, shredded
- Bell pepper, diced
- 1 can of corn, drained
- 1 can of black beans, drained and rinsed
- 1 cup tomatoes, diced
- 2 cups Romaine lettuce, chopped
- Box Jiffy cornbread

Directions:
Dressing:

1. Place all of the ingredients for the dressing in your blender and pulse them until the cilantro is well blended into the avocado and lime juice.

Salad:

1. First, preparation time the cornbread according to the directions on the box.
2. Once it has cooked through, set it aside and allow it to cool completely.
3. Once it is cooled, cut the cornbread in half and then break half of it up into little crumbs.
4. Put the crumbled cornbread into the bottom of your dish.
5. Using a trifle dish is best because you will be able to see all of the beautiful layers. You can use any bowl that you want if you don't have a trifle dish.
6. Place half of the Romaine lettuce on top of the crumbled cornbread. Make sure you evenly spread it across. It is your second layer.
7. Top the lettuce with half of the black beans, ensuring they are evenly distributed.
8. Add half of the corn evenly on top of the beans.
9. Top the corn with half of the chopped bell peppers.
10. Add half of the tomatoes to the bell peppers, ensuring they are evenly distributed.
11. Sprinkle half of the Cheddar cheese on top of the tomatoes.
12. Now drizzle on half of the salad dressing that you made earlier.
13. Repeat this process, starting with the lettuce through the dressing.
14. To finish the recipe, top everything with the green onions and enjoy.
15. You can reserve the rest of the cornbread for another meal, or you can make another salad. The choice is yours.

Nutrition: Calories: 148 kcal; **Fat:** 8.4 g; **Protein:** 4 g; **Carb:** 16.8 g

227. Asparagus Salad

Preparation Time: 5 minutes
Cooking Time: 5 minutes
Servings: 2–3
Ingredients:

- 1 cup baby arugula
- 1 bunch asparagus; trimmed
- 1 tbsp. balsamic vinegar
- 1 tbsp. Cheddar cheese, grated
- A pinch salt and black pepper
- Cooking spray

Directions:

1. Put the asparagus in your air fryer's basket, grease with cooking spray, season with salt and pepper, and cook at 360°F for 10 minutes.
2. Take a bowl and mix the asparagus with the arugula and the vinegar, toss, divide between plates and serve hot with cheese sprinkled on top

Nutrition: Calories: 200 kcal; **Fat:** 5 g; **Fiber:** 1 g; **Carbs:** 4 g; **Protein:** 5 g

228. Mushrooms and Cheese Spread

Preparation Time: 5 minutes
Cooking Time: 10 minutes
Servings: 2–3
Ingredients:

- ¼ cup mozzarella; shredded
- ½ cup coconut cream
- 1 cup white mushrooms
- A pinch salt and black pepper
- Cooking spray

Directions:

1. Put the mushrooms in your air fryer's basket, grease with cooking spray, and cook at 370°F for 20 minutes.
2. Transfer to a blender, add the remaining ingredients, pulse well, divide into bowls and serve as a spread

Nutrition: Calories: 202 kcal; **Fat:** 12 g; **Fiber:** 2 g; **Carbs:** 5 g; **Protein:** 7 g

229. Zoodles with "Meat" Sauce

Preparation Time: 5 minutes
Cooking Time: 30 minutes
Servings: 2–3
Ingredients:
For the Zoodles:

- 1 tbsp. extra-virgin olive oil
- 2 medium zucchinis, peeled and spiralized

For the "Meat" Sauce:

- 1 tbsp. extra-virgin olive oil
- 1 cup soy protein crumbles
- 1 cup yellow onion, diced
- 2 cups tomato, chopped
- 2 tsp. garlic powder
- 2 tsp. Italian seasoning
- ¼ tsp. salt
- 1 cup mozzarella cheese, shredded

Directions:
To make the zoodles:

1. In a large skillet, heat the oil over medium heat.
2. Put the zucchini in the skillet and cook, stirring every 30 seconds or so, for 4 to 6 minutes, until softened. Remove from the heat and place the zucchini in a serving bowl.

To make the "meat" sauce:

1. In the same skillet, heat the oil over medium. Add the soy protein crumbles and cook for 5 to 7 minutes. Add the onion and cook for 5 to 7 minutes, stirring frequently, or until translucent.
2. Add the tomato, garlic powder, Italian seasoning, and salt, and mix well. Reduce the heat to medium-low and simmer for 7 to 10 minutes, stirring regularly, until the sauce thickens.
3. Remove from the heat and pour the sauce over the zoodles. Top with Mozzarella cheese before serving.

Nutrition: Calories: 217 kcal; **Total Carbs:** 11.0 g; **Protein:** 15.0 g; **Total Fat:** 13.0 g; **Sugar:** 4.0 g; **Fiber:** 4.0 g; **Sodium:** 435 mg

230. Tempeh, Mushroom, and Broccoli Bowl

Preparation Time: 5 minutes
Cooking Time: 20 minutes
Servings: 2–3
Ingredients:

- 8 oz. (227 g) tempeh
- ½ cup water
- 4 oz. (113 g) Portobello mushroom, sliced in strips (1 to 2 mushrooms)
- 2 cups broccoli florets, chopped
- ½ cup vegetable broth
- 1 tbsp. extra-virgin olive oil
- ¼ tsp. cilantro, dried
- ¼ tsp. cumin, ground
- ⅛ tsp. salt

Directions:

1. In a small skillet, cook the tempeh and water over medium heat for 8 to 10 minutes to soften. Remove from the skillet and set aside. Discard the water.
2. While the tempeh cooks, in a large skillet, combine the mushrooms, broccoli, and broth over medium heat. Cover and steam the vegetables for 8 to 10 minutes, until tender.
3. Once the broth has mostly evaporated, add the tempeh and oil. Mash the tempeh into small morsels and stir the vegetables and tempeh frequently while cooking for 10 minutes. Add the cilantro, cumin, and salt. Stir well and serve warm.

Nutrition: Calories: 114 kcal; **Total Carbs:** 8.0 g; **Protein:** 9.0 g; **Total Fat:** 6.0 g; **Sugar:** 1.0 g; **Fiber:** 3.0 g; **Sodium:** 154 mg

231. Zucchini Squash Mix

Preparation Time: 10 minutes
Cooking Time: 35 minutes
Servings: 2–3
Ingredients:

- 1 lb. zucchini, sliced
- 1 tbsp. parsley, chopped
- 1 yellow squash, halved, deseeded, and chopped
- 1 tbsp. olive oil

- Pepper
- Salt

Directions:

1. Add all ingredients into the large bowl and mix well.
2. Transfer bowl mixture into the air fryer basket and cook at 400°F for 35 minutes.
3. Serve and enjoy.

Nutrition: Calories: 49 kcal; **Fat:** 3 g; **Carbohydrate:** 4 g; **Sugar:** 2 g; **Protein:** 1.5 g; **Cholesterol:** 0 mg

232. Tomatoes with Basil and Garlic

Preparation Time: 10 minutes
Cooking Time: 14 minutes
Servings: 2–3
Ingredients:

- 1 bunch basil, chopped
- 3 garlic cloves, minced
- A drizzle olive oil
- Salt and black pepper to the taste
- 2 cups cherry tomatoes, halved

Directions:

1. In a pan that fits your air fryer, combine tomatoes with garlic, salt, pepper, basil, and oil, toss, introduce it to your air fryer and cook at 320°F for 12 minutes.
2. Divide between plates and serve as a side dish.

Nutrition: Calories: 140 kcal; **Fat:** 1 g; **Fiber:** 1 g; **Carbs:** 2 g; **Protein:** 10 g

233. Potatoes with Green Beans

Preparation Time: 10 minutes
Cooking Time: 8 minutes
Servings: 2–3
Ingredients:

- 1 lb. red potatoes, cut into wedges
- 1 lb. green beans
- 2 garlic cloves, minced
- 2 tbsp. olive oil
- Salt and black pepper to the taste
- ½ tsp. oregano, dried

Directions:

1. In a pan that fits your air fryer, combine potatoes with green beans, garlic, oil, salt, pepper, and oregano, toss, introduce it to your air fryer and cook at 380°F for 15 minutes.
2. Divide between plates and serve as a side dish.

Nutrition: Calories: 201 kcal; **Fat:** 6 g; **Fiber:** 4 g; **Carbs:** 8 g; **Protein:** 5 g

234. Herbed Tomatoes with Jalapeño

Preparation Time: 10 minutes
Cooking Time: 8 minutes
Servings: 2–3
Ingredients:

- 1 Jalapeño pepper, chopped
- 4 garlic cloves, minced
- 2 lb. cherry tomatoes, halved
- Salt and black pepper to the taste
- ¼ cup olive oil
- ½ tsp. oregano, dried
- ¼ cup basil, chopped

Directions:

1. In a bowl, mix tomatoes with garlic, Jalapeño, salt, pepper, oregano, and the oil, toss to coat, transfer them to your air fryer and cook at 380°F for 15 minutes.
2. Divide fried tomatoes between plates, sprinkle basil on top, and serve as a side dish.

Nutrition: Calories: 140 kcal; **Fat:** 2 g; **Fiber:** 2 g; **Carbs:** 6 g; **Protein:** 8 g

235. Mushrooms with Veggies and Avocado

Preparation Time: 30 minutes
Cooking Time: 8 minutes
Servings: 2–3
Ingredients:

- 10 oz. mushrooms, halved
- 1 broccoli head, florets separated
- 1 garlic clove, minced
- 1 tbsp. balsamic vinegar
- 1 yellow onion, chopped
- 1 tbsp. olive oil
- Salt and black pepper
- 1 tsp. basil, dried
- 1 avocado, peeled, pitted and roughly cubed
- A pinch of red pepper flakes

Directions:

1. Mix mushrooms with broccoli, onion, garlic, and avocado in a bowl.
2. Mix vinegar, oil, salt, pepper, and basil in another bowl and whisk well.
3. Pour this over veggie, toss to coat, leave aside for 30 minutes, transfer to your air fryer's basket and cook at 350°F for 8 minutes,
4. Divide between plates and serve with pepper flakes on top as a side dish.

Nutrition: Calories: 182 kcal; **Fat:** 3 g; **Fiber:** 3 g; **Carbs:** 5 g; **Protein:** 8 g

236. Soft Tofu with Veggies

Preparation Time: 10 minutes
Cooking Time: 14 minutes
Servings: 2–3
Ingredients:

- 1 broccoli head, florets separated and steamed
- 1 tomato, chopped
- 3 carrots, chopped and steamed
- 2 oz. soft tofu, crumbled
- 1 tsp. parsley, chopped
- 1 tsp. thyme, chopped
- Salt and black pepper to the taste

Directions:

1. In a pan that fits your air fryer, combine broccoli with tomato, carrots, thyme, parsley, salt, and pepper, toss, introduce the fryer and cook at 350°F for 10 minutes.
2. Add tofu, toss, introduce it in the fryer for 4 minutes more, divide between plates and serve as a side dish.

Nutrition: Calories: 174 kcal; **Fat:** 4 g, **Fiber:** 7 g, **Carbs:** 12 g, **Protein:** 3 g

237. Lemony Baby Potatoes

Preparation Time: 10 minutes
Cooking Time: 25 minutes
Servings: 2–3
Ingredients:

- 2 tbsp. olive oil
- 2 springs rosemary, chopped
- 2 tbsp. parsley, chopped
- 2 tbsp. oregano, chopped
- Salt and black pepper to the taste
- 1 tbsp. lemon rind, grated
- 3 garlic cloves, minced
- 2 tbsp. lemon juice
- 2 lb. baby potatoes

Directions:

1. In a bowl, mix baby potatoes with oil, rosemary, parsley, oregano, salt, pepper, lemon rind, garlic, and lemon juice, toss, transfer potatoes to your air fryer's basket and cook at 356°F for 25 minutes.
2. Divide potatoes between plates and serve as a side dish.

Nutrition: Calories: 204 kcal; **Fat:** 4 g, **Fiber:** 5 g, **Carbs:** 17 g, **Protein:** 6 g

238. Green Beans Side Salad

Preparation Time: 10 minutes
Cooking Time: 8 minutes
Servings: 2–3
Ingredients:

- 1 pint cherry tomatoes
- 1 lb green beans
- 2 tbsp. olive oil
- Salt and black pepper to the taste

Directions:

1. Mix cherry tomatoes with green beans, olive oil, salt, and pepper in a bowl, toss and transfer to a pan that fits your air fryer and cook at 400°F for 15 minutes.
2. Divide between plates and serve as a side dish.

Nutrition: Calories: 142 kcal; **Fat:** 6 g, **Fiber:** 5 g, **Carbs:** 8 g, **Protein:** 9 g

239. Gold Potatoes and Bell Pepper Mix

Preparation Time: 10 minutes
Cooking Time: 25 minutes
Servings: 2–3
Ingredients:

- 4 gold potatoes, cubed
- 1 yellow onion, chopped
- 2 tsp. olive oil
- 1 green bell pepper, chopped
- Salt and black pepper to the taste
- ½ tsp. thyme, dried

Directions:

1. Heat your air fryer at 350°F, add oil, add onion, bell pepper, salt, and pepper, stir, and cook for 5 minutes.
2. Add potatoes and thyme, stir, cover, and cook at 360°F for 20 minutes.
3. Divide between plates and serve as a side dish.

Nutrition: Calories: 201 kcal; **Fat:** 4 g, **Fiber:** 4 g, **Carbs:** 12 g, **Protein:** 7 g

240. Colored Veggie Mix

Preparation Time: 10 minutes
Cooking Time: 12 minutes
Servings: 2–3
Ingredients:

- 1 zucchini, sliced in half and roughly chopped
- 1 orange bell pepper, roughly chopped
- 1 green bell pepper, roughly chopped
- 1 red onion, roughly chopped
- 4 oz. brown mushrooms, halved
- Salt and black pepper to the taste
- 1 tsp. Italian seasoning
- 1 cup cherry tomatoes, halved
- ½ cup kalamata olives, pitted and halved
- ¼ cup olive oil
- 3 tbsp. balsamic vinegar
- 2 tbsp. basil, chopped

Directions:

1. Mix zucchini with mushrooms, orange bell pepper, green bell pepper, red onion, salt, pepper, Italian seasoning, and oil, toss well, transfer to preheated air fryer at 380°F and cook them for 12 minutes.
2. In a large bowl, combine mixed veggies with tomatoes, olives, vinegar, and basil, toss, divide between plates and serve cold as a side dish.

Nutrition: Calories: 180 kcal; **Fat:** 5 g, **Fiber:** 8 g, **Carbs:** 10 g, **Protein:** 6 g

241. Oregano Bell Peppers

Preparation Time: 10 minutes
Cooking Time: 8 minutes
Servings: 2–3
Ingredients:

- 1 tbsp. olive oil
- 1 sweet onion, chopped
- 1 red bell pepper, chopped
- 1 orange bell pepper, chopped
- 1 green bell pepper, chopped
- Salt and black pepper to the taste
- ½ cup cashew cheese, shredded
- 1 tbsp. oregano, chopped

Directions:

1. In a pan that fits your air fryer, combine onion with red bell pepper, green bell pepper, orange bell pepper, salt, pepper, oregano, and oil, toss, introduce it into the fryer and cook at 320°F for 10 minutes.
2. Add cashew cheese, toss, introduce it in the fryer for 4 minutes more, divide between plates and serve as a side dish.

Nutrition: Calories: 172 kcal; **Fat:** 4 g, **Fiber:** 6 g, **Carbs:** 8 g, **Protein:** 7 g

242. Corn with Tomatoes Salad

Preparation Time: 10 minutes
Cooking Time: 5 minutes
Servings: 2–3
Ingredients:

- 3 cups corn
- A drizzle olive oil
- Salt and black pepper to the taste
- 1 tsp. sweet paprika
- 1 tbsp. stevia
- ½ tsp. garlic powder
- ½ iceberg lettuce head, cut into medium strips
- ½ Romaine lettuce head, cut into medium strips
- 1 cup black beans, canned, drained
- 3 tbsp. cilantro, chopped
- 4 green onions, chopped
- 12 cherry tomatoes, sliced

Directions:

1. Put the corn in a pan that fits your air fryer, drizzle the oil, add salt, pepper, paprika, stevia, and garlic powder, introduce it to your air fryer and cook at 350°F for 10 minutes.
2. Transfer corn to a salad bowl, add lettuce, black beans, tomatoes, green onions, and cilantro, toss, divide between plates and serve as a side salad.

Nutrition: Calories: 162 kcal; **Fat:** 6 g, **Fiber:** 4 g, **Carbs:** 7 g, **Protein:** 6 g

243. Crispy Zucchini Wedges

Preparation Time: 10 minutes
Cooking Time: 12 minutes
Servings: 2–3
Ingredients:

- Cooking spray
- ½ cup all-purpose flour
- 2 vegan eggs
- 2 tbsp. water
- 1 ½ cup breadcrumbs
- 1 zucchini, sliced into wedges
- ½ tbsp. red-wine vinegar
- 2 tbsp. tomato paste
- Salt and pepper to taste

Directions:

1. Spray the air fryer basket with oil.
2. Put the flour in a dish.
3. In another dish, combine vegan eggs and water.
4. In a third dish, put the breadcrumbs.
5. Dip each zucchini strip into the 3 dishes: the flour, the eggs and water, and the breadcrumbs.
6. Cook in the air fryer at 360°F for 12 minutes, shaking once.
7. Mix the rest of the ingredients in a bowl.
8. Serve zucchini fries with dipping sauce.

Nutrition: Calories: 235 kcal; Total **Fat:** 12 g; **Saturated Fat:** 1 g; **Cholesterol:** 66 mg; **Sodium:** 232 mg; **Total Carbohydrate:** 26 g; **Dietary Fiber:** 2 g; **Total Sugar:** 2 g; **Protein:** 6 g; **Potassium:** 435 mg

244. Tomatoes and Basil Mix

Preparation Time: 10 minutes
Cooking Time: 14 minutes
Servings: 2–3
Ingredients:

- 1 bunch basil, chopped
- 3 garlic cloves, minced
- A drizzle olive oil
- Salt and black pepper to the taste
- 2 cups cherry tomatoes, halved

Directions:

1. In a pan that fits your Air Fryer, combine tomatoes with garlic, salt, pepper, basil, and oil, toss, introduce it to your Air Fryer and cook at 320°F for 12 minutes.
2. Divide between plates and serve as a side dish.

Nutrition: Calories: 140 kcal; **Fat:** 1 g; **Fiber:** 1 g; **Carbs:** 2 g; **Protein:** 10 g

245. Minty Leeks Medley

Preparation Time: 10 minutes
Cooking Time: 12 minutes
Servings: 2–3
Ingredients:

- 6 leeks, roughly chopped
- 1 tbsp. cumin, ground
- 1 tbsp. mint, chopped
- 1 tbsp. parsley, chopped
- 1 tsp. garlic, minced
- A drizzle olive oil
- Salt and black pepper to the taste

Directions:

1. In a pan that fits your air fryer, combine leeks with cumin, mint, parsley, garlic, salt, pepper, and the oil, toss, introduce it to your air fryer and cook at 350°F for 12 minutes.
2. Divide Minty Leeks Medley between plates and serve as a side dish.

Nutrition: Calories: 131 kcal; **Fat:** 7 g, **Fiber:** 3 g, **Carbs:** 10 g, **Protein:** 6 g

246. Yellow Lentils Herbed Mix

Preparation Time: 10 minutes
Cooking Time: 8 minutes
Servings: 2–3
Ingredients:

- 1 cup yellow lentils, soaked in water for 1 hour and drained
- 1 hot chili pepper, chopped
- 1-inch ginger piece, grated
- ½ tsp. turmeric powder
- 1 tsp. garam masala
- Salt and black pepper to the taste
- 2 tsp. olive oil
- ½ cup cilantro, chopped
- 1 and ½ cup spinach, chopped
- 4 garlic cloves, minced
- ¾ cup red onion, chopped

Directions:

1. In a pan that fits your air fryer, mix lentils with chili pepper, ginger, turmeric, garam masala, salt, pepper, olive oil, cilantro, spinach, onion, and garlic, toss, introduce it to your air fryer and cook at 400°F for 15 minutes.
2. Divide lentils mix between plates and serve as a side dish.

Nutrition: Calories: 202 kcal; **Fat:** 2 g, **Fiber:** 8 g, **Carbs:** 12 g, **Protein:** 4 g

247. Summer Squash Mix

Preparation Time: 10 minutes
Cooking Time: 10 minutes
Servings: 2–3
Ingredients:

- 3 oz. coconut cream
- ½ tsp. oregano, dried
- Salt and black pepper
- 1 big yellow summer squash, peeled and cubed
- ⅓ cup carrot, cubed
- 2 tbsp. olive oil

Directions:

1. In a pan that fits your air fryer, combine squash with carrot, oil, oregano, salt, pepper, and coconut cream, toss, transfer to your air fryer and cook at 400°F for 10 m.
2. Divide between plates and serve as a side dish.

Nutrition: Calories: 170 kcal; **Fat:** 4 g, **Fiber:** 7 g, **Carbs:** 8 g, **Protein:** 6 g

248. Creamy Zucchini and Sweet Potatoes

Preparation Time: 10 minutes
Cooking Time: 16 minutes
Servings: 2–3
Ingredients:

- 1 cup veggie stock
- 2 tbsp. olive oil
- 2 sweet potatoes, peeled and cut into medium wedges
- 8 zucchinis, cut into medium wedges
- 2 yellow onions, chopped
- 1 cup coconut milk
- Salt and black pepper to the taste
- 1 tbsp. coconut aminos
- ¼ tsp. thyme, dried
- ¼ tsp. rosemary, dried
- 4 tbsp. dill, chopped
- ½ tsp. basil, chopped

Directions:

1. Heat a pan that fits your air fryer with the oil over medium heat, add onion, stir and cook for 2 minutes.

2. Add zucchinis, thyme, rosemary, basil, potato, salt, pepper, stock, milk, aminos, and dill, stir, introduce it to your air fryer, and cook at 360°F for 14 minutes, divide between plates and serve as a side dish.

Nutrition: Calories: 133 kcal; **Fat:** 3 g, **Fiber:** 4 g, **Carbs:** 10 g, **Protein:** 5 g

249. Corn and Tomatoes

Preparation Time: 10 minutes
Cooking Time: 13 minutes
Servings: 2–3
Ingredients:

- 2 cups corn
- 4 tomatoes, roughly chopped
- 1 tbsp. olive oil
- Salt and black pepper to the taste
- 1 tbsp. oregano, chopped
- 1 tbsp. parsley, chopped
- 2 tbsp. soft tofu, pressed and crumbled

Directions:

1. In a pan that fits your air fryer, combine corn with tomatoes, oil, salt, pepper, oregano, and parsley, toss, introduce the pan into your air fryer and cook at 320°F for 10 minutes.
2. Add tofu, toss, introduce it in the fryer for 3 minutes more, divide between plates and serve as a side dish.

Nutrition: Calories: 171 kcal; **Fat:** 7 g; **Fiber:** 8 g; **Carbs:** 9 g; **Protein:** 6 g

250. Onion Soup

Preparation Time: 5 minutes
Cooking Time: 35 minutes
Servings: 2–3
Ingredients:

- 2 large white onions, peeled, sliced
- ½ cup squash, cubed
- 1 sprig thyme
- 1 tbsp. grapeseed oil
- 2 cups spring water

Extra:

- ½ tsp. salt
- ¼ tsp. cayenne pepper

Directions:

1. Take a medium pot, place it over medium heat, add oil, and when hot, add onion and cook for 10 minutes.
2. Add thyme sprig, switch heat to the low level and then cook onions for 15 to 20 minutes until soft, covering the pan with its lid.
3. Add remaining ingredients stir until mixed, and simmer for 5 minutes.
4. Ladle soup into bowls and then serve.

Nutrition: Calories: 182 kcal; **Fat:** 3 g; **Fiber:** 3 g; **Carbs:** 5 g; **Protein:** 8 g

251. Basil Parmesan Tomatoes

Preparation Time: 30 minutes
Cooking Time: 20 minutes
Servings: 2–3
Ingredients:

- ½ tsp. oregano, dried
- 4 roam tomatoes
- Spices: onion powder, garlic powder, sea salt, and black pepper
- ½ cup Parmesan cheese, shredded
- 12 small fresh basil leaves

Directions:

1. Preheat the oven to 425°F and grease a baking sheet lightly.
2. Mix dried oregano, onion powder, garlic powder, sea salt, and black pepper in a small bowl.
3. Arrange the tomato slices on a baking sheet and sprinkle with the seasoning blend.
4. Top with Parmesan cheese and basil leaves and transfer to the oven.
5. Bake for about 20 minutes and remove from the oven to servings.

Nutrition: Calories: 49 kcal; **Total Fat:** 2.2 g; **Saturated Fat:** 1.4 g; **Cholesterol:** 7 mg; **Sodium:** 91 mg; **Total Carbohydrate:** 4.3 g; **Dietary Fiber:** 1.2 g; **Total Sugars:** 2.4 g; **Protein:** 3.9 g

252. Roasted Veggies

Preparation Time: 5 minutes
Cooking Time: 30 minutes
Servings: 2–3
Ingredients:

- 1 medium bell pepper, cut into strips
- 1 small onion, halved then sliced
- 1 small zucchini, sliced into rounds
- 2 tbsp. extra-virgin olive oil
- Salt
- 1 pint grape tomatoes
- Black pepper, freshly ground

Directions:

1. Preheat the oven to 400°F.
2. Using 1 or 2 large baking sheets, arrange the vegetables to lie flat, lightly touching each other.
3. Evenly pour the olive oil over the vegetables and gently toss to coat, using either a spoon or your hands. Add salt and pepper to taste.
4. Roast for 20 to 30 minutes, or until soft and lightly charred, stirring halfway through, and servings.

Seasonal substitution: choose seasonal vegetables for variety throughout the year: cauliflower, Brussels sprouts, asparagus, sweet potatoes, broccoli, summer squash, butternut squash, and carrots. Prepare using the same method, keeping in mind that harder veggies like butternut squash may require additional time in the oven.
Nutrition: Calories: 75 kcal; **Total Fat:** 5 g; **Protein:** 0 g; **Carbohydrate:** 8 g; **Fiber:** 1 g; **Sugar:** 4 g; **Sodium:** 2 mg

253. Cabbage Salad

Preparation Time: 10 minutes
Cooking Time: 15 minutes
Servings: 2–3
Ingredients:

- 2 ½ cups cabbage, shredded
- 1 tsp. salt
- Low-fat mayonnaise, as needed to coat

Directions:

1. Mix all ingredients.

Nutrition: Protein: 3 kcal; **Fat:** 55 g; **Carb:** 50 g

254. Potato Salad

Preparation Time: 20 minutes
Cooking Time: 1 hour
Servings: 2–3
Ingredients:

- 3 cups potatoes, cubed, boiled, cold
- 1 tbsp. onion, finely chopped
- dash salt
- A dash black pepper
- Pimiento, to taste, optional
- Parsley, to taste, optional
- ¼ cup French dressing
- ¾ cup low-fat mayonnaise

Directions:

1. Boil the eggs. Let cool. Chill.
2. Peel, cube, and boil the potatoes until soft but not falling apart. Cool.
3. Chop the onions.
4. Put the cooled potatoes and the onions together in a bowl.
5. Season with salt and pepper. Mix gently.
6. Add the French dressing, and mix gently; chill for 1–2 hours.
7. Add the mayonnaise, pimiento, and parsley. Mix gently.
8. Dice and add the chilled eggs. Mix gently.
9. Add extra seasonings to taste.
10. Dish up into individual bowls. For more variety, place on individual plates surrounded with salad greens, cucumber sticks, slices of boiled eggs, and/or tomato pieces.

Nutrition: Protein: 11 kcal; **Fat:** 74 g; **Carb:** 45 g

255. Spaghetti Squash Chow Mein

Preparation Time: 10 minutes
Cooking Time: 55 minutes; **Servings:** 2–3
Ingredients:

- Nonstick cooking spray
- 1 small (3-to 4-lb.) spaghetti squash
- ¼ cup low-sodium soy sauce
- 3 garlic cloves, minced
- 1 tbsp. oyster sauce
- 1-inch ginger root, peeled and minced
- 2 tbsp. extra-virgin olive oil
- 1 small white onion, diced
- 3 celery stalks, thinly sliced
- 2 cups shredded cabbage (or coleslaw mix)

Directions:

1. Preheat the oven to 350°F. Coat a baking sheet with cooking spray.
2. Halve the spaghetti squash, remove and discard the seeds, and place the halves cut-side down on the prepared baking sheet. Bake for 30 to 45 minutes or until the flesh is tender and can be scraped with a fork.
3. Remove from the oven, and let cool. Scrape out the flesh with a fork, creating small noodles. Set aside.
4. Whisk together the soy sauce, garlic, oyster sauce, and ginger in a small bowl.
5. In a large skillet over medium heat, heat the oil.
6. Add the onion and celery and cook, stirring, until tender, 3 to 4 minutes. Add the cabbage and cook, stirring, until heated through, 1 to 2 minutes. Then, add the spaghetti squash and sauce mixture. Continue cooking for another 2 minutes.
7. Serve immediately.

Nutrition: Calories: 252 kcal; **Total Fat:** 11 g; **Protein:** 6 g; **Carbohydrate:** 39 g; **Fiber:** 9 g; **Sugar:** 15 g; **Sodium:** 950 mg

256. Zucchini Lasagna Roll-Ups

Preparation Time: 30 minutes
Cooking Time: 15 minutes
Servings: 2–3
Ingredients:

- 3 large zucchinis, trimmed and sliced lengthwise into -inch-thick strips
- 1 tsp. salt
- Nonstick cooking spray
- 1 (10-oz.) bag fresh spinach
- 1 cup part-skim ricotta
- ½ cup Parmesan cheese
- 1 large egg

- 2 garlic cloves, minced
- 2 tsp. Italian seasoning
- 1 ½ cup marinara sauce, divided
- 1 cup part-skim shredded mozzarella

Directions:

1. Preheat the oven to 400°F.
2. Lay the zucchini slices flat on a paper towel-lined baking sheet, and sprinkle with salt. Let it sit for 15 minutes.
3. Meanwhile, spray a small skillet with nonstick cooking spray, and set over medium heat.
4. Add the spinach and cook for 2 minutes, or until wilted. Remove from the heat.
5. In a medium bowl, mix the ricotta, Parmesan, egg, garlic, and Italian seasoning until well combined.
6. Pat the zucchini dry, removing excess salt.
7. Spread 1 cup of marinara in the bottom of a 9-by-9-inch baking dish.
8. Spread each zucchini slice with a spoonful of ricotta mixture, then gently roll up and place in the prepared baking dish, seam-side down. Repeat with the remaining zucchini and filling.
9. Top with the remaining ½ cup of marinara, and sprinkle with the mozzarella cheese.
10. Bake for 25 to 30 minutes, or until the lasagna rolls are heated through, and the cheese begins to brown.
11. Serve immediately.

Nutrition: Calories: 240 kcal; **Total Fat:** 13 g; **Protein:** 18 g; **Carbohydrate:** 16 g; **Fiber:** 5 g; **Sugar:** 7 g; **Sodium:** 1019 mg

257. Roasted Vegetable Quinoa Salad with Chickpeas

Preparation Time: 15 minutes
Cooking Time: 15 minutes
Servings: 2–3
Ingredients:

- 1 small eggplant, diced
- 1 small zucchini, diced
- 1 small yellow summer squash, diced
- ½ cup grape tomatoes, halved
- 1 (15-oz.) can chickpeas, drained and rinsed
- 3 tbsp. extra-virgin olive oil, divided
- ⅓ cup packaged quinoa
- 1 cup low-sodium vegetable or chicken broth
- 2 tbsp. lemon juice, freshly squeezed
- 1 tsp. fresh garlic, minced; or 1 garlic clove, minced
- 1 tbsp. basil, dried
- 1 tsp. dried oregano

Directions:

1. Preheat the oven to 425°F. Line a 9-x-13-inch baking sheet with parchment paper.
2. Spread the eggplant, zucchini, yellow squash, tomatoes, and chickpeas across the baking sheet and toss them with 1 tablespoon of olive oil.
3. Bake for 30 minutes, stirring once halfway through. The finished vegetables should be tender, and the tomatoes should be juicy. The chickpeas will be firm and crispy.
4. While the vegetables and chickpeas are roasting, place the quinoa and broth in a small saucepan over medium-high heat. Cover and bring to a boil. Reduce the heat to low and cook for about 15 minutes until all liquid has been absorbed. Remove the pan from the heat and fluff the quinoa with a fork. (Otherwise, make the quinoa according to the package instructions.)
5. Whisk together the lemon juice, garlic, and 2 tablespoons of olive oil in a small dish. Mix in the basil and oregano.
6. Combine the quinoa, and roasted vegetables with chickpeas, and dress in a large bowl. Gently stir to combine. Serve and enjoy!

Nutrition: Calories: 200 kcal; **Total Fat:** 9 g; **Protein:** 7 g; **Carbs:** 27 g; **Fiber:** 8 g; **Sugar:** 4 g; **Sodium:** 160 mg

258. Mexican Stuffed Summer Squash

Preparation Time: 5 minutes
Cooking Time: 33 minutes; **Servings:** 2–3
Ingredients:

- Nonstick cooking spray
- 1 yellow summer squash
- ½ cup Black Beans, Refried or Fat-free pinto beans, canned and refried with 1 tsp. taco seasoning mixed in (for flavor)
- ½ cup quinoa, cooked
- ¼ cup Colby Jack cheese, shredded
- 1 small tomato, diced
- 2 tbsp. black olives, sliced
- 2 scallions, chopped, for garnish

Directions:

1. Preheat the oven to 400°F. Coat an 8-by-8-inch baking dish with the cooking spray.
2. Cut the ends off of the summer squash and discard. Cut lengthwise, then use a spoon to remove and discard the seeds. Place the squash halves cut-side down in the baking dish. Gently poke a couple of holes in the squash to vent. Add 1 tablespoon of water to the dish. Microwave for about 3 minutes or until slightly tender. Discard any leftover water.
3. When cool enough to handle, turn the squash so they are skin-side down and spaced evenly in the dish.

4. Layer ¼ cup of the beans in each squash, then ¼ cup of the quinoa. Top the whole thing with the Colby Jack cheese. Cover with aluminum foil and bake for 25 minutes. Remove the foil and bake for 5 minutes until the cheese is bubbly and the squash is tender.
5. Garnish each squash with the tomatoes, olives, and scallions before serving.

Nutrition: Calories: 190 kcal; Total **Fat:** 8 g; **Protein:** 9 g; **Carbs:** 21 g; **Fiber:** 4 g; **Sugar:** 3 g; **Sodium:** 40 mg

259. Roasted Garlic Zucchini and Tomatoes

Preparation Time: 15 minutes
Cooking Time: 9 minutes; **Servings:** 2–3
Ingredients:

- 2 zucchinis cut in half lengthwise, then cut into ½-inch half-moons
- 2 cups ripe tomatoes, quartered
- ½ onion, minced
- 3 garlic cloves, minced
- ½ tsp. red pepper flakes, crushed
- ¼ cup olive oil
- salt and pepper, as needed
- ½ cup Parmesan cheese, grated
- 1 tbsp. fresh basil, chopped

Directions:

1. Heat the oven to 450°F. Lightly grease a baking dish measuring 9x13 inches.
2. Combine the zucchini, tomatoes, onion, garlic, and red pepper flakes in the prepared baking dish. Add the olive oil and sprinkle, season with salt and pepper, and blend well.
3. Set in a preheated oven. Roast for about 18 minutes until the vegetables are tender and slightly golden. Remove from the oven; sprinkle with basil and Parmesan cheese.

Nutrition: Calories: 204 kcal; **Protein:** 5.9 g; **Carbohydrate:** 9.5 g; **Fat:** 16.8 g; **Cholesterol:** 8.8 mg; **Sodium:** 165.2 mg

260. Acorn Squash- Stuffed with Cheese

Preparation Time: 5 minutes
Cooking Time: 40 minutes
Servings: 2–3
Ingredients:

- 2 lb. turkey breast, ground (extra-lean)
- 1 acorn squash
- 1 can (8 oz.) tomato sauce
- 1 cup each:
- 1 cup fresh mushrooms, sliced
- 1 onion, chopped
- 1 stalk celery, diced
- 1 tsp. each: garlic powder, basil, oregano
- 1 pinch black pepper
- ⅛ tsp. salt
- 1 cup Cheddar cheese, shredded (reduced-fat)

Directions:

1. Program the oven temperature to 350°F.
2. Slice the squash in half and remove the seeds. Arrange the squash, cut side down, in a dish, and microwave on high for 20 minutes.
3. Brown the turkey in a skillet and add the onion and celery. Sauté 2 to 3 minutes. Blend in the mushrooms, and add the sauce and seasonings. Divide into quarters and spoon into the squash.
4. Cover and bake for 15 minutes.
5. Garnish with the cheese and bake until the cheese has melted.

Nutrition: Calories: 299 kcal; **Protein:** 30 g; Fat: 4 g; **Carbohydrate:** 38 g

261. Soba Noodle and Edamame Salad with Grilled Tofu

Preparation Time: 15 minutes
Cooking Time: 8 minutes; **Servings:** 2–3
Ingredients:

- 140 g soba noodles
- 300 g podded edamame, fresh or frozen (soy) beans
- 4 spring onions, shredded
- 300 g bag beansprouts
- 1 cucumber, peeled, halved lengthways, deseeded with a tsp, and sliced
- 250 g block firm tofu, patted dry and thickly sliced
- 1 tsp. oil
- a handful of coriander leaves, to serve

For the dressing:

- 3 tbsp. mirin
- 2 tsp. tamari
- 2 tbsp. orange juice
- 1 red chili, deseeded, if you like, and finely chopped

Directions:

1. In your smallest saucepan, heat the dressing ingredients, boil for 30 seconds and then set aside.
2. Boil noodles according to the instructions for the box, adding the edamame beans for the final cooking time of 2 mins. Rinse under freezing water, drain thoroughly, and pour the spring onions, beansprouts, cucumbers, sesame oil, and warm dressing into a large bowl. If you like, season.

3. For 2–3 minutes per hand, brush tofu with the veg oil, season, and grill-the tofu is very delicate, so turn carefully. Cover the tofu salad, scatter with cilantro and serve.

Nutrition: Calories: 331 kcal; **Fat:** 7 g; **Saturates Fat:** 1 g; **Carbs:** 48 g; **Sugars:** 7 g; **Fiber:** 5 g; **Protein:** 21 g; **Low in Salt:** 1.24 g

262. Broccoli Casserole

Preparation Time: 1 minute
Cooking Time: 10 min
Servings: 2–3
Ingredients:

- 4 cups cut-up broccoli
- Ritz crackers, as needed
- 2 cups Cheddar cheese

Directions:

1. Add the casserole ingredients into a Pyrex dish with the crumbled crackers.
2. Bake long enough to melt the cheese at 375°F.

Nutrition: Calories: 90.5 kcal; **Protein:** 10.3 g; **Carbohydrate:** 9.8 g; **Fat:** 2.3 g

263. Chickpea and Feta Salad

Preparation Time: 7 min
Cooking Time: 0 min
Servings: 2–3
Ingredients:

- ¾ cup raw vegetables, chopped
- ¼ cup each:
- 1 can fresh chickpeas
- Feta cheese, crumbled
- 2 tbsp. lemon juice
- 2 tbsp. olive oil
- 1 tsp. oregano, dried
- Dash of pepper, salt

Directions:

1. Use your imagination for the chopped veggies. Include peppers, avocado, tomatoes, onions, celery, or your favorites.
2. Rinse and drain the chickpeas.
3. Combine all ingredients and chill in the fridge until ready to serve.

Nutrition: Calories: 285.2 kcal; **Protein:** 10.2 g; **Carbohydrate:** 22.2 g; **Fat:** 18.4 g

264. Eggplant Pesto Mini Pizza

Preparation Time: 10 min
Cooking Time: 45 min; **Servings:** 2–3
Ingredients:

- 1 bell pepper
- 1 tomato
- 1 eggplant
- 1 medium red onion, sliced
- ⅛ tsp. salt
- 2 garlic cloves
- Pinch oregano
- ¼ cup each: extra-virgin olive oil, pesto sauce, hummus, vegan Parmesan cheese
- Sandwich thins Arnold Oroweat
- Optional: Pepper flakes

Directions:

1. Set the oven to 400°F.
2. If desired, chop the vegetables and combine the oil, pepper, salt, oregano, and pepper flakes. Arrange on a baking tin and toast for approximately 30 to 45 min or until they are done the way you like them.
3. Toast the buns and spread the hummus; add the veggies and a bit of pesto sauce. Sprinkle with the vegan cheese, and enjoy.

Nutrition: Calories: 405 kcal; **Protein:** 11.4 g; **Carbohydrate:** 40.6 g; **Fat:** 24.5 g

265. Spinach Lasagna

Preparation Time: 10 min
Cooking Time: 45 min; **Servings:** 2–3
Ingredients:

- 1 large egg
- 2 cups cottage cheese (1% fat milk)
- 2 cups part-skim mozzarella cheese
- 10 oz. baby spinach
- 1 jar spaghetti/marinara tomato sauce
- 1 cup water
- 9 lasagna noodles
- ⅛ tsp. black pepper

Directions:

1. Program the oven temperature to 350°F.
2. Combine the thawed, drained spinach, 1 cup of mozzarella, cottage cheese, egg, and the seasonings in a large mixing bowl.
3. Spray a 9x13x2-inch casserole dish with some cooking spray.
4. Layer ½ cup of the sauce, 3 noodles, and ½ of the cheese mixture. Repeat, and top with the noodles one cup of mozzarella. Pour water around the edges and toothpicks on top to place a piece of foil over the noodles.
5. Bake covered for one hour to 1 ½ hour. Let it rest for 15 min.

Nutrition: Calories: 316.8 kcal; **Protein:** 26.4 g; **Carbohydrate:** 24.3 g; **Fat:** 12.6 g

266. Vegetarian Frittata

Preparation Time: 15 min
Cooking Time: 30–35 min; **Servings:** 2–3
Ingredients:

- 6 oz. button mushrooms
- 1 lb. asparagus
- 1 shallot
- 1 garlic clove
- 1 tbsp. olive oil
- 1 small zucchini
- 6 large eggs
- ⅓ cup 1% milk
- ¼ tsp. black pepper, freshly ground
- 1 tsp. salt
- 1 tbsp. chives, chopped
- A dash nutmeg
- 1 medium/large tomato
- ¼ cup Parmesan cheese, freshly grated

Directions:

1. Set the oven temperature to 350°F.
2. Prepare the Asparagus: Wash and trim, cutting it into 1-inch pieces. Blanche cut asparagus for 1 to 2 min. Shock it by adding it to ice water. Drain and set to the side.
3. Wash and slice the mushrooms. Sauté them in the oil for 10 min using medium heat. Mince the shallots and garlic and add—cooking 2 more min. Transfer the mushrooms to a plate and set them aside.
4. Slice the zucchini lengthwise and into half-moon shapes.
5. Whisk the eggs, milk, chives, pepper, salt, and nutmeg in a large mixing dish. Add the mushroom mixture, asparagus, and zucchini.
6. Spray a 2/4 baking dish with cooking spray and add the egg/veggie mixture.
7. Arrange the thinly sliced tomatoes on top and sprinkle them with the Parmesan cheese.
8. Bake 30–35 min. You can place the frittata under the broiler for 2 to 3 min to brown the top.
9. Cool and serve at room temperature or straight from the fridge.

Nutrition: Calories: 146.2 kcal; **Protein:** 10.6 g; **Carbohydrate:** 7.4 g; **Fat:** 8.8 g

267. Power Pesto Zoodles

Preparation Time: 10 min
Cooking Time: 5 min; **Servings:** 2
Ingredients:

- 2 zucchinis
- 1 avocado, peeled, pitted
- ½ cup cherry tomatoes
- 2 tbsp. walnuts
- ½ of key lime, juiced

Extra:

- ¼ tsp. salt
- ⅛ tsp. cayenne pepper
- 2 tsp. grapeseed oil
- 2 tbsp. olive oil

Directions:

1. Prepare the zucchini noodles and for this, cut them into thin strips by using a vegetable peeler or use a spiralizer.
2. Then take a medium skillet pan, add oil, and when hot, add zucchini noodles and cook for 3 to 5 min until tender-crisp.
3. Meanwhile, place the remaining ingredients in a food processor and then pulse until the creamy paste comes together.
4. When zucchini noodles are sautéed, drain and place them in a large bowl and add the blended sauce.
5. Add 2 tablespoons of water, and then toss until well combined.
6. Garnish the zoodles with grated coconut, and then serve.

Nutrition: Calories: 214 kcal; **Fat:** 1017.10 g; **Protein:** 4.8 g; **Carbohydrate:** 13.2 g; **Fiber:** 6.1 g

268. Spinach with Chickpeas

Preparation Time: 5 minutes
Cooking Time: 10 min; **Servings:** 2
Ingredients:

- 3 tbsp. oil
- 1 onion, thinly sliced
- 4 garlic cloves, minced
- 1 tbsp. ginger, grated
- ½ container cherry tomatoes
- 1 tbsp. red pepper flakes, crushed
- 1 can chickpeas
- Salt to taste

Directions:

1. Add oil to a skillet and cook onions until browned. Add garlic cloves, ginger, tomatoes, and pepper flakes. Cook for 4 min.
2. Add chickpeas and cook for 3 more minutes. Add spinach and cook until they start to wilt.
3. Season with salt to taste. Cook for 2 more min.
4. Serve and enjoy.

Nutrition: Calories: 209 kcal; **Fat:** 8.1 g; **Total Carbohydrate:** 28.5 g; **Protein:** 22.5 g; **Fiber:** 6 g

269. Mushroom Sauce

Preparation Time: 5 min
Cooking Time: 12 min; **Servings:** 2
Ingredients:

- ¾ tbsp. spelt flour

- ¼ onion, peeled, diced
- 4 oz. mushrooms, sliced
- ½ cup walnut milk, homemade
- 1 tbsp. walnuts, chopped

Extra:

- ¼ tsp. salt
- ⅛ tsp. cayenne pepper
- ½ tsp. thyme, dried
- 1 tbsp. grapeseed oil
- ¼ cup vegetable broth, homemade

Directions:

1. Take a medium skillet pan, place it over medium heat, add oil, and when hot, add onion and mushrooms, and season with 1/16 teaspoon of salt and cayenne pepper, and then cook for 4 minutes until tender.
2. Stir in spelt flour until coated, cook for 1 minute, slowly whisk in milk and vegetable broth and then season with remaining salt and cayenne pepper.
3. Switch heat to low-level, cook for 5 to 7 min until the sauce has thickened slightly, and then stir in walnuts and thyme.
4. Serve straight away with spelt flour bread.

Nutrition: Calories: 65.3 kcal; **Fat:** 1.6 g; **Protein:** 3.5 g; **Carbohydrate:** 9.6 g; **Fiber:** 1 g;

270. Vegetable Fajitas

Preparation Time: 10 min
Cooking Time: 8 min; **Servings:** 2
Ingredients:

- 2 Portobello mushroom caps, ⅓-inch sliced
- ¾ red bell pepper, sliced
- ½ onion, peeled, sliced
- ½ of key lime, juiced
- 2 spelt flour tortillas

Extra:

- ⅓ tsp. salt
- ¼ tsp. cayenne pepper
- ¼ tsp. onion powder
- 1 tbsp. grapeseed oil

Directions:

1. Take a medium skillet pan, place it over medium heat, add oil, and when hot, add onion and red pepper, and then cook for 2 min until tender-crisp.
2. Add mushrooms slices, sprinkle with all the seasoning, stir until mixed, and then cook for 5 min until vegetables turn soft.
3. Heat the tortilla until warm, distribute vegetables in their center, drizzle with lime juice, and then roll tightly.

Nutrition: Calories: 337 kcal; **Fat:** 3.7 g; **Protein:** 2.6 g; **Carbohydrate:** 73.3 g; **Fiber:** 21.3 g

271. Chickpea and Mushroom Curry

Preparation Time: 5 min
Cooking Time: 12 min; **Servings:** 2
Ingredients:

- 1 cup chickpea, cooked
- 1 small white onion, peeled, diced
- ½ medium green bell pepper, cored, chopped
- 1 cup mushrooms, diced
- 8 cherry tomatoes, chopped

Extra:

- ½ tsp. salt
- ¼ tsp. cayenne pepper
- 1 tsp. grapeseed oil

Directions:

1. Take a medium skillet pan, place it over medium heat, add oil, and when hot, add onion, tomatoes, and bell pepper, and then cook for 2 minutes.
2. Add chickpeas and mushrooms, season with cayenne pepper, stir until combined, switch heat to medium-low level, and then simmer for 10 min until cooked, covering the pan with its lid.

Nutrition: Calories: 194.7 kcal; **Fat:** 8.5 g; **Protein:** 5.8 g; **Carbohydrate:** 25.7 g; **Fiber:** 5.4 g

272. Vegetable Low Mein

Preparation Time: 5 min
Cooking Time: 10 min; **Servings:** 2
Ingredients:

- 2 cups spelt noodles, cooked
- ½ medium green bell pepper, cored, sliced
- ½ medium red bell pepper, cored, sliced
- 1 medium white onion, cored, sliced
- ½ cup mushrooms, sliced

Extra:

- ⅔ tsp. salt
- ¼ tsp. onion powder
- ⅓ tsp. cayenne pepper
- 1 key lime juiced
- 1 tbsp. sesame oil

Directions:

1. Take a large skillet pan, place it over medium heat, add oil, and when hot, add all the vegetables and cook for 3 to 5 min until tender-crisp.
2. Add all the spices, drizzle with lime juice, stir until mixed, and then cook for 1 minute.
3. Add noodles, toss until well mixed, and cook for 2 to 3 min until hot.

Nutrition: Calories: 330 kcal; **Fat:** 11 g; **Protein:** 10 g; **Carbohydrate:** 48 g; **Fiber:** 4 g

273. Spiced Okra Curry

Preparation Time: 5 min
Cooking Time: 10 min; **Servings:** 2
Ingredients:

- 1 ½ cup okra
- 8 cherry tomatoes, chopped
- 1 medium onion, peeled, sliced
- ¾ cup vegetable broth, homemade

Extra:

- 6 tsp. spice mix
- ¼ tsp. salt
- ½ tbsp. grapeseed oil
- ¼ tsp. cayenne pepper
- ¾ cup tomato sauce, alkaline
- 6 tbsp. soft-jelly coconut milk

Directions:

1. Take a large skillet pan, place it over medium heat, add oil and warm, add onion, and then cook for 5 min until golden brown.
2. Add spice mix, add ingredients into the pan except for okra, stir until mixed, and then bring the mixture to a simmer.
3. Add okra, stir until mixed, and then cook for 10 to 15 min over medium-low heat setting until cooked.

Nutrition: Calories: 137 kcal; **Fat:** 8.4 g; **Protein:** 4 g; **Carbohydrate:** 15 g; **Fiber:** 5.6 g

274. Baked Portobello Mushrooms

Preparation Time: 10 min
Cooking Time: 30 min; **Servings:** 2
Ingredients:

- 2 caps Portobello mushrooms, destemmed
- ⅔ tsp. onion, minced
- ⅔ tsp. sage, minced
- ⅔ tsp. thyme
- ⅔ tbsp. key lime juice

Extra:

- 2 tbsp. alkaline soy sauce

Directions:

1. Switch on the oven set it to 400°F, and let it preheat.
2. Take a baking dish, arrange mushroom caps in it, and cut side up.
3. Take a small bowl, place remaining ingredients in it, stir until mixed, brush the mixture over inside and outside mushrooms, and then let them marinate for 15 min.
4. Bake the mushrooms for 30 min, flipping halfway, and then serve.

Nutrition: Calories: 72 kcal; **Fat:** 2 g; **Protein:** 6 g; **Carbohydrate:** 10 g; **Fiber:** 2 g

275. Chard and Lime Pasta

Preparation Time: 5 min
Cooking Time: 5 min
Servings: 2
Ingredients:

- 1 head Swiss chard, cut into ½-inch pieces
- 1 cup spelt pasta, cooked
- 2 green onions, sliced
- ¼ cup cilantro
- 1 key lime, juiced, zested

Extra:

- ¼ tsp. salt
- ¼ tsp. cayenne pepper
- 1 tbsp. olive oil

Directions:

1. Take a large skillet pan, place it over medium heat, add oil, and when hot, add chard pieces and cook for 4 min or more until wilted.
2. Remove pan from heat, transfer chards to a large bowl, add remaining ingredients and then toss until combined.

Nutrition: Calories: 224 kcal; **Fat:** 7 g; **Protein:** 7 g; **Carbohydrate:** 33 g; **Fiber:** 2 g

276. Roasted Squash and Apples

Preparation Time: 10 min
Cooking Time: 35 min; **Servings:** 2
Ingredients:

- 1 ½ lb. butternut squash, peeled, deseeded, cut into chunks
- 2 apples, cored, cut into ½-inch pieces
- 2 tbsp. agave syrup
- ½ tsp. sea salt

Extra:

- 2 tbsp. grapeseed oil

Directions:

- Switch on the oven set it to 375°F, and let it preheat.
- Meanwhile, take a baking sheet and then spread squash pieces on it.
- Take a small bowl, pour in oil, stir in salt and allspice until mixed, and then drizzle over squash pieces.
- Cover the pan with foil, then bake for 20 min.
- Meanwhile, place apple pieces in a medium bowl, drizzle with agave syrup, and toss until coated.
- When squash has baked, unwrap the baking sheet, and spoon it into the bowl containing apple, then stir until mixed.
- Spread the apple-squash mixture evenly on the baking sheet and then continue baking for 15 min.

Nutrition: Calories: 126.4 kcal; **Fat:** 4.9 g; **Protein:** 1.1 g; **Carbohydrate:** 22.2 g; **Fiber:** 5.1 g

277. Mushroom Steak

Preparation Time: 10 min
Cooking Time: 10 min; **Servings:** 2
Ingredients:

- 2 Portabello mushroom caps, ⅛-inch thick sliced
- ½ cup green bell peppers, sliced
- ½ cup white onions, sliced
- ½ cup red bell peppers, sliced
- ¼ cup alkaline sauce

Extra:

- ½ tsp. sea salt
- ½ tbsp. onion powder
- ½ tsp. oregano, dried
- ½ tsp. thyme, dried
- ½ tbsp. grapeseed oil
- 2 spelt flatbread, toasted

Directions:

1. Take a medium bowl, place sauce, add all the seasoning, and then whisk until combined.
2. Add mushroom slices, toss until coated, and then let them marinate for a minimum of 30 min, tossing halfway.
3. Then take a pan, place it over medium-high heat, add oil, and when hot, add onion and pepper and cook for 3 to 5 min until tender-crisp.
4. Add mushroom slices, stir until mixed and continue cooking for 5 min.
5. Distribute vegetables evenly between flatbread, roll them, and then serve.

Nutrition: Calories: 302 kcal; **Fat:** 18 g; **Protein:** 2 g; **Carbohydrate:** 27 g; **Fiber:** 3 g

278. Chayote Mushroom Stew

Preparation Time: 10 min
Cooking Time: 40 min; **Servings:** 2
Ingredients:

- ⅔ cup chayote squash cubes
- 1 cups mushroom, sliced
- ⅓ cup white onions, diced
- ½ cup chickpea flour
- ⅓ cup vegetable broth, homemade

Extra:

- ⅓ tbsp. onion powder
- ⅔ tsp. sea salt
- ⅔ tsp. basil, dried
- ⅓ tsp. red pepper, crushed
- 2 cups spring water
- ½ tbsp. grapeseed oil
- ⅓ cup hemp milk, homemade

Directions:

1. Take a medium pot, place it over medium-high heat, add oil, and when hot, add onion and mushroom, and then cook for 5 min.
2. Switch heat to medium level, pour in 1 cup of water, milk, and broth, add chayote and all the seasoning, stir until mixed, and then bring it to a simmer, covering the pan with a lid.
3. Pour remaining water into a food processor, add chickpea flour, pulse until blended, add to the pot and then stir until mixed.
4. Switch heat to the low level, simmer for 30 min, and then serve.

Nutrition: Calories: 173 kcal; **Fat:** 9 g; **Protein:** 2 g; **Carbohydrate:** 20 g; **Fiber:** 2 g

279. Veggie Lettuce Wraps

Preparation Time: 10 min
Cooking Time: 0 min; **Servings:** 2
Ingredients:

- ½ cup cherry tomatoes, halved
- 1 avocado, peeled, pitted, sliced
- ½ cup sprouts
- ½ of medium white onion, peeled, sliced
- 2 large lettuce leaves

Extra:

- 2 tbsp. key lime juice
- ½ tbsp. raisins
- ¼ tsp. salt
- ⅛ tsp. cayenne pepper

Directions:

1. Add lime juice, salt, and pepper to a small bowl, and stir until mixed.
2. Take a medium bowl, place all the vegetables except for lettuce, drizzle with the lime juice mixture, and then toss until mixed.
3. Place lettuce leaves on a plate, top with half of the vegetable mixture, and then roll it tightly.
4. Repeat with the other lettuce wrap and then serve.

Nutrition: Calories: 155 kcal; **Fat:** 10.5 g; **Protein:** 4.8 g; **Carbohydrate:** 13.2 g; **Fiber:** 3.5 g

280. Zucchini Linguine

Preparation Time: 10 min
Cooking Time: 8 min; **Servings:** 2
Ingredients:

- 2 zucchini, spiralized
- ½ cup mushrooms, sliced
- ½ tsp. thyme, dried
- ½ cup alkaline Avocado sauce
- ¼ cup cilantro, chopped

Extra:

- ⅓ tsp. salt
- ⅛ tsp. cayenne pepper
- 1 tbsp. grapeseed oil
- ½ tsp. oregano, dried

Directions:

1. Take a skillet pan, place it over medium heat, add oil and when hot, add mushrooms and cilantro and then cook for 3 to 5 min until tender.
2. Add avocado sauce, season with salt, pepper, oregano, and thyme, stir until mixed and cook for 1 to 2 min until warmed.
3. Place zucchini noodles in a large bowl, drizzle with some oil, and then toss until well coated.
4. Add avocado mixture, toss until combined, and then serve.

Nutrition: Calories: 284 kcal; **Fat:** 23.6 g; **Protein:** 5.7 g; **Carbohydrate:** 18.8 g; **Fiber:** 9.7 g

281. Spiced Mushroom Bowl

Preparation Time: 5 min
Cooking Time: 10 min; **Servings:** 2
Ingredients:

- 1 ½ cup mushrooms, sliced
- 8 cherry tomatoes, chopped
- 1 medium onion, peeled, sliced
- ¾ cup vegetable broth, homemade

Extra:

- 6 tsp. spice mix
- ¼ tsp. salt
- ½ tbsp. grapeseed oil
- ¼ tsp. cayenne pepper
- ¾ cup tomato sauce, alkaline
- 6 tbsp. soft-jelly coconut milk

Directions:

1. Take a large skillet pan, place it over medium heat, add oil and warm, add onion, and then cook for 5 min until golden brown.
2. Add spice mix, add ingredients into the pan except for okra, stir until mixed, and then bring the mixture to a simmer.
3. Add mushrooms, stir until mixed, and then cook for 10 to 15 min over medium-low heat until cooked.

Nutrition: Calories: 186 kcal; **Fat:** 3.4 g; **Protein:** 2.1 g; **Carbohydrate:** 36.7 g; **Fiber:** 3.5 g

282. Chickpea and Kale Curry

Preparation Time: 5 min
Cooking Time: 10 min
Servings: 2
Ingredients:

- 2 cups chickpeas, cooked
- ⅔ tsp. salt
- 1 cup Kale leaves
- ⅔ cup soft-jelly coconut cream
- 2 tbsp. grapeseed oil

Extra:

- ⅓ tsp. cayenne pepper

Directions:

1. Switch on the oven, set it to 425°F, and let it preheat.
2. Then take a medium baking sheet, spread chickpeas on it, and drizzle with 1 tbsp. oil, sprinkle with all the seasonings, and then bake for 15 min until roasted.
3. Then take a frying pan, place it over medium heat, add remaining oil and when hot, add kale and cook for 5 min.
4. Add roasted chickpeas, pour in the cream, stir until mixed, and then simmer for 4 min, squashing chickpeas slightly.

Nutrition: Calories: 522 kcal; **Fat:** 38 g; **Protein:** 15 g; **Carbohydrate:** 26 g; **Fiber:** 8 g

283. Hummus Wrap

Preparation Time: 10 min
Cooking Time: 8 min
Servings: 2
Ingredients:

- ½ cup iceberg lettuce
- 1 zucchini, sliced
- 2 cherry tomatoes, sliced
- 2 spelt flour tortillas
- 4 tbsp. homemade hummus

Extra:

- ¼ tsp. salt
- ⅛ tsp. cayenne pepper
- 1 tbsp. grapeseed oil

Directions:

1. Take a grill pan, grease it with oil, and let it preheat over medium-high heat.
2. Meanwhile, place zucchini slices in a large bowl, sprinkle with salt and cayenne pepper, drizzle with oil and then toss until coated.
3. Arrange zucchini slices on the grill pan and then cook for 2 to 3 min per side until developed grill marks.
4. Assemble tortillas; heat the tortilla on the grill pan until warm and develop grill marks. Spread 2 tablespoons of hummus over each tortilla.
5. Distribute grilled zucchini slices over the tortillas, top with lettuce and tomato slices, and then wrap tightly.
6. Storage instructions:
7. Cover each wrap with plastic and foil, and then refrigerate for up to 5 days.
8. Reheating instructions:

9. When ready to eat, bring the wrap to room temperature or reheat in the oven for 1 to 2 min until hot and then serve.

Nutrition: Calories: 264.5 kcal; **Fat:** 5.1 g; **Protein:** 8.5 g; **Carbohydrate:** 34.5 g; **Fiber:** 5 g

284. Tomato Sauce

Preparation Time: 15 min
Cooking Time: 50 min
Servings: 24
Ingredients:

- 18 plum tomatoes, halved
- ½ red bell pepper, seeded and halved
- ½ red onion, halved
- ½ sweet onion, halved
- 1 medium shallot, halved
- 2 tbsp. grapeseed oil
- 3 tsp. basil, dried and divided
- 3 tsp. sea salt
- 1 tbsp. agave nectar
- 2 tsp. oregano, dried
- 2 tsp. onion powder
- ⅛ tsp. cayenne powder

Directions:

1. Preheat your oven to 400°F.
2. Line a baking sheet with parchment paper.
3. Add tomatoes, bell pepper, onions, shallot, oil, 1 teaspoon of basil, and 1 teaspoon of salt, and toss to coat well.
4. Arrange the vegetables onto the prepared baking sheet, cut-side down.
5. Roast for about 30 min, flipping the vegetables once halfway through.
6. Remove the baking sheet from the oven and set it aside to cool slightly.
7. In a high-powered blender, add the roasted vegetables and pulse at high speed until smooth.
8. In a pan, add the puréed vegetables and remaining ingredients over low heat and simmer for about 20 min.
9. Remove from the heat and set aside to cool completely before serving.

Nutrition: Calories: 33 kcal; **Fat:** 0.1 g; **Cholesterol:** 0 mg; **Carbohydrate:** 5.3 g; **Fiber:** 4 g; **Protein:** 0.9 g

285. Lettuce Wraps

Preparation Time: 15 min
Cooking Time: 15 min
Servings: 3
Ingredients:

- ¾ cup fresh kale, tough ribs removed and torn
- 1 cup cucumber, sliced
- 1 cup cherry tomatoes, halved
- Sea salt, as needed
- 6 large lettuce leaves

Directions:

1. Add the kale, cucumber, tomato, and salt to a large bowl and mix well.
2. Arrange the lettuce leaves onto serving plates.
3. Divide the kale mixture onto each lettuce leaf evenly.
4. Serve immediately.

Nutrition: Calories: 26 kcal; **Fat:** 0 g; **Cholesterol:** 0 mg; **Carbohydrate:** 5.4 g; **Fiber:** 1.2 g; **Protein:** 1.3 g

286. Veggies Burgers

Preparation Time: 15 min
Cooking Time: 20 min
Servings: 4
Ingredients:

- ½ cup fresh kale, tough ribs removed and chopped
- ½ cup green bell peppers, seeded and chopped
- ½ cup onions, chopped
- 1 plum tomato, chopped
- 2 tsp. fresh oregano, chopped
- 2 tsp. fresh basil, chopped
- 1 tsp. dill, dried
- 1 tsp. onion powder
- ½ tsp. ginger powder
- ½ tsp. cayenne powder
- Sea salt, as needed
- 1 cup chickpeas flour
- ¼–½ cup spring water
- 2 tbsp. grapeseed oil
- 4 cups fresh arugula

Directions:

1. Add all vegetables, herbs, spices, and salt to a bowl and mix well.
2. Add the flour and mix well.
3. Slowly add the water and mix until a thick mixture is formed.
4. Make desired-sized patties from the mixture.
5. In a skillet, heat the grapeseed oil over medium-high heat and cook the patties for about 2–3 min per side.
6. Divide the arugula onto serving plates and top each with 2 burgers.
7. Serve immediately.

Nutrition: Calories: 177 kcal; **Fat:** 0.9 g; **Cholesterol:** 0 mg; **Carbohydrate:** 19.2 g; **Fiber:** 4.1 g; **Protein:** 6.6 g

287. Veggie Balls in Tomato Sauce

Preparation Time: 20 min
Cooking Time: 15 min

Servings: 8
Ingredients:

- 1 ½ cup chickpeas, cooked
- 2 cups fresh button mushrooms
- ½ cup onions, chopped
- ¼ cup green bell peppers, seeded and chopped
- 2 tsp. oregano
- 2 tsp. fresh basil
- 1 tsp. savory
- 1 tsp. sage, dried
- 1 tsp. dill, dried
- 1 tbsp. onion powder
- ½ tsp. cayenne powder
- ½ tsp. ginger powder
- Sea salt, as needed
- ½–1 cup chickpea flour
- 6 cups homemade tomato sauce
- 2 tbsp. grapeseed oil

Directions:

1. In a food processor, add the chickpeas, veggies, herbs, and spices and pulse until well combined.
2. Transfer the mixture into a large bowl with flour and mix until well combined.
3. Make desired-sized balls from the mixture.
4. In a skillet, heat the grapeseed oil over medium-high heat and cook the balls in 2 batches for about 4–5 min or until golden brown from all sides.
5. In a large pan, add the tomato sauce and veggie balls over medium heat and simmer for about 5 min.
6. Serve hot.

Nutrition: Calories: 247 kcal; **Fat:** 0.7 g; **Cholesterol:** 0 mg; **Carbohydrate:** 38.8 g; **Fiber:** 10.7 g; **Protein:** 11.8 g

288. Garden Vegetables and Chickpeas Salad

Preparation Time: 10 minutes (or you can refrigerate it overnight)
Cooking time: 0 minutes
Servings: 4
Ingredients

- 2 tablespoons freshly squeezed lemon juice
- 1/8 teaspoon freshly ground pepper
- 1 cup cubed part-skim mozzarella cheese
- 1 tablespoon fresh basil leaf, snipped
- 1 (15-ounce) can chickpeas, rinsed and well drained
- 2 cups coarsely chopped fresh broccoli
- 2 cloves fresh garlic, finely minced
- ½ cup sliced fresh carrots
- 1 7½-ounce can dice tomatoes, undrained

Direction:

1. Use a large bowl and add garlic, basil, lemon juice, and ground pepper. Mix them well.
2. Add the chickpeas, carrots, tomatoes with juice, broccoli, and mozzarella cheese. Toss all the ingredients well.
3. You can serve immediately, or you can keep it refrigerated overnight.

Nutrition: Calories: 195 calories Protein: 16 g Total Fat: 7 g Carbohydrate: 24 g

289. Peppered Watercress Salad

Preparation Time: 5 minutes (or less)
Cooking time: 0 minutes
Servings: 4
Ingredients

- 2 teaspoons champagne vinegar
- 2 bunches (about 8 cups) watercress, rinsed and rough stems removed
- 2 tablespoons extra-virgin olive oil
- salt and freshly ground pepper to taste

Direction:

1. Drain the watercress properly.
2. Take out a small bowl and then add salt, pepper, vinegar, and olive oil. Mix them well together.
3. Transfer the watercress to a bowl. Add the vinegar mixture into it and toss well.
4. Serve immediately.

Nutrition: Calories: 67 calories **Protein**: 4 g **Total Fat**: 7 g **Carbohydrate:** 1 g

290. Creamy Broccoli Soup

Preparation Time: 5 min
Cooking Time: 5 min; **Servings:** 2–3
Ingredients:

- 2 cups vegetable stock
- 4 cups broccoli, chopped
- 1 red pepper, chopped
- 1 avocado
- 2 onions, chopped
- 2 celery stalks, sliced
- Ginger, to taste
- 1 tbsp. salt

Directions:

1. Warm vegetable stock in a small pot. Add broccoli and season with salt to taste. Simmer for 5 min.
2. Add the broccoli into a blender with pepper, avocado, onions, and celery stalks. Add some water for thinning, then blend until smooth.
3. Serve when warm with ginger to your liking. Garnish with a lemon slice. Enjoy.

Nutrition: Calories: 270 kcal; **Fat:** 18 g; **Carbohydrate:** 17 g; **Protein:** 12 g; **Fiber:** 3.5 g

291. Beef, White Bean, and Spinach Soup

Preparation Time: 10 min
Cooking Time: 40 min;
Servings: 2–3
Ingredients:

- 1 tsp. extra-virgin olive oil
- 1 medium onion, chopped
- 2 (4-oz.) Beef chops, boneless, cut into 1-inch cubes
- 1 (14.5 oz.) can diced tomatoes
- 3 cups low-sodium chicken broth
- ½ tsp. thyme, dried
- ¼ tsp. red pepper flakes, crushed
- 1 (15-oz.) can great northern beans, drained and rinsed
- 8 oz. fresh spinach leaves

Directions:

1. Place a large soup pot or Dutch oven over medium heat and heat the olive oil.
2. Add the onion and sauté for 2 to 3 minutes or until tender. Add the beef and brown it for 4 to 5 min on each side.
3. Mix in the tomatoes, broth, thyme, red pepper flakes, and beans. Boil and minimize heat to simmer, covered, for 30 min.
4. Add the spinach and stir until wilted, about 5 min, and serve immediately.

Nutrition per serving (1 cup): Calories: 156 kcal; Total **Fat:** 4 g; **Protein:** 17 g; **Carbs:** 17 g; **Fiber:** 4 g; **Sugar:** 6 g; **Sodium:** 600 mg

292. Spaghetti Squash Casserole with Ground Beef

Prep Time: 10 min
Cooking Time: 75 min
Servings: 2–3
Ingredients:

- Nonstick cooking spray
- 2 medium spaghetti squash (2 ½ to 3 lb.)
- 1 lb supreme lean ground beef
- 1 large onion, minced
- 2 tsp. garlic, minced
- 1 (8-oz.) can tomato sauce
- 1 (10-oz.) can tomatoes, diced
- 1 tsp. basil, dried
- 1 tsp. oregano, dried
- 1 cup mozzarella cheese, shredded
- ½ cup Parmigiano-Reggiano cheese, shredded

Directions:

1. Preheat the oven to 350°F. Coat a baking sheet with the cooking spray.

2. Halve the spaghetti squash, remove and discard the stem, pulp, and seeds, and place the halves cut-side down on the baking sheet. Bake till the flesh is tender and for 35 min.
3. While the squash bakes, spray a large skillet with the cooking spray and place it over medium heat. Add the ground beef, onion, garlic, and sauté for about 10 minutes or until the beef is no longer pink and the onion is tender. Add the tomato sauce, diced tomatoes, basil, and oregano, and stir to combine well. Remove the pan from the heat and set it aside.
4. When the spaghetti squash is cool enough to handle, carefully use a fork to pull the flesh from the outer skin and make "spaghetti." Set aside in a bowl.
5. In a 9-x-13-inch baking dish, layer one-third of the meat-and-tomato mixture at the bottom of the dish. Evenly spread half of the squash over the meat layer. Layer another one-third of the meat mixture over the squash. Finish the last layer with the second half of the squash and the last one-third of the meat mixture, and sprinkle the mozzarella and Parmigiano-Reggiano cheeses over the top.
6. Cover with aluminum foil and bake for 30 min. Remove the foil and bake for 10 min more, or until the cheese begins to brown. Serve.

Nutrition per serving (1 cup): Calories: 229 kcal; **Total Fat:** 10 g; **Protein:** 20 g; **Carbs:** 16 g; **Fiber:** 3 g; **Sugar:** 11 g; **Sodium:** 511 mg

293. Ham and Bean Soup

Preparation Time: 10 min
Cooking Time: 4 hours
Servings: 2–3
Ingredients:

- 125 g celery, chopped fine
- 125 g carrots, chopped fine
- 125 g onion, minced
- 1 garlic clove, minced
- 350 g ham, cubed
- ⅛ tsp. pepper, cayenne
- ¼ tsp. cumin, dried
- ¼ tsp. sea salt
- 1 can beans, navy
- 250 ml broth, chicken or veggie
- 250 ml water

Directions:

1. Brown ham in a soup pot or large saucepan on medium heat.
2. Pour in water, scraping the glaze off the bottom of the pan.
3. Pour in the broth.
4. Add the beans. Drain the liquid from the can and rinse the beans before adding.
5. Add the remaining ingredients and stir well.
6. Bring soup to a boil, turn heat to simmer, and let it be for one to 3 hours (the longer it cooks, the better it tastes), stirring occasionally.

Nutrition: Calories: 240 kcal; **Carbohydrate:** 25.8 g; **Protein:** 24.4 g; **Fat:** 4.1 g; **Saturated Fat:** 1.5 g; **Polyunsaturated Fat:** 3.6 g; **Trans Fat:** 0 g; **Cholesterol:** 30 mg; **Sodium:** 1044 mg; **Fiber:** 7 g; **Sugar:** 4.1 g

294. Potato Broccoli Soup

Preparation Time: 10 min
Cooking Time: 30 min
Servings: 2–3
Ingredients:

- 1 cup broth
- Half a cup broccoli, chopped
- 1 small-sized potato, chopped
- 1 tbsp. corn starch
- Half a cup milk
- 2 tbsp. Cheddar cheese, shredded
- 1 tsp. garlic powder
- Pepper and salt according to taste

Directions:

1. Peel and cut the potato. Then boil it till it becomes soft.
2. Steam the broccoli till it is tender.
3. Put the potato and broccoli in one food processor and make a purée.
4. Mix 1 tbsp. corn starch in a ¼th cup of broth in a saucepan and heat it for one minute till it starts boiling. Slowly add the remaining broth and let it cook till it starts boiling again. The liquid will become thick and creamy because of the corn starch.
5. Put milk, garlic powder, and the purée and stir. Then add the pepper and salt according to taste.
6. Remove it from heat. Put the Cheddar cheese and stir till it melts.

7. Serve when it is warm. You can keep the leftovers in the fridge for 3 days.

Nutrition: Calories: 171 kcal; **Carbohydrate:** 22.5 g; **Protein:** 14.4 g; **Fat:** 2.5 g; **Saturated Fat:** 0.4 g; **Polyunsaturated Fat:** 2.1 g; **Trans-Fat:** 0 g; **Cholesterol:** 31 mg; **Sodium:** 521 mg; **Fiber:** 4.6 g; **Sugar:** 3 g

295. Creamy Chicken Vegetable Soup

Preparation Time: 10 min
Cooking Time: 20 min ; **Servings:** 2–3
Ingredients:

- 2 tbsp. olive oil
- ½ cup onions, finely chopped
- ½ cup carrots, thinly sliced or shredded
- ½ cup potatoes, diced
- ½ cup green beans
- ½ cup peas
- 1 cup chicken, finely chopped
- 1 (14-oz.) can chicken broth
- ¼ tsp. black pepper
- 1 ¼ cup milk
- 1 (10 ¾-oz.) can cream celery soup
- 1 (10 ¾-oz.) can cream Cheddar cheese soup

Directions:

1. In a large saucepan, heat oil; add onions and carrots; cook and stir until softened, about 5 min.
2. Add potatoes, green beans, peas, chicken, broth, and pepper. Cover, and cook over low heat for 1 ½ hour, or until vegetables are soft; stir occasionally.
3. Add milk, celery soup, and Cheddar cheese soup; stir and continue cooking time until heated throughout.

Nutrition: Calories: 125 kcal; **Total Fat:** 3.6 g; **Total Carbohydrate:** 15.6 g; **Protein:** 7.6 g

296. Cucumber and Basil Gazpacho

Preparation Time: 5 min
Cooking Time: 0 mi; **Servings:** 2
Ingredients:

- 1 avocado, peeled, pitted, cold
- 1 cucumber, deseeded, unpeeled, cold
- ½ cup basil leaves, cold
- ½ of key lime, juiced
- 2 cups spring water, chilled

Extra:

- 1 ½ tsp. sea salt

Directions:

1. Place all the ingredients into a high-speed food processor or blender jar and then pulse until smooth.
2. Tip the soup into a medium bowl and then chill for 1 hour.
3. Divide the soup evenly between 2 bowls, top with some more basil, and serve.

Nutrition: Calories: 190 kcal; **Fat:** 15 g; **Protein:** 4 g; **Carbohydrate:** 15 g; **Fiber:** 6 g

297. Orange Fidelity Soup

Preparation Time: 20 min
Cooking Time: 45 min; **Servings:** 2–3
Ingredients:

- 1 onion, medium and sliced
- 2 pears, small, halved, unpeeled, cored, and chopped small
- 3 sprigs thyme
- 2 tbsp. olive oil, extra-virgin
- 1-kilo butternut squash, halved, seeded, unpeeled
- 250 ml broth, chicken or vegetable
- 500 ml milk, non-fat
- Garnish: 75 ml pecan pieces, toasted or almonds

Directions:

1. Heat oven to 400°F.
2. On a cookie sheet covered with parchment paper, place the pears, onions, and thyme. Sprinkle with olive oil.
3. On top of this, place the 2 squash halves.

4. Roast for 50–60 min. It is done when you can pierce the squash with a fork. Remove from oven and let cool.
5. Scoop the flesh from the squash, discarding the peel.
6. Place squash flesh and pan contents (without the parchment paper) into a blender or food processor. Blend.
7. Pour this into a large soup pot, add the broth, and simmer for 10 min.
8. Stir in the milk and continue to simmer for another 8 min.
9. Garnish with the nut pieces and servings.
10. Do not add the pecans as garnish unless you are more than six months post-directions.

Nutrition: Calories: 144 kcal; **Carbohydrate:** 20.5 g; **Protein:** 0.5 g; **Fat:** 0.2 g; **Saturated Fat:** 0 g; **Polyunsaturated Fat:** 0 g; **Trans Fat:** 0 g; **Cholesterol:** 0 mg; **Sodium:** 41 mg; **Fiber:** 0.2 g; **Sugar:** 18 g

298. Zoodle Vegetable Soup

Preparation Time: 5 min
Cooking Time: 12 min; **Servings:** 2
Ingredients:

- ½ onion, peeled, cubed
- ½ green bell pepper, chopped
- ½ zucchini, grated
- 4 oz. mushrooms, sliced and chopped
- ½ cup cherry tomatoes

Extra:

- ¼ cup basil leaves
- 1 pack spelt noodles, cooked
- ¼ tsp. salt
- ⅛ tsp. cayenne pepper
- ½ key lime, juiced
- 1 tbsp. grapeseed oil
- 2 cups spring water

Directions:

1. Take a medium saucepan, place it over medium heat, add oil, and when hot, add onion and then cook for 3 min or more until tender.
2. Add cherry tomatoes, bell pepper, and mushrooms, stir until mixed, and then continue cooking for 3 min until soft.
3. Add grated zucchini, season with salt, and cayenne pepper, pour in the water, and then bring the mixture to a boil.
4. Then switch heat to the low level, add cooked noodles and then simmer the soup for 5 min.
5. When done, ladle soup into 2 bowls, top with basil leaves, drizzle with lime juice and then serve.

Nutrition: Calories: 265 kcal; **Fat:** 2 g; **Protein:** 4 g; **Carbohydrate:** 57 g; **Fiber:** 13.6 g

299. Delicious Chickpea and Mushroom Bowl

Preparation Time: 5 min
Cooking Time: 5 min; **Servings:** 2–3
Ingredients:

- 1 ½ cup chickpeas, cooked
- 2 zucchinis, spiralized
- 4 small oyster mushrooms, destemmed, diced
- ¼ white onion, peeled, chopped
- ¼ of red bell pepper, cored, chopped

Extra:

- ⅓ tsp. sea salt; 1 tsp. basil, dried
- ¼ tsp. cayenne pepper
- 1 tsp. oregano, dried
- 1 tbsp. grapeseed oil
- 2 ½ cups vegetable broth, homemade

Directions:

1. Take a medium pot, place it over medium-high heat, add oil, and when hot, add red pepper, onion, and mushrooms, season with salt and cayenne pepper, and then cook for 5 min until tender.
2. Switch heat to medium-low level, add remaining ingredients except for zucchini noodles, stir until mixed, and then simmer the soup for 15 to 20 minutes.
3. Then add zucchini noodles into the pan, stir until mixed, and cook for 1 minute or more until thoroughly warmed.

Nutrition: Calories: 242 kcal; **Fat:** 9 g; **Protein:** 10 g; **Carbohydrate:** 34 g; **Fiber:** 9 g

300. Zoodle Chickpea Soup

Preparation Time: 5 min
Cooking Time: 25 min; **Servings:** 2–3
Ingredients:

- ½ cup chickpeas, cooked
- ½ white onion, peeled, diced
- ½ large zucchini, chopped
- 1 cup kale leaves
- 1 cup squash cubes

Extra:

- ¾ tsp. salt
- ¾ tbsp. thyme, chopped and fresh
- ¾ tbsp. tarragon, fresh
- 2 cups vegetable broth, homemade
- 1 ½ cup spring water

Directions:

1. Take a saucepan, place it over medium-high heat, pour in the ¼ cup broth, add zucchini, onion, and thyme and then cook for 4 minutes.

2. Pour in the remaining broth and water, bring it to a boil, switch heat to the low level, and then simmer for 10 to 15 min until tender.
3. Add the remaining ingredients, stir until mixed, and then continue cooking for 10 minutes or more.

Nutrition: Calories: 184.5 kcal; **Fat:** 0.3 g; **Protein:** 6.8 g; **Carbohydrate:** 31 g; **Fiber:** 6 g

301. Frank Sinatra Soup

Preparation Time: 10 min
Cooking Time: 20 min; **Servings:** 2–3
Ingredients:

- 1 tbsp. olive oil
- 1 onion, diced
- 4 garlic cloves, minced
- 250 g carrots, diced
- 500 g broccoli florets, chopped into small pieces
- 750 g cauliflower florets, chopped into small pieces
- 1 ½ liter vegetable broth
- 4 tomatoes, medium, diced
- 1 tbsp. Italian herb mix, dried
- Pinch red pepper flakes, crushed, a pinch
- Black pepper and salt, for taste
- Parmesan cheese, grated, for sprinkling on top
- Fresh parsley, chopped, for sprinkling on top

Directions:

1. Heat the oil in a large soup pot over medium heat.
2. Add the garlic and onion. Cook until fragrant for about 2 min.
3. Stir in the carrot. Continue cooking time for another 2–3 min.
4. Pour in the broth, stir in the tomatoes, herbs, pinch of red pepper flakes, black pepper, and salt.
5. Bring the ingredients to a boil. Lower the heat and simmer for 5 min.
6. Add the broccoli and cauliflower, and simmer until the vegetables are cooked but still crunchy. This may take 5 minutes.
7. Taste and adjust your seasoning.
8. Serve yourself a bowl, sprinkling the cheese and parsley on top.
9. If you want to enjoy this as a slightly thicker soup, stir 1 tablespoon of coconut flour or cornstarch into 75 ml of cold water. Add this to the soup and continue to cook for an additional 5 min after the vegetables have finished cooking time.

Nutrition: Calories: 329 kcal; **Carbohydrate:** 43.6 g; **Protein:** 28.9 g; **Fat:** 4.9 g; **Saturated Fat:** 0.9 g; **Polyunsaturated Fat:** 4 g; **Trans-Fat:** 0 g; **Cholesterol:** 64 mg; **Sodium:** 992 mg; **Fiber:** 9.3 g; **Sugar:** 5.8 g

302. Healthy Alkaline Green Soup

Preparation Time: 10 min
Cooking Time: 5 min; **Servings:** 2–3
Ingredients:

- 2 cups leafy greens
- 1 small zucchini, sliced
- 1 small white onion, peeled, sliced
- 1 medium green bell pepper, cored, sliced
- 2 ½ cups spring water

Extra:

- ¾ tsp. salt
- ¼ tsp. cayenne pepper
- 1 tsp. basil, dried

Directions:

1. Take a medium pot, place it over medium heat, add all the ingredients, stir until mixed, and then cook for 5 to 10 min until the vegetables turn tender-crisp.
2. Remove pot from heat, purée the soup using an immersion blender and then serve.

Nutrition: Calories: 129 kcal; **Fat:** 0.2 g; **Protein:** 1.1 g; **Carbohydrate:** 28 g; **Fiber:** 4.5 g

303. Kamut Squash Soup

Preparation Time: 5 min
Cooking Time: 32 min; **Servings:** 2–3
Ingredients:

- 6 tbsp. Kamut berries
- 1 cup white onion, chopped
- ½ cup squash, chopped
- ½ cup chickpeas, cooked
- 1 cup vegetable broth, homemade

Extra:

- ¼ tsp. cayenne pepper
- ½ tbsp. tarragon, chopped
- 1 bay leaf
- 1 tsp. thyme, chopped
- 1 tbsp. olive oil
- 1 cup spring water, boiling

Directions:

1. Place Kamut in a small bowl, pour in the boiling water, and let it stand for 30 min.
2. Then take a medium pot, place it over medium heat, add oil, and when hot, add onion, stir in thyme and tarragon and then cook for 5 min until tender.
3. Drain Kamut, add to the pot, add bay leaves, pour in the vegetable broth, and then bring it to boil.
4. Cover the pot with its lid, simmer for 20 to 30 minutes, then stir in cayenne pepper and cook for 5 minutes.
5. Remove bay leaf, add chickpeas, and then cook for 2 min.

Nutrition: Calories: 348.8 kcal; **Fat:** 8.8 g; **Protein:** 11.3 g; **Carbohydrate:** 57.2 g; **Fiber:** 7.8 g

304. Creamy Mushroom Soup

Preparation Time: 5 min
Cooking Time: 10 min; **Ingredients**:

- 2 cups Baby Bella mushrooms, diced
- ½ cup red onions, diced
- 1 cup vegetable broth
- 1 ½ cup soft-jelly coconut milk

Extra:

- ½ tsp. sea salt
- ¼ tsp. cayenne pepper
- 2 tsp. grapeseed oil

Directions:

1. Take a medium saucepan, place it over medium-high heat, add oil, and when hot, add onion, and mushrooms, season with salt and pepper, and then cook for 3 to 4 min until vegetables turn tender.
2. Then add soy sauce, pour in milk and broth, stir until mixed and bring it to a boil.
3. Switch heat to medium-low level, and then simmer the soup for 15 min until it thickens to the desired level.

Nutrition: Calories: 100 kcal; **Fat:** 2 g; **Protein:** 2 g; **Carbohydrate:** 18 g; **Fiber:** 2 g

305. Basil Tomato Soup with Avocado Oil

Preparation Time: 15 min
Cooking Time: 8 min;
Servings: 2–3
Ingredients:

- 2 tsp. avocado oil
- 1 medium white onion, chopped
- 3 garlic cloves, minced
- 7 cups fresh plum tomatoes, chopped
- ½ cup fresh sweet basil, chopped
- Sea salt, as needed
- ¼ tsp. cayenne powder

Directions:

1. In a pan, heat the oil over medium heat and sauté the onion and garlic for about 5–6 min.
2. Add the tomatoes and cook for about 6–8 min, crushing with the back of a spoon occasionally.
3. Stir in the basil, salt, and cayenne powder and remove from the heat.
4. With a hand blender, purée the soup mixture until smooth.
5. Serve immediately.

Nutrition: Calories: 75 kcal; **Fat:** 0.2 g; **Cholesterol:** 0 mg; **Carbohydrate:** 15.8 g; **Fiber:** 4.6 g; **Protein:** 3.5 g

306. Mushroom Soup

Preparation Time: 15 min
Cooking Time: 25 min;
Servings: 2–3
Ingredients:

- 2 tsp. avocado oil
- 1 ¼ cup fresh Portobello mushrooms, sliced
- 1 ¼ cup fresh button mushrooms, sliced
- ½ cup white onion, chopped
- 1 garlic clove, crushed
- ½ tsp. thyme, dried
- Sea salt and cayenne powder, as needed
- 1¾ cups coconut milk, unsweetened
- 1 ½ cup spring water

Directions:

1. In a soup pan, heat the avocado oil over medium-high heat and cook the mushrooms, onions, garlic, thyme, salt, and black pepper for about 5–6 min.
2. Add the coconut milk and water and bring to a boil.
3. Now, adjust the heat to medium-low and simmer for about 10–15 min, stirring occasionally.
4. Serve hot.

Nutrition: Calories: 177 kcal; **Fat:** 13.2 g; **Cholesterol:** 0 mg; **Carbohydrate:** 5.9 g; **Fiber:** 0.9 g; **Protein:** 2.9 g

307. Mixed Greens Soup

Preparation Time: 15 min
Cooking Time: 5 min;
Servings: 2–3
Ingredients:

- 2 cups fresh kale, tough ribs removed and chopped
- 2 cups fresh watercress
- 2 cups dandelion greens
- 2 garlic cloves, peeled
- 2 cups spring water
- 1 cup coconut milk, unsweetened
- 1 tbsp. fresh key lime juice
- ½ tsp. cayenne powder
- Sea salt, as needed

Directions:

1. Place all soup ingredients in a high-powered blender and pulse at high speed until smooth.
2. Transfer the soup into a pan over medium heat and cook for about 3–5 min or until heated.
3. Serve hot.

Nutrition: Calories: 168 kcal; **Fat:** 10.1 g; **Cholesterol:** 0 mg; **Carbohydrate:** 11 g; **Fiber:** 2.4 g; **Protein:** 4.2 g

308. Squash and Apple Soup

Preparation Time: 15 min
Cooking Time: 45 min;
Servings: 2–3

Ingredients:

- 2 tbsp. avocado oil
- 1 cup white onion, chopped
- 2 garlic cloves, minced
- 1 tsp. thyme, dried
- 3 cups butternut squash, peeled and cubed
- 2 apples, cored and chopped
- 4 cups spring water
- Sea salt, as needed

Directions:

1. In a soup pan, heat avocado oil over medium heat and sauté the onion for about 5 min.
2. Add the garlic and thyme and sauté for about 1 minute.
3. Add the squash, apple, and ginger, and cook for about 1–2 min.
4. Stir in the water and bring to a boil.
5. Now, adjust the heat to low and simmer covered for about 30 min.
6. Stir in the salt and remove from the heat.
7. With a hand blender, purée the soup mixture until smooth.
8. Serve immediately.

Nutrition: Calories: 129 kcal; **Fat:** 0.2 g; **Cholesterol:** 0 mg; **Carbohydrate:** 31.4 g; **Fiber:** 5.9 g; **Protein:** 1.9 g

309. Chickpeas and Squash Stew

Preparation Time: 15 min
Cooking Time: 1 ¼ hour;
Servings: 2–3
Ingredients:

- 2 tbsp. avocado oil
- 1 large white onion, chopped
- 4 garlic cloves, minced
- ½ tbsp. cayenne powder
- 4 large plum tomatoes, seeded and chopped finely
- 1 lb. butternut squash; peeled, seeded, and chopped
- 1 ½ cup spring water
- 1 cup chickpeas, cooked
- 2 tbsp. fresh key lime juice
- Sea salt, as needed
- 2 tbsp. fresh parsley, chopped

Directions:

1. In a soup pan, heat the avocado oil over medium heat and sauté the onion for about 4–6 min.
2. Add the garlic and cayenne powder and sauté for about 1 minute.
3. Add the tomatoes and cook for about 2–3 min.
4. Add the squash and water and bring to a boil.
5. Now, adjust the heat to low and simmer, covered for about 50 min.
6. Add the chickpeas and cook for about 10 min.
7. Stir in lime juice and salt and remove from heat.
8. Serve hot with the garnishing of parsley.

Nutrition: Calories: 150 kcal; **Fat:** 0.3 g; **Cholesterol:** 0 mg; **Carbohydrate:** 21.5 g; **Protein:** 5.2 g

310. Chickpeas and Kale Stew

Preparation Time: 15 min
Cooking Time: 15 min;
Servings: 2–3
Ingredients:

- 1 tbsp. avocado oil
- 1 large onion, chopped
- 2 garlic cloves, minced
- 3 cups cherry tomatoes, chopped finely
- 2 cups spring water
- 2 cups cooked chickpeas
- 2 cups fresh kale, tough ribs removed and chopped
- 1 tbsp. fresh key lime juice
- Sea salt, as needed
- ¼ tsp. cayenne powder

Directions:

1. In a soup pan, heat avocado oil over medium heat and sauté the onion for about 6 min.
2. Stir in the garlic and sauté for about 1 minute.
3. Add the tomatoes and cook for about 2–3 min.
4. Add the water and bring to a boil.
5. Now, adjust the heat to low and simmer for about 10 min.
6. Stir in the chickpeas and simmer for about 5 min.
7. Stir in the spinach and simmer for 3–4 min more.
8. Stir in the lime juice and seasoning and remove from the heat.
9. Serve hot.

Nutrition: Calories: 206 kcal; **Fat:** 0.3 g; **Cholesterol:** 0 mg; **Carbohydrate:** 40.1 g; **Fiber:** 8.4 g; **Protein:** 8.7 g

311. Chickpeas and Veggie Stew

Preparation Time: 20 min
Cooking Time: 1 hour 5 min;
Servings: 2–3
Ingredients:

- 3 cups portabella mushrooms, chopped
- 4 cups spring water
- 1 cup cooked chickpeas
- 1 cup fresh kale, tough ribs removed and chopped
- 1 cup white onion, chopped
- 1 cup green bell peppers, seeded and chopped
- ½ cup butternut squash; peeled, seeded, and chopped
- 2 plum tomatoes, chopped
- 2 tbsp. grapeseed oil

- 1 tsp. oregano, dried
- 1 tsp. basil, dried
- ½ tsp. thyme, dried
- 2 tsp. onion powder
- 1 tsp. cayenne powder
- ½ tsp. ginger powder
- Sea salt, as needed

Directions:

1. In a soup pan, add all ingredients over high heat and bring to a rolling boil.
2. Now, adjust the heat to low and simmer, covered for about 1 hour, stirring occasionally.
3. Serve hot.

Nutrition: Calories: 75 kcal; **Total Fat:** 5 g; **Protein:** 0 g; **Carbohydrate:** 8 g; **Fiber:** 1 g; **Sugar:** 4 g; **Sodium:** 2 mg

312. Quinoa and Veggie Stew

Preparation Time: 15 min
Cooking Time: 1 hour;
Servings: 2–3
Ingredients:

- 2 tbsp. grapeseed oil
- 1 large onion, chopped
- Sea salt, as needed
- 2 cups butternut squash, peeled and cubed
- 3 garlic cloves, minced
- 1 tsp. ground cumin
- 1 tsp. cayenne powder
- 2½ cups plum tomatoes, chopped finely
- ½ cup dry quinoa, rinsed
- 3 cups spring water
- 3 cups fresh kale, tough ribs removed and chopped
- 1 tbsp. fresh key lime juice

Directions:

1. In a soup pan, heat the grapeseed oil over medium heat and cook the onion with a few pinches of salt for about 4–5 min, stirring occasionally.
2. Add the butternut squash and cook for about 3–4 min.
3. Stir in the garlic and spices and cook for about 1 minute.
4. Stir in the tomatoes, quinoa, and water and bring to a boil.
5. Now, adjust the heat to low and simmer, covered for about 35 min.
6. Stir in the kale and cook for about 10 min.

Nutrition: Calories: 237 kcal; **Fat:** 0.9 g; **Cholesterol:** 0 mg; **Carbohydrate:** 36.2 g; **Fiber:** 6 g; **Protein:** 6.9 g

313. Creamy Squash Soup

Preparation Time: 5 min
Cooking Time: 25 min; **Servings:** 2–3
Ingredients:

- ½ of medium white onion, peeled, cubed
- 2 cups cubed squash
- ¼ cup basil leaves
- ½ cup soft-jelly coconut cream

Extra:

- ⅛ tsp. sea salt
- ⅛ tsp. cayenne pepper
- 1 tbsp. grapeseed oil
- 1 cup vegetable broth, homemade

Directions:

1. In a medium saucepan, place it over medium heat, add oil and when hot, add onion, and then cook for 5 min or until softened.
2. Add squash, cook for 10 min until golden and begin to soften, pour in the vegetable broth, season with salt and pepper and then bring the soup to boil.
3. Switch heat to medium level and then simmer the soup for 10 min until squash turns very soft.
4. Remove pan from heat, purée it with a stick blender until smooth, and then garnish with basil.

Nutrition: Calories: 183 kcal; **Fat:** 14.4 g; **Protein:** 1.9 g; **Carbohydrate:** 13.4 g; **Fiber:** 2.7 g

314. Healing Ginger Carrot Soup

Preparation Time: 10 min
Cooking Time: 8 min; **Servings:** 2–3
Ingredients:

- 1 tbsp. fresh ginger
- Sea salt and pepper, to taste
- 2 garlic cloves
- ½ onion, quartered
- 4 carrots, washed and peeled
- 2 cups vegetable stock
- 1 tsp. turmeric

Directions:

1. Add all your ingredients to a huge pot and bring to a boil. Once boiled, let it simmer for an hour. When the carrots are soft, blend using an immersion blender until smooth.
2. Garnish with some hemp seeds on top if desired.

Nutrition: Calories: 443 kcal; **Fat:** 8 g; **Fiber:** 1 g; **Carbohydrate:** 8 g; **Protein:** 3 g

315. Caramelized Salmon Fillet

Preparation Time: 5 min
Cooking Time: 25 min; **Servings:** 2
Ingredients:

- 2 salmon fillets
- 60 g cane sugar
- 4 tbsp. soy sauce
- 50 g sesame seeds
- Ginger, unlimited

Directions:

1. Preheat the air fryer to 180°C for 5 min.
2. Put the sugar and soy sauce in the basket.
3. Cook everything for 5 minutes.
4. In the meantime, wash the fish well, pass it through sesame to cover it completely and place it inside the tank and add the fresh ginger.
5. Cook for 12 minutes.
6. Turn the fish over and finish cooking for another 8 min.

Nutrition: Calories: 569 kcal; **Fat:** 14.9 g; **Carbohydrate:** 40 g; **Sugar:** 27.6 g; **Protein:** 66.9 g; **Cholesterol:** 165.3 mg

316. Salmon Butter Crumbed

Preparation Time: 5–10 min.
Cooking Time: 10 min.
Servings: 2
Ingredients:

- 1 tbsp. thyme, chopped
- 2 garlic cloves, minced
- 1 ½ cup soft bread crumbs
- 2 tbsp. parsley, minced
- 1 tsp. lemon zest, grated
- ½ tsp. salt
- ¼ tsp. paprika
- 1 tbsp. butter, melted
- ¼ tsp. lemon-pepper seasoning
- 2 salmon fillets (6 oz. each)

Directions:

1. In a mixing bowl, add bread crumbs, fresh parsley thyme, garlic, lemon zest, salt, lemon-pepper seasoning, and paprika. Combine to mix well with each other.
2. Place Instant Pot over kitchen platform. Place Air Fryer Lid on top. Press Air Fry, set the temperature to 375°F and set the timer to 5 minutes to preheat. Press "Start" and allow it to preheat for 5 min.
3. Take Air Fryer Basket and grease it with some cooking spray. Add salmon fillets skin side down in the basket and top with the crumb mixture.
4. Place the basket in the inner pot of the Instant Pot and close the Air Fryer Lid on top.
5. Press the "Bake" setting. Set temperature to 390°F and set the timer to 10 min. Press "Start."
6. Open the Air Fryer Lid after cooking time is over. Serve warm.

Nutrition: Calories: 308 kcal; **Fat:** 17 g; **Saturated Fat:** 2.5 g; **Trans Fat:** 0 g; **Carbohydrate:** 11.5 g; **Fiber:** 1 g; **Sodium:** 347 mg; **Protein:** 9 g

317. Cajun Shrimp

Preparation Time: 5 min
Cooking Time: 5 min
Servings: 2–3
Ingredients:

- 16–20/(1.25 lb.) tiger shrimp
- 1 tbsp. olive oil
- ½ tsp. old bay seasoning
- ¼ tsp. paprika, smoked
- ¼ tsp. cayenne pepper

Directions:

1. Set the Air Fryer at 390° F.
2. Cover the shrimp using the oil and spices.
3. Toss them into the Air Fryer basket and set the timer for 5 min.
4. Serve with your favorite side dish.

Nutrition: Calories: 356 kcal; **Fat:** 18 g; **Carbohydrate:** 5 g; **Protein:** 34 g

318. Vegetable Egg Halibut

Preparation Time: 5–10 min.
Cooking Time: 15 min.; **Servings:** 3–4
Ingredients:

- 2 lb. mixed vegetables
- 4 cups torn lettuce leaves
- 1 cup cherry tomatoes, halved
- 1 ½ lb. halibut fillets
- Black pepper, ground, and salt to taste
- 2 tbsp. olive oil
- 4 large hard-boiled eggs, sliced

Directions:

1. Rub the halibut with salt and black pepper. Coat fish with oil.
2. Place Instant Pot over kitchen platform. Place Air Fryer Lid on top. Press Air Fry, set the temperature to 375°F, and set the timer to 5 min to preheat. Press "Start" and allow it to preheat for 5 min.
3. Take Air Fryer Basket and grease it with some cooking spray. In the basket, add fish and arrange vegetables around.
4. Place the basket in the inner pot of the Instant Pot and close the Air Fryer Lid on top.
5. Press the "Air Fry" setting. Set temperature to 375°F and set the timer to 15 min. Press "Start." Stir the mixture halfway down.
6. Open Air Fryer Lid after cooking time is over. Serve warm in a bowl mixed with eggs, lettuce, and tomatoes.

Nutrition: Calories: 336 kcal; **Fat:** 11 g; **Saturated Fat:** 3 g; **Trans Fat:** 0 g; **Carbohydrate:** 16 g; **Fiber:** 2 g; **Sodium:** 658 mg; **Protein:** 20.5 g

319. Deep-Fried Prawns

Preparation Time: 15 min
Cooking Time: 10 min; **Servings:** 2–3
Ingredients:

- 12 prawns
- 2 eggs
- Flour to taste
- Breadcrumbs
- 1 tsp. oil

Directions:

1. Remove the head of the prawns and shell carefully.
2. Pass the prawns first in the flour, then in the beaten egg, and then in the breadcrumbs.
3. Preheat the air fryer for 1 minute at 150°C.
4. Add the prawns and cook for 4 min. If the prawns are large, it will be necessary to cook 6 at a time.
5. Turn the prawns and cook for another 4 min.
6. They should be served with a yogurt or mayonnaise sauce.

Nutrition: Calories: 2385.1 kcal; **Fat:** 23 g; **Carbohydrate:** 52.3 g; **Sugar:** 0.1 g; **Protein:** 21.4 g

320. Salmon with Pistachio Bark

Preparation Time: 10 min
Cooking Time: 15 min
Servings: 2–3
Ingredients:

- 600 g salmon fillet
- 50 g pistachios
- Salt to taste

Directions:

1. Put the parchment paper on the bottom of the air fryer basket and place the salmon fillet in it (it can be cooked whole or already divided into four portions).
2. Cut the pistachios into thick pieces; grease the top of the fish, salt (little because the pistachios are already salted), and cover everything with the pistachios.

3. Set the air fryer to 180°C, and simmer for 25 min.

Nutrition: Calories: 371.7 kcal; **Fat:** 21.8 g; **Carbohydrate:** 9.4 g; **Sugar:** 2.2 g; **Protein:** 34.7 g; **Cholesterol:** 80.5 mg

321. Grilled Sardines

Preparation Time: 5 min
Cooking Time: 10 min
Servings: 2–3
Ingredients:

- 5 sardines
- Herbs of Provence

Directions:

1. Preheat the air fryer to 160°C.
2. Spray the basket and place your sardines in the basket of your fryer.
3. Set the timer for 14 min. After 7 min, remember to turn the sardines, so that they are roasted on both sides.

Nutrition: Calories: 189 kcal; **Fat:** 10 g; **Carbohydrate:** 0 g; **Sugar:** 0 g; **Protein:** 22 g; **Cholesterol:** 128 mg

322. Rangoon Crab Dip

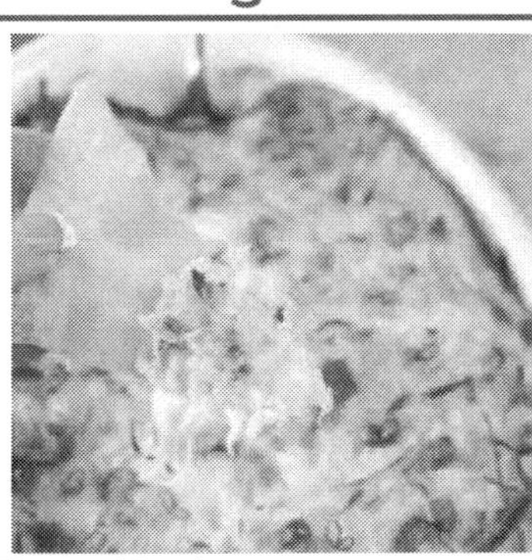

Preparation Time: 10 min
Cooking Time: 16 min; **Servings:** 2–3
Ingredients:

- 2 cups crab meat
- 1 cup mozzarella cheese, shredded
- ½ tsp. garlic powder
- ¼ cup pimentos, drained and diced
- ¼ tsp. stevia
- ½ lemon juice
- 2 tsp. coconut amino
- 2 tsp. mayonnaise
- 8 oz. cream cheese, softened
- 1 tbsp. green onion
- ¼ tsp. pepper
- Salt

Directions:

1. Preheat the air fryer to 325°F.
2. Add all ingredients except half mozzarella cheese into the large bowl and mix until well combined.
3. Transfer bowl mixture into the air fryer baking dish and sprinkle with remaining mozzarella cheese.
4. Place into the air fryer and cook for 16 min.
5. Serve and enjoy.

Nutrition: Calories: 141 kcal; **Fat:** 11.5 g; **Carbohydrate:** 4.9 g; **Sugar:** 1.7 g; **Protein:** 4.9 g; **Cholesterol:** 38 mg

323. Perfect Crab Dip

Preparation Time: 5 min
Cooking Time: 7 min; **Servings:** 2–3
Ingredients:

- 1 cup crabmeat
- 2 tbsp. parsley, chopped
- 2 tbsp. fresh lemon juice
- 2 tbsp. hot sauce
- ½ cup green onion, sliced
- 2 cups cheese, grated
- ¼ cup mayonnaise
- ¼ tsp. pepper
- ½ tsp. salt

Directions:

1. In a 6-inch dish, mix crabmeat, hot sauce, cheese, mayo, pepper, and salt.
2. Place dish in air fryer basket and cook dip at 400°F for 7 min.
3. Remove dish from air fryer.
4. Drizzle dip with lemon juice and garnish with parsley.
5. Serve and enjoy.

Nutrition: Calories: 313 kcal; **Fat:** 23.9 g; **Carbohydrate:** 8.8 g; **Sugar:** 3.1 g; **Protein:** 16.2 g; **Cholesterol:** 67 mg

324. Herb-Crusted Salmon

Preparation Time: 10 min
Cooking Time: 10 min; **Servings:** 2–3
Ingredients:

- 2 (4-oz.) salmon fillets
- 2 tsp. minced garlic
- 1 tbsp. parsley, dried
- ½ tsp. thyme, dried
- 2 tsp. lemon, freshly squeezed
- 4 tbsp. Parmigiano-Reggiano cheese, grated

Directions:

1. Preheat the oven to 425°F. Line a rimmed baking sheet with parchment paper.
2. Place the salmon skin-side on the baking sheet and cover with a second piece of parchment paper. Bake for 10 min.
3. Meanwhile, mix the garlic, parsley, thyme, lemon juice, and Parmigiano-Reggiano cheese in a small dish.
4. Discard the parchment paper covering the salmon. Use a pastry brush to cover the fillets with the herb-cheese mixture carefully.
5. Bake the uncovered salmon for about 5 min more. The salmon is done when the fish flakes easily with a fork.
6. Serve immediately.

Cooking tips: Don't overcook the salmon. Overcooked fish turns rubbery, and the "fishy" flavor tends to be emphasized. Fish is safely cooked when the internal temperature measures 145°F with a meat thermometer.

Nutrition per serving (4 oz.): Calories: 197 kcal; **Total Fat:** 10 g; **Protein:** 27 g; **Carbs:** 9 g; **Fiber:** 1 g; **Sugar:** 3 g; **Sodium:** 222 mg

325. Shrimp Kabobs

Preparation Time: 10 min
Cooking Time: 8 min
Servings: 2–3
Ingredients:

- 1 cup shrimp
- 1 lime juice
- 1 garlic clove, minced
- ¼ tsp. pepper
- ⅛ tsp. salt

Directions:

1. Preheat the air fryer to 350°F.
2. Add shrimp, lime juice, garlic, pepper, and salt into the bowl and toss well.
3. Thread shrimp onto the soaked wooden skewers and place them into the air fryer basket.
4. Cook for 8 min and turn halfway through.
5. Serve and enjoy.

Nutrition: Calories: 75 kcal; **Fat:** 1 g; **Carbohydrate:** 4 g; **Sugar:** 0.5 g; **Protein:** 13 g; **Cholesterol:** 160 mg

326. Crab Mushrooms

Preparation Time: 10 min
Cooking Time: 8 min; **Servings:** 2–3
Ingredients:

- 16 mushrooms, clean and chop stems
- ¼ tsp. chili powder
- ¼ tsp. onion powder
- ¼ cup mozzarella cheese, shredded
- 2 oz. crab meat, chopped
- 8 oz. cream cheese, softened
- 2 tsp. garlic, minced
- ¼ tsp. pepper

Directions:

1. In a mixing bowl, mix stems, chili powder, onion powder, pepper, cheese, crabmeat, cream cheese, and garlic until well combined.
2. Stuff mushrooms with bowl mixture and place into the air fryer basket.
3. Cook mushrooms at 370°F for 8 min.
4. Serve and enjoy.

Nutrition: Calories: 59 kcal; **Fat:** 5.1 g; **Carbohydrate:** 1.2 g; **Sugar:** 0.4 g; **Protein:** 2.2 g; **Cholesterol:** 18 mg

327. Tuna Noodle-Less Casserole

Preparation Time: 15 min
Cooking Time: 40 min
Servings: 2–3
Ingredients:

- Nonstick cooking spray
- 1 medium red onion, chopped
- 1 red bell pepper, chopped
- 1 ½ cup tomato, diced
- 3 cups fresh green beans
- ⅓ cup olive oil-based mayonnaise
- 1 (14.5-oz.) can condensed cream of mushroom soup
- ½ cup low-fat milk
- 1 cup Cheddar cheese, shredded
- ½ tsp. black pepper, freshly ground
- 8 (5-oz.) cans water-packed albacore tuna, drained

Directions:

1. Preheat the oven to 425°F.
2. Coat a large skillet with the cooking spray and place it over medium heat. Add the onion, red bell pepper, and tomatoes and sauté for about 5 min, or until the vegetables are tender and the tomatoes start to soften. Remove the skillet from the heat and set it aside.
3. Cut off the stem ends of the green beans, and snap them into 3- to 4-inch pieces.
4. Fill a large saucepot ⅓ full with water, and place a steamer basket inside. Place the pot over high heat, and bring the water to a boil.
5. Add the green beans to the steamer basket, cover the pot, and reduce the heat to medium. Steam the green beans for 5 min. Immediately, remove them from the heat, drain them, and set them aside.
6. Coat a 9-by-13-inch baking dish with the cooking spray.
7. Mix the mayonnaise, condensed soup, milk, and cheese in a large bowl. Season the mixture with black pepper.

8. Add the tuna, green beans, and sautéed vegetables to the bowl, and combine. Pour the mixture into the baking dish.
9. Serve after baking for 30 min and brown.

Cooking tips: It's easy to shake up this standby recipe. To boost protein and reduce fat, add ½ cup of nonfat cottage cheese and reduce the mayonnaise to 2 tbsp. Use an immersion blender to purée until smooth. To change the flavor profile, first, sauté the diced tomatoes in 1 teaspoon of extra-virgin olive oil for 5 min before cooking the rest of the vegetables.

Set the sautéed tomatoes aside, and mix them in with the tuna. Then follow the rest of the directions to put together the casserole. The tomatoes become almost sun-dried and help attenuate some of the fishiness of the tuna.

Nutrition per serving (1 cup): Calories: 147 kcal; **Total Fat:** 7 g; **Protein:** 15 g; **Carbs:** 6 g; **Fiber:** 2 g; **Sugar:** 2 g; **Sodium:** 318 mg

328. Slow-Roasted Pesto Salmon

Preparation Time: 5 min
Cooking Time: 10 min; **Servings:** 4
Ingredients:

- 4 (6-oz.) salmon fillets
- 1 tsp. extra-virgin olive oil
- 4 tbsp. Perfect Basil Pesto

Directions:

1. Preheat the oven to 275°F. Brush the foil with olive oil.
2. Place the salmon fillets skin-side down on the baking sheet.
3. Spread 1 tablespoon of pesto on each fillet.
4. Roast the salmon for about 20 minutes or until opaque in the center.
5. Serve immediately.

Cooking tips: Enjoy a gourmet meal any night of the week by keeping a bag of freshly frozen wild Alaskan salmon fillets on hand. Look for the kinds that are perfectly portioned into individual fillets for easy meal prep—just thaw in the fridge a day or 2 before needed.

Nutrition per serving (3 oz.): Calories: 182 kcal; Total **Fat:** 10 g; **Protein:** 20 g; **Carbs:** 1 g; **Fiber:** 0 g; **Sugar:** 0 g; **Sodium:** 90 mg

329. Baked Halibut with Tomatoes and White Wine

Preparation Time: 5 min
Cooking Time: 15 min; **Servings:** 2–3
Ingredients:

- 3 tbsp. extra-virgin olive oil
- 1 Vidalia onion, chopped
- 1 tbsp. garlic, minced
- 1 (10-oz.) container grape tomatoes
- ¾ cup dry white wine, divided
- 3 tbsp. capers
- 1 ½ lb. thick-cut halibut fillet, deboned
- ½ tsp. oregano, dried
- Salt
- Black pepper, freshly ground

Directions:

1. Preheat the oven to 350°F.
2. In a pan, heat the olive oil. Add the onion and sauté until browned and softened, 3 to 5 min.
3. Add the garlic and cook until fragrant, 1 to 2 min.
4. Add the tomatoes and cook for 5 minutes or until they soften. Once the tomatoes start to soften, carefully use a potato masher to crush the tomatoes just enough to release their juices gently.
5. Add ½ cup of the wine to the pan and stir. Cook 2 to 3 min until slightly thickened. Stir in the capers.
6. Push the vegetables to the sides of the pan, leaving the center of the pan open for the fish. Place the fish in the pan and sprinkle it with the oregano, salt, and pepper, then scoop the tomato mixture over the fish.
7. Pour in the remaining ¼ cup of wine.
8. Place in the oven and bake for about 20 min, uncovered, or until the fish flakes easily with a fork or reaches an internal temperature of 145°F. Serve.

Nutrition per serving (4 oz.): Calories: 237 kcal; **Total Fat:** 10 g; **Protein:** 24 g; **Carbs:** 6 g; **Fiber:** 1 g; **Sugar:** 2 g; **Sodium:** 166 mg

330. Baked Cod with Fennel and Kalamata Olives

Preparation Time: 10 min
Cooking Time: 35 min; **Servings:** 4
Ingredients:

- 2 tsp. extra-virgin olive oil
- 1 fennel bulb, sliced paper-thin
- ¼ cup dry white wine
- ⅛ cup orange juice, freshly squeezed
- 1 tsp. black pepper, freshly ground
- 4 (4-oz.) cod fillets
- 4 slices fresh orange (with rind)
- ¼ cup Kalamata olives, pitted
- 2 bay leaves

Directions:

1. Preheat the oven to 400°F.
2. Place a pan on medium heat and add the olive oil. Add the fennel and cook, occasionally stirring, until softened, 8 to 10 min.
3. Add the wine. Bring it to a simmer and cook for 1 to 2 min. Stir in the orange juice and pepper and simmer for 2 min more.

4. Remove the pan from the heat and arrange the cod on top of the fennel mixture. Place the orange slices over the fillets. Position the olives and bay leaves around the fish.
5. Roast for 20 minutes or until the fish is opaque. The fish is done when it flakes easily with a fork or reaches an internal temperature of 145°F. Remove the bay leaves before serving.

Nutrition: Calories: 186 kcal; **Total Fat:** 5 g; **Protein:** 21 g; **Carbs:** 8 g; **Fiber:** 3 g; **Sugar:** 4 g; **Sodium:** 271 mg

331. Shrimp, Zucchini, and Cherry Tomato Sauce

Preparation Time: 5 min
Cooking Time: 15 min; **Servings:** 2–3
Ingredients:

- 2 zucchinis
- 300 shrimp
- 7 cherry tomatoes
- Salt and pepper to taste
- 1 garlic clove

Directions:

1. Pour the oil into the air fryer, and add the garlic clove and diced zucchini.
2. Cook for 15 min at 150°C.
3. Add the shrimp and the pieces of tomato, salt, and spices.
4. Cook for another 5 to 10 min or until the shrimp water evaporates.

Nutrition: Calories: 214.3 kcal; **Fat:** 8.6 g; **Carbohydrate:** 7.8 g; **Sugar:** 4.8 g; **Protein:** 27.0 g; **Cholesterol:** 232.7 mg

332. Monkfish with Olives and Capers

Preparation Time: 25 min
Cooking Time: 20 min ; **Servings:** 2–3
Ingredients:

- 1 monkfish
- 10 cherry tomatoes
- 50 g cailletier olives
- 5 capers

Directions:

1. Spread aluminum foil inside the air fryer basket and place the monkfish clean and skinless.
2. Add chopped tomatoes, olives, capers, oil, and salt.
3. Set the temperature to 160°C.
4. Cook the monkfish for about 40 min.

Nutrition: Calories: 404 kcal; **Fat:** 29 g; **Carbohydrate:** 36 g; **Sugar:** 7 g; **Protein:** 24 g **Cholesterol:** 36 mg

333. Baked Garlic Scallops

Preparation Time: 5–10 min.
Cooking Time: 10 min.; **Servings:** 2–3
Ingredients:

- 5 garlic cloves, minced
- 2 shallots, chopped
- 16 sea scallops, rinsed and drained
- 5 tbsp. butter, melted
- 3 pinches nutmeg, ground
- 1 cup bread crumbs
- 4 tbsp. olive oil
- ¼ cup parsley, chopped
- Black pepper, ground, and salt to taste

Directions:

1. In a mixing bowl, put the shallots, garlic, melted butter, scallops, salt, nutmeg, and pepper. Combine to mix well with each other.
2. In another bowl, add oil and bread crumbs. Combine to mix well with each other.
3. Place Instant Pot over kitchen platform. Place Air Fryer Lid on top. Press Air Fry, set the temperature to 375°F, and set the timer to 5 min to preheat. Press "Start" and allow it to preheat for 5 min.
4. Take the Air Fryer Basket and grease it with some cooking spray. In the basket, add a scallop mixture and top with the crumb mixture.
5. Place the basket in the inner pot of the Instant Pot and close the Air Fryer Lid on top.
6. Press the "Bake" setting. Set temperature to 390°F and set the timer to 10 min. Press "Start." Cook until the top is light brown.
7. Open the Air Fryer Lid after cooking time is over. Serve warm with the parsley on top.

Nutrition: Calories: 407 kcal; **Fat:** 21 g; **Saturated Fat:** 2 g; **Trans Fat:** 0 g; **Carbohydrate:** 28.5 g; **Fiber:** 4 g; **Sodium:** 358 mg; **Protein:** 15 g

334. Ranch Tilapia

Preparation Time: 15 min
Cooking Time: 13 min
Servings: 2–3
Ingredients:

- ¾ cup cornflakes, crushed
- 1 (1-oz.) packet dry ranch-style dressing mix
- 2 ½ tbsp. vegetable oil
- 2 eggs
- 4 (6-oz.) tilapia fillets

Directions:

1. In a shallow bowl, beat the eggs.
2. In another bowl, add the cornflakes, ranch dressing, and oil and mix until a crumbly mixture forms.
3. Dip the fish fillets into the egg and then coat with the bread crumbs mixture.

4. Press the "Power Button" of the Air Fry Oven and turn the dial to select the "Air Fry" mode.
5. Press the Time button and again turn the dial to set the Cooking Time to 13 min.
6. Now push the Temp button and rotate the dial to set the temperature at 356°F.
7. Press the "Start/Pause" button to start.
8. Open the lid when the unit beeps to show that it is preheated.
9. Arrange the tilapia fillets in greased "Air Fry Basket" and insert them in the oven.
10. Serve hot.

Nutrition: Calories: 267 kcal; **Fat:** 12.2 g; **Carbs:** 5.1 g; **Protein:** 34.9 g

335. Easy Crab Sticks

Preparation Time: 5 min
Cooking Time: 5 min
Servings: 2–3
Ingredients:

- 1 package Crab sticks
- Cooking oil spray, as needed

Directions:

1. Take each stick out of the package and unroll it until the stick is flat. Tear the sheets into thirds.
2. Arrange them on the air fryer basket and lightly spritz using cooking spray. Set the timer for 10 min.

Note: If you shred the crab meat, you can cut the time in half, but they will also easily fall through the holes in the basket.

Nutrition: Calories: 285 kcal; **Fat:** 12.8 g; **Carbohydrate:** 3.7 g; **Protein:** 38.1 g

336. Vinegar Spice Prawns

Preparation Time: 5 min.
Cooking Time: 8 min.; **Servings:** 3–4
Ingredients:

- 1 tbsp. ketchup
- 12 prawns, shelled and deveined
- 1 tbsp. white wine vinegar
- ½ tsp. black pepper
- ½ tsp. sea salt
- 1 tsp. chili flakes
- 1 tsp. chili powder

Directions:

1. Place the Instant Pot over the kitchen platform. Place the Air Fryer Lid on top. Press Air Fry, set the temperature to 375°F, and set the timer to 5 min to preheat. Press "Start" and allow it to preheat for 5 min.
2. Take Air Fryer Basket and grease it with some cooking spray. In the basket, add all ingredients and combine well.
3. Place the basket in the inner pot of the Instant Pot and close the Air Fryer Lid on top.
4. Press the "Air Fry" setting. Set temperature to 390°F and set the timer to 8 min. Press "Start." Stir mixture halfway down.
5. Open the Air Fryer Lid after cooking time is over. Serve warm.

Nutrition: Calories: 178 kcal; **Fat:** 3.5 g; **Saturated Fat:** 1 g; **Trans Fat:** 0 g; **Carbohydrate:** 9 g; **Fiber:** 1 g; **Sodium:** 581 mg; **Protein:** 21 g

337. Herbed Baked Shrimp

Preparation Time: 5–10 min.
Cooking Time: 10 min.; **Servings:** 2–3
Ingredients:

- 1 tbsp. garlic, minced
- 2 tsp. red pepper flakes
- 4 tbsp. butter
- 1 tbsp. lemon juice
- 1 tbsp. chives, chopped
- 1 tbsp. basil leaves, minced
- 2 tbsp. chicken stock (or white wine)
- 1 lb shrimp, defrosted

Directions:

1. Place Instant Pot over kitchen platform. Place the Air Fryer Lid on top. Press Air Fry, set the temperature to 375°F, and set the timer to 5 min to preheat. Press "Start" and allow it to preheat for 5 min.
2. Take Air Fryer Basket and grease it with some cooking spray. In the basket, add shrimp and butter.
3. Place the basket in the inner pot of the Instant Pot and close the Air Fryer Lid on top.
4. Press the "Bake" setting. Set temperature to 330°F and set the timer to 2 min. Press "Start."
5. Open the Air Fryer Lid after cooking time is over. Mix in red pepper flakes and garlic.
6. Press the "Bake" setting. Set temperature to 330°F and set the timer to 3 min. Press "Start." Add other ingredients and combine them.
7. Press the "Bake" setting. Set temperature to 330°F and set the timer to 5 min. Press "Start." Serve warm.

Nutrition: Calories: 233 kcal; **Fat:** 12 g; **Saturated Fat:** 2.5 g; **Trans Fat:** 0 g; **Carbohydrate:** 3 g; **Fiber:** 0.5 g; **Sodium:** 394 mg; **Protein:** 23 g

338. Breaded Coconut Shrimp

Preparation Time: 5 min
Cooking Time: 8 min; **Servings:** 2–3
Ingredients:

- 1 lb. shrimp
- 1 cup panko breadcrumbs

- 1 cup coconut, shredded
- 2 eggs
- ⅓ cup all-purpose flour

Directions:

1. Fix the temperature of the Air Fryer to 360°F.
2. Peel and devein the shrimp.
3. Whisk the seasonings with the flour as desired. In another dish, whisk the eggs, and in the third container, combine the breadcrumbs and coconut.
4. Dip the cleaned shrimp into the flour and egg wash, and finish it with the coconut mixture.
5. Lightly spray the fryer basket and set the timer for 10–15 min.
6. Air fry until it's a golden brown before serving.

Nutrition: Calories: 285 kcal; **Fat:** 12.8 g; **Carbohydrate:** 3.7 g; **Protein:** 38.1 g

339. Lemon Cod Meal

Preparation Time: 5 min
Cooking Time: 15 min; **Servings:** 4
Ingredients:

- A bunch basil, torn
- Juice from 1 lemon
- ¼ cup olive oil
- 4 cod fillets
- Black pepper, ground, and salt to taste

Directions:

1. Season cod fillets with salt and black pepper to taste.
2. In a mixing bowl, add other ingredients. Combine to mix well with each other. Add fish and coat well.
3. Place the Instant Pot over the kitchen platform. Place the Air Fryer Lid on top. Press Air Fry, set the temperature to 375°F, and set the timer to 5 min to preheat. Press "Start" and allow it to preheat for 5 min.
4. Take Air Fryer Basket and grease it with some cooking spray. In the basket, add fish.
5. Place the basket in the inner pot of the Instant Pot and close the Air Fryer Lid on top.
6. Press the "Air Fry" setting. Set temperature to 350°F and set the timer to 15 min. Press "Start." Flip cod halfway down.
7. Open the Air Fryer Lid after cooking time is over. Serve warm with the vinaigrette on top.

Nutrition: Calories: 326 kcal; **Fat:** 15 g; **Saturated Fat:** 2 g; **Trans Fat:** 0 g; **Carbohydrate:** 2 g; **Fiber:** 0.5 g; **Sodium:** 290 mg; **Protein:** 16 g

340. Oregano Scallops

Preparation Time: 5 min
Cooking Time: 10 min
Servings: 2–3
Ingredients:

- 2 tbsp. thyme, dried
- 1 tbsp. oregano, dried
- 2 tsp. chipotle pepper
- 1 tbsp. coriander, ground
- 1 tbsp. fennel, ground
- 1 lb. sea scallops, cleaned and patted dry
- Black pepper, ground, and salt to taste
- 3 chilies, dried

Directions:

1. In a mixing bowl, add scallops and other ingredients. Combine to mix well with each other.
2. Place the Instant Pot over the kitchen platform. Place the Air Fryer Lid on top. Press Air Fry, set the temperature to 375°F, and set the timer to 5 min to preheat. Press "Start" and allow it to preheat for 5 min.
3. Take Air Fryer Basket and grease it with some cooking spray. In the basket, add scallops.
4. Place the basket in the inner pot of the Instant Pot and close the Air Fryer Lid on top.
5. Press the "Air Fry" setting. Set temperature to 390°F and set the timer to 10 min. Press "Start."
6. Open the Air Fryer Lid after cooking time is over. Serve warm.

Nutrition: Calories: 297 kcal; **Fat:** 3 g; **Saturated Fat:** 0.5 g; **Trans Fat:** 0 g; **Carbohydrate:** 19 g; **Fiber:** 6 g; **Sodium:** 588 mg; **Protein:** 46.5 g

341. Raba's

Preparation Time: 5 min
Cooking Time: 12 min; **Servings:** 2–3
Ingredients:

- 16 rabbis
- 1 egg
- Breadcrumbs
- Salt, pepper, sweet paprika

Directions:

1. Put the rabbis in the air fryer to boil for 2 min.
2. Remove and dry well.
3. Beat the egg and season to taste. You can put salt, pepper, and sweet paprika. Place in the egg.
4. Bread with breadcrumbs. Place in sticks.

Nutrition: Calories: 356 kcal; **Fat:** 18 g; **Carbohydrate:** 5 g; **Protein:** 34 g;

342. Sweet and Sour Glazed Salmon

Preparation Time: 12 min
Cooking Time: 10 min; **Servings:** 4
Ingredients:

- ⅓ cup soy sauce
- ⅓ cup honey
- 3 tsp. rice wine vinegar

- 1 tsp. water
- 4 (3½-oz.) salmon fillets

Directions:

1. Mix the soy sauce, honey, vinegar, and water in a bowl.
2. In another small bowl, reserve about half of the mixture.
3. Add salmon fillets into the remaining mixture and coat well.
4. Cover the bowl and refrigerate to marinate for about 2 hours.
5. Press the "Power Button" of the Air Fry Oven and turn the dial to select the "Air Fry" mode.
6. Press the Time button and again turn the dial to set the cooking time to 12 min.
7. Now push the Temp button and rotate the dial to set the temperature at 355°F.
8. Press the "Start/Pause" button to start.
9. Open the lid when the unit beeps to show that it is preheated.
10. Arrange the salmon fillets in a greased "Air Fry Basket" and insert them in the oven.
11. Flip the salmon fillets halfway through and coat with the reserved marinade every 3 min.
12. Serve hot.

Nutrition: Calories: 462 kcal; **Fat:** 12.3 g; **Carbs:** 49.8 g; **Protein:** 41.3 g

343. Fried Catfish

Preparation Time: 5 min
Cooking Time: 8 min; **Servings:** 4
Ingredients:

- 1 tbsp. olive oil
- ¼ cup fish fry, seasoned
- 4 catfish fillets

Directions:

1. Heat the Air Fryer to reach 400°F before fry time.
2. Rinse the catfish and pat dry using a paper towel.
3. Dump the seasoning into a sizeable zipper-type bag. Add the fish and shake to cover each fillet. Spray with a spritz of cooking oil spray and add to the basket.
4. Set the timer for 10 min. Flip and reset the timer for ten additional min. Turn the fish once more and cook for 2–3 min.
5. Once it reaches the desired crispiness, transfer it to a plate, and serve.

Nutrition: Calories: 376 kcal; **Fat:** 9 g; **Carbohydrate:** 10 g; **Protein:** 28 g

344. Baked Tilapia Cheese

Preparation Time: 5–10 min.
Cooking Time: 15 min.
Servings: 2
Ingredients:

- 2 tsp. Dijon mustard
- 1 tsp. prepared horseradish
- 3 tbsp. mayonnaise
- 1 tbsp. lemon juice
- ¼ cup dry bread crumbs
- 2 tsp. butter, melted
- 2 tbsp. Parmesan cheese, grated
- 2 tilapia fillets (5-6 oz. each)

Directions:

1. Add mayo, lemon juice, mustard, 1 tablespoon cheese, and horseradish to a mixing bowl. Combine to mix well with each other.
2. Combine the remaining cheese, melted butter, and bread crumbs in another bowl.
3. Place Instant Pot over kitchen platform. Place the Air Fryer Lid on top. Press Air Fry, set the temperature to 375°F, and set the timer to 5 min to preheat. Press "Start" and allow it to preheat for 5 min.
4. Take Air Fryer Basket and grease it with some cooking spray. In the basket, add fish and top with the mayo mixture. Add the crumb mixture on top.
5. Place the basket in the inner pot of the Instant Pot and close the Air Fryer Lid on top. Press the "Bake" setting. Set temperature to 390°F and set the timer to 15 min. Press "Start."
6. Open the Air Fryer Lid after cooking time is over. Serve warm.

Nutrition: Calories: 268 kcal; **Fat:** 7.5 g; **Saturated Fat:** 2 g; **Trans Fat:** 0 g; **Carbohydrate:** 8 g; **Fiber:** 0.5 g; **Sodium:** 624 mg; **Protein:** 28 g

345. Breaded Cod Sticks

Preparation Time: 5 min
Cooking Time: 10 min; **Servings:** 2–3
Ingredients:

- 2 large eggs
- 3 tbsp. milk
- 2 cups breadcrumbs
- 1 cup almond flour
- 1 lb. cod

Directions:

1. Preheat the Air Fryer to 350°F.
2. Prepare 3 bowls; one with the milk and eggs, one with the breadcrumbs (salt and pepper if desired), and another with almond flour.
3. Dip the sticks in the flour, egg mixture, and breadcrumbs.
4. Place in the basket and set the timer for 12 min. Toss the basket halfway through the cooking process.
5. Serve with your favorite sauce.

Nutrition: Calories: 254 kcal; **Fat:** 14.2 g; **Carbohydrate:** 5.7 g; **Protein:** 39.1 g

346. Honey Glazed Salmon

Preparation Time: 10 min
Cooking Time: 8 min; **Servings:** 2
Ingredients:

- 2 (6-oz.) salmon fillets
- Salt, as required
- 2 tbsp. honey

Directions:

1. Sprinkle the salmon fillets with salt and then coat with honey.
2. Press the "Power Button" of the Air Fry Oven and turn the dial to select the "Air Fry" mode.
3. Press the Time button and again turn the dial to set the Cooking Time to 8 min.
4. Now push the Temp button and rotate the dial to set the temperature at 355°F.
5. Press the "Start/Pause" button to start.
6. Open the lid when the unit beeps to show that it is preheated.
7. Arrange the salmon fillets in a greased "Air Fry Basket" and insert them in the oven.
8. Serve hot.

Nutrition: Calories: 289 kcal; **Fat:** 10.5 g; **Carbs:** 17.3 g; **Protein:** 33.1 g

347. Crumbled Fish

Preparation Time: 5 min
Cooking Time: 8 min; **Servings:** 4
Ingredients:

- ½ cup breadcrumbs
- 4 tbsp. vegetable oil
- 1 egg
- 4 fish fillets
- 1 lemon

Directions:

1. Heat the Air Fryer to reach 356°F.
2. Whisk the oil and breadcrumbs until crumbly.
3. Dip the fish into the egg, then the crumb mixture.
4. Arrange the fish in the cooker and Air fry for 12 min.
5. Garnish using the lemon.

Nutrition: Calories: 320 kcal; **Carbs:** 8 g; **Fat:** 10 g; **Protein:** 28 g

348. Salted Marinated Salmon

Preparation Time: 10 min
Cooking Time: 15 min; **Servings:** 2–3
Ingredients:

- 500 g salmon fillet
- 1 kg coarse salt

Directions:

1. Place the baking paper on the air fryer basket and the salmon on top (skin side up) covered with coarse salt.
2. Set the air fryer to 150°C.
3. Cook everything for 25 to 30 min. At the end of cooking, remove the salt from the fish and serve with a drizzle of oil.

Nutrition: Calories: 290 kcal; **Fat:** 13 g; **Carbohydrate:** 3 g; **Fiber:** 0 g; **Protein:** 40 g; **Cholesterol:** 196 mg

349. Cod Fish Nuggets

Preparation Time: 5 min
Cooking Time: 10 min; **Servings:** 2–3
Ingredients:

- 1 lb. cod fillet
- 3 eggs
- 4 tbsp. olive oil
- 1 cup almond flour
- 1 cup gluten-free breadcrumbs

Directions:

1. Warm the Air Fryer at 390°F.
2. Slice the cod into nuggets.
3. Prepare 3 bowls, whisk the eggs in one, and combine the salt, oil, and breadcrumbs in another. Sift the almond flour into the third one.
4. Cover each nugget with flour, and dip in the eggs and the breadcrumbs.
5. Arrange the nuggets in the basket and set the timer for 20 min.
6. Serve the fish with your favorite dips or sides.

Nutrition: Calories: 334 kcal; **Fat:** 10 g; **Carbohydrate:** 8 g; **Protein:** 32 g

350. Creamy Salmon

Preparation Time: 5 min
Cooking Time: 10 min; **Servings:** 6
Ingredients:

- 1 tbsp. dill, chopped
- 1 tbsp. olive oil
- 3 tbsp. sour cream
- 1.76 oz. plain yogurt
- 6 pieces salmon (¾ lb.)

Directions:

1. Heat the Air Fryer and wait for it to reach 285°F.
2. Shake the salt over the salmon and add them to the fryer basket with the olive oil to Air fry for 10 min.
3. Whisk the yogurt, salt, and dill.
4. Serve the salmon with the sauce with your favorite sides.

Nutrition: Calories: 340 kcal; **Carbs:** 5 g; **Fat:** 16 g; **Protein:** 32 g

351. Baked Onion Cod

Preparation Time: 10 min.
Cooking Time: 12 min.; **Servings:** 2–3
Ingredients:

- ½ lb. thick-cut cod loin
- Juice of ¼ lemon
- 2 tbsp. butter, melted
- ¼ sleeve round crackers, crushed
- 1 ½ tsp. parsley, chopped
- 1 ½ tsp. green onion, chopped
- ½ lemon, cut into wedges
- 2 tbsp. dry white wine

Directions:

1. In a mixing bowl, add half butter and crackers. Combine to mix well with each other.
2. Add lemon juice, white wine, parsley, and green onion to another bowl. Combine to mix well with each other. Coat cod with remaining butter.
3. Place the Instant Pot over the kitchen platform. Place the Air Fryer Lid on top. Press Air Fry, set the temperature to 375°F, and set the timer to 5 min to preheat. Press "Start" and allow it to preheat for 5 min.
4. Take the Air Fryer Basket and grease it with some cooking spray. In the basket, add cod. Top with the dressing and add the cracker mixture.
5. Place the basket in the inner pot of the Instant Pot and close the Air Fryer Lid on top. Press the "Bake" setting. Set temperature to 390°F and set the timer to 10 min. Press "Start."
6. Open the Air Fryer Lid after cooking time is over. Serve warm.

Nutrition: Calories: 290 kcal; **Fat:** 15 g; **Saturated Fat:** 3 g; **Trans Fat:** 0 g; **Carbohydrate:** 10 g; **Fiber:** 2 g; **Sodium:** 624 mg; **Protein:** 21 g

352. Mussels with Pepper

Preparation Time: 15 min
Cooking Time: 10 min;
Servings: 2–3
Ingredients:

- 700 g mussels
- 1 garlic clove
- 1 tsp. oil
- Pepper to taste
- Parsley Taste

Directions:

1. Clean and scrape the mold cover and remove the byssus (the "beard" that comes from the mold).
2. Pour the oil, clean the mussels and the crushed garlic in the air fryer basket. Set the temperature to 200°C and simmer for 12 min.
3. Towards the end of cooking, add black pepper and chopped parsley.
4. Finally, distribute the mussel juice well at the bottom of the basket, stirring the basket.

Nutrition: Calories: 150 kcal; **Carbohydrate:** 2 g; **Fat:** 8 g; **Sugar:** 0 g; **Protein:** 15 g; **Cholesterol:** 0 mg

353. Cajun Salmon

Preparation Time: 5 min
Cooking Time: 5 min; **Servings:** 2–3
Ingredients:

- 1-7 oz. salmon fillet, 0.75-inches thick
- Cajun seasoning
- ¼ juice of a lemon

5. **Optional:** Sprinkle of sugar

Directions:

1. Set the Air Fryer at 356°F to preheat for 5 min.
2. Rinse and dry the salmon with a paper towel. Cover the fish with the Cajun coating mix.
3. Place the fillet in the air fryer for 7 min with the skin side up.
4. Serve with a sprinkle of lemon and a dusting of sugar if desired.

Nutrition: Calories: 285 kcal; **Fat:** 17.8 g; **Carbohydrate:** 6.8 g; **Protein:** 42.1 g

354. Breaded Flounder

Preparation Time: 15 min
Cooking Time: 12 min
Servings: 2–3
Ingredients:

- 1 egg
- 1 cup dry breadcrumbs
- ¼ cup vegetable oil
- 3 (6-oz.) flounder fillets
- 1 lemon, sliced

Directions:

1. In a shallow bowl, beat the egg.
2. Add the breadcrumbs and oil to another bowl until a crumbly mixture is formed.
3. Dip flounder fillets into the beaten egg and coat with the breadcrumb mixture.
4. Press the "Power Button" of the Air Fry Oven and turn the dial to select the "Air Fry" mode.
5. Press the Time button and again turn the dial to set the Cooking Time to 12 min.
6. Now push the Temp button and rotate the dial to set the temperature at 356°F.
7. Press the "Start/Pause" button to start.
8. Open the lid when the unit beeps to show that it is preheated.
9. Arrange the flounder fillets in greased "Air Fry Basket" and insert them in the oven.
10. Plate with lemon slices and serve hot.

Nutrition: Calories: 524 kcal; **Total Fat:** 24.2 g; **Saturated Fat:** 5.1 g; **Cholesterol:** 170 mg; **Sodium:** 463 mg; **Total Carbs:** 26.5 g; **Fiber:** 1.5 g; **Sugar:** 2.5 g; **Protein:** 47.8 g

Review this Book

Thank you for reading this far!
We worked hard for almost a year to complete this 500-recipes cookbook, even comparing ourselves with different doctors. Rachel put in all the effort she could, thanks in part to her experience with daddy troubles. We are very pleased with this book, but now **what matters most is your feedback!**

If you enjoyed this book, please take a few moments **to leave a review on Amazon** about this work, or rating (it takes less than 5 seconds) hoose your amazon marketplace below).

We appreciate your time!

Scan this QR code to review on Amazon.com

Scan this QR code to review on Amazon.co.uk

Scan this QR code to review on Amazon.co.au

Scan this QR code to review on Amazon.ca

355. Thanksgiving Turkey with Mustard Gravy

Preparation Time: 50 min
Cooking Time: 45 min
Servings: 2–3
Ingredients:

- 2 tsp. butter, softened
- 1 tsp. sage, dried
- 2 sprigs rosemary, chopped
- 1 tsp. salt
- ¼ tsp. black pepper, freshly ground, or more to taste
- 1 whole turkey breast
- 2 tbsp. turkey broth
- 2 tbsp. whole-grain mustard
- 1 tbsp. butter

Directions:

1. Start by preheating your air fryer to 360°F.
2. To make the rub, combine 2 tablespoons of butter, sage, rosemary, salt, and pepper; mix well to combine and spread it evenly over the surface of the turkey breast.
3. Roast for 20 min in an air fryer cooking basket. Flip the turkey breast over and cook for a further 15 to 16 min. Now, flip it back over and roast for 12 min more.
4. While the turkey is roasting, whisk the other ingredients in a saucepan. After that, spread the gravy all over the turkey breast.
5. Let the turkey rest for a few min before carving.

Nutrition: Calories: 415 kcal; **Fat:** 19.4 g; **Fiber:** 12.1 g; **Carbs:** 31 g; **Protein:** 27.1 g

356. Dry-Rubbed Chicken Wings

Preparation Time: 5 min
Cooking Time: 15 min; **Servings:** 2–3
Ingredients:

- 12 chicken wings
- 1 tsp. garlic powder
- 1 tsp. chili powder
- ½ tsp. Kosher salt
- ½ black pepper, paprika

Directions:

1. Preheat the air fryer to 180°C.
2. Mix garlic powder, chili powder, paprika, salt, and pepper in a large bowl.
3. Rinse and pat every chicken wing dry and toss into a bowl to cover uniformly.
4. Place wings in air fryer crate and cook for 15 min, turning at interims.
5. Cool again for an additional 5 min.
6. Serve hot.

Nutrition: Calories: 315 kcal; **Fat:** 3.4 g; **Fiber:** 7.1 g; **Carbs:** 25.7 g; **Protein:** 19.1 g

357. Herbed Roast Chicken

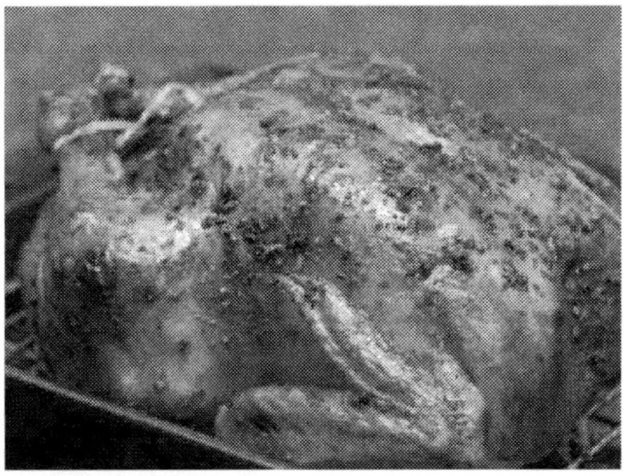

Preparation Time: 35 min
Cooking Time: 1 hr. 30 min
Servings: 2–3

Ingredients:

- 1 (3.5 lb.) whole chicken
- 2 tbsp. olive oil
- 1 tsp. garlic powder
- 1 tsp. paprika
- ½ tsp. oregano
- Salt and black pepper to taste
- 1 lemon, cut into quarters
- 5 garlic cloves

Directions:

1. In a bowl, combine olive oil, garlic powder, paprika, oregano, salt, and pepper, and mix well to make a paste. Rub the chicken with the paste and stuff lemon and garlic cloves into the cavity.
2. Place the chicken in the air fryer, breast side down, and tuck the legs and wings tips under. Bake for 45 min at 360°F. Flip the chicken breast side up and cook for another 15–20 min. Let rest for 5-6 min, then carve and serve.

Nutrition: Calories: 280 kcal; **Fat:** 5.7 g; **Fiber:** 12.1 g; **Carbs:** 40.7 g; **Protein:** 12.9 g

358. Za'atar Chicken

Preparation Time: 15 min
Cooking Time: 20–30 min
Servings: 2–3
Ingredients:

- 4 chicken thighs
- 2 sprigs thyme
- 1 onion, cut into chunks
- 2 ½ tbsp. za'atar
- ½ tsp. cinnamon
- 2 garlic cloves, smashed
- 1 lemon juice
- 1 lemon zest
- ¼ cup olive oil
- ¼ tsp. pepper
- 1 tsp. salt

Directions:

1. Add oil, lemon juice, zest, cinnamon, garlic, pepper, 2 tbsp. za'atar, and salt in a large zip-lock bag and shake well.
2. Add chicken, thyme, and onion into the bag and shake well to coat. Place in refrigerator overnight.
3. Preheat the air fryer to 380°F.
4. Add marinated chicken to the air fryer basket and cook at 380°F for 15 min.
5. Turn chicken to another side and sprinkle with remaining za'atar spice and cook at 380°F for 15-18 min more.
6. Serve and enjoy.

Nutrition: Calories: 399 kcal; **Fat:** 15.7 g; **Fiber:** 19.5 g; **Carbs:** 67 g; **Protein:** 21.1 g

359. Spicy Asian Chicken

Preparation Time: 10 min
Cooking Time: 20 min
Servings: 2–3
Ingredients:

- 4 chicken thighs, skin-on and bone-in
- 2 tsp. ginger, grated
- 1 lime juice
- 2 tbsp. chili garlic sauce
- ¼ cup olive oil
- ⅓ cup soy sauce

Directions:

1. Whisk together ginger, lime juice, chili garlic sauce, oil, and soy sauce in a large bowl.
2. Add the chicken into a bowl, coat well with the marinade, and place in the refrigerator for 30 minutes.
3. Place marinated chicken in the air fryer basket and cook at 400°F for 15–20 min or until the internal temperature of the chicken reaches 165°F. Turn chicken halfway through.
4. Serve and enjoy.

Nutrition: Calories: 318 kcal; **Fat:** 6.7 g; **Fiber:** 11.5 g; **Carbs:** 49.9 g; **Protein:** 18.4 g

360. Turkey Loaf

Preparation Time: 20 min
Cooking Time: 40 min; **Servings:** 2–3
Ingredients:

- 1 egg
- ½ tsp. savory dill, dried
- ⅔ cup walnuts, finely chopped
- 1 ½ lb. turkey breast, diced
- ½ tsp. allspice, ground
- ¼ tsp. black pepper
- 1 garlic clove, minced
- 1 tbsp. Dijon mustard
- 1 tbsp. liquid Aminos
- 1 tbsp. tomato paste

- 2 tbsp. Parmesan cheese, grated
- 1 tbsp. onion flakes

Directions:

1. Preheat your air fryer to 375°F.
2. Grease a baking dish using cooking spray.
3. Whisk dill, egg, tomato paste, liquid aminos, mustard, garlic, allspice, salt, and pepper.
4. Mix well and add diced turkey. Mix again and add cheese, walnuts, and onion flakes.
5. Put mixture into baking dish and bake for 40-min in the air fryer. Serve hot!

Nutrition: Calories: 277 kcal; **Fat:** 5.7 g; **Fiber:** 4.51 g; **Carbs:** 45.6 g; **Protein:** 10.6 g

361. Cheesy Turkey Calzone

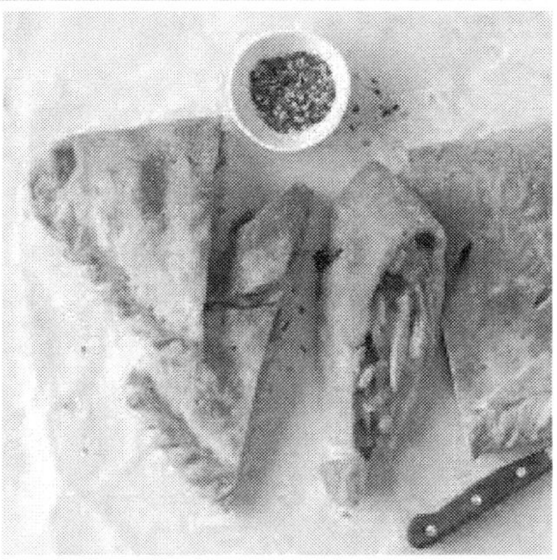

Preparation Time: 20 min
Cooking Time: 10–15 min; **Servings:** 2–3
Ingredients:

- 1 free-range egg, beaten
- ¼ cup mozzarella cheese, grated
- 1 cup Cheddar cheese, grated
- Turkey, cooked and shredded
- 4 tbsp. tomato sauce
- Salt and pepper to taste
- 1 tsp. thyme
- 1 tsp. basil
- 1 tsp. oregano
- 1 package pizza dough, frozen

Directions:

1. Roll the pizza dough out into small circles, the same size as a small pizza. Add thyme, oregano, and basil into a bowl with tomato sauce and mix well.
2. Pour a small amount of sauce onto your pizza bases and spread it across the surface. Add the turkey and cheese.
3. Brush the edge of the dough with beaten egg, then fold over and pinch to seal. Brush the outside with more egg.
4. Place into the air fryer and cook at 350°F for 10-min. Serve warm.

Nutrition: Calories: 265 kcal; **Fat:** 8.5 g; **Fiber:** 7.1 g; **Carbs:** 39.7 g; **Protein:** 12.5 g

362. Korean Chicken Wings

Preparation Time: 10 min
Cooking Time: 15 min
Servings: 2–3
Ingredients:

- 8 chicken wings
- Salt to taste
- 1 tsp. sesame oil
- Juice from half lemon
- ¼ cup sriracha chili sauce
- 1-inch piece ginger, grated
- 1 tsp. garlic powder
- 1 tsp. sesame seeds

Directions:

1. Preheat the air fryer to 370°F. Grease the air fryer basket with cooking spray.
2. Mix salt, ginger, garlic, lemon juice, sesame oil, and chili sauce in a bowl. Add the wings and coat them well. Air Fry for 15 min, flipping once. Sprinkle with sesame seeds and serve.

Nutrition: Calories: 154 kcal; **Fat:** 2.8 g; **Fiber:** 9.1 g; **Carbs:** 22.1 g; **Protein:** 10.4 g

363. Curry Chicken Wings

Preparation Time: 30 min
Cooking Time: 20 min
Servings: 2–3
Ingredients:

- 1 cup rice milk
- 1 tbsp. soy sauce
- 1 tbsp. red curry paste
- 1 tbsp. sugar
- 8 chicken wings
- 2 tbsp. fresh parsley, chopped

Directions:

1. Preheat the air fryer to 380°F.
2. In a bowl, mix all the ingredients, except for the parsley. Marinate for 20 min. Grease the air fryer basket with cooking spray. After 20 min, drain the wings and reserve the marinade.
3. Place wings in the frying basket and Air Fry for 18-20 min, flipping once. Add the marinade to a saucepan over medium heat, and cook until

thickened, 8 min. Pour this sauce over the chicken and top with parsley to serve

Nutrition: Calories: 212 kcal; **Fat:** 4.5 g; **Fiber:** 9.4 g; **Carbs:** 23.8 g; **Protein:** 10.4 g

364. Coconut Chicken Meatballs

Preparation Time: 30 min
Cooking Time: 10–15 min
Servings: 2–3
Ingredients:

- 1 lb. chicken, ground
- 1 ½ tsp. sriracha
- ½ tbsp. soy sauce
- ½ tbsp. hoisin sauce
- ¼ cup coconut, shredded
- 1 tsp. sesame oil
- ½ cup fresh cilantro, chopped
- 2 green onions, chopped
- Pepper
- Salt

Directions:

1. Spray the air fryer basket with cooking spray.
2. Add all ingredients into the large bowl and mix until well combined.
3. Make small balls from the meat mixture and place them into the air fryer basket.
4. Cook at 350°F for 10 min. Turn halfway through. Serve and enjoy.

Nutrition: Calories: 241 kcal; **Fat:** 2.8 g; **Fiber:** 8.1 g; **Carbs:** 21.7 g; **Protein:** 11.5 g

365. Whole Roasted Turkey

Preparation Time: 35 min
Cooking Time: 3 hrs. Min
Servings: 2–3
Ingredients:

- 1 clean turkey with about 8.8 lbs.
- 2 large onions, cut into small pieces
- ½ tbsp. hot sauce
- 1 tbsp. French mustard
- 1 bottle dry white wine
- 3 cups chicken broth
- 1 cup butter, melted
- Salt, to taste
- Butter, melted, for injection

Directions:

1. Preheat the air fryer to 360°F.
2. Place the onions, garlic, pepper sauce, mustard, 1 cup of wine, 1 cup of chicken stock, butter, and salt and beat in a blender.
3. Transfer to a bowl, add the remaining wine and chicken stock, and mix well.
4. Fill the turkey and place it on an ungreased baking sheet.
5. Hold the skin of the turkey breast with one hand and remove it from the meat with the other.
6. Prick the meat with a fork and, with the help of a seasoning injector, inject the melted butter at several points on the turkey breast.
7. Rub the prepared seasoning onto the surface of the turkey and inject a little into the meat.
8. Pull the skin back, cover the turkey again, and sew with a thick thread.
9. Cover with aluminum foil and put in the air fryer for about 3 hours, basting the turkey every 20 minutes with the sauce that falls into the pan.
10. When the paper is dark, remove it and leave the turkey in the air fryer until golden.

Nutrition: Calories: 267 kcal; **Fat:** 5.6 g; **Fiber:** 12.9 g; **Carbs:** 59.6 g; **Protein:** 21.8 g

366. Sundried Tomato and Goat Cheese Turkey Roll

Preparation Time: 15 min
Cooking Time: 20 min
Servings: 4
Ingredients:

- 4 fillets turkey breast
- 4 halves tomatoes, sun-dried
- 200 g goat cheese
- Salt
- Pepper, to season

Directions:

1. Beat the fillets with the meat whisk (to soften to taste). Season with salt, pepper, and oil to taste.
2. Place half a slice of tomato and 50 g of goat cheese on each fillet.
3. Roll them up and then wrap them in aluminum foil.
4. Arrange the rolls in a pan and bake in the preheated air fryer at 420°F for 20 to 30 min.
5. Remove from the air fryer, open the rollers, and spread a little butter/margarine on them.
6. Put them back in the pan and back in the air fryer until golden.
7. Serve hot with rice and arugula salad, or serve cold with mayonnaise-based sauces.

Nutrition: Calories: 310 kcal; **Fat:** 8.6 g; **Fiber:** 12.9 g; **Carbs:** 55.9 g; **Protein:** 19.5 g

367. Creole Cornish Hen

Preparation Time: 10 min
Cooking Time: 40 min
Servings: 2–3
Ingredients:

- 2 tbsp. olive oil, plus more for spraying
- ½ tbsp. Creole seasoning
- ½ tbsp. garlic powder
- ½ tbsp. onion powder
- ½ tbsp. black pepper, freshly ground
- ½ tbsp. paprika
- 2 Cornish hens

Directions:

1. Set to 370°F. Spray a fryer basket lightly with olive oil.
2. Mix Creole seasoning, garlic powder, onion powder, pepper, and paprika in a small bowl.
3. Pat the Cornish hens, dry, and brush each hen all over with 2 tablespoons of olive oil. Rub each hen with the seasoning mixture.
4. Place the Cornish hens in the fryer basket. Air fry for 15 min. Flip the hens over and baste with any drippings collected in the bottom drawer of the air fryer. Lightly spray them with olive oil.
5. Air fry for 15 min. Flip the hens back over and cook until a thermometer inserted into the thickest part of the thigh reaches at least 165°F and it's crispy and golden, an additional 5 to 10 min.
6. Let the hens rest for 10 min before carving.

Nutrition: Calories: 315 kcal; **Fat:** 9.6 g; **Fiber:** 12.8 g; **Carbs:** 32 g; **Protein:** 11 g

368. Caribbean Chicken Thighs

Preparation Time: 30 min
Cooking Time: 10 min; **Servings:** 2–3
Ingredients:

- 3 lbs. chicken thigh fillets, boneless and skinless
- Black pepper, ground
- 1 tbsp. coriander seed, ground
- Salt
- 1 tbsp. cinnamon, ground
- 1 tbsp. cayenne pepper
- 1 ½ tsp. ginger, ground
- 1 ½ tsp. nutmeg, ground
- 3 tbsp. coconut oil

Directions:

1. Take chicken off the packaging and pat dry. Place any residual liquid on a large baking sheet covered with paper towels to soak up. Chicken is salted and peppered on both sides. Let the chicken sit for 30 minutes, so it isn't that cold when you enter the air fryer.
2. Combine cilantro, cinnamon, cayenne, ginger, and nutmeg in a small bowl. Coat the spice mixture on each piece of chicken and brush both sides with coconut oil.
3. Place 4 pieces of chicken in your air fryer basket (they shouldn't overlap). Air fry for 10 min at 390°F. Remove the chicken from the basket and place it in a safe stove dish, tightly covered with foil.
4. Keep the chicken in the oven to keep it warm until the remaining chicken is done—repeat the instructions for air frying with the rest of the chicken.

Nutrition: Calories: 276 kcal; **Fat:** 6.4 g; **Fiber:** 12.1 g; **Carbs:** 56.5 g; **Protein:** 13.1 g

369. Greek Style Chicken

Preparation Time: 15 min
Cooking Time: 30 min; **Servings:** 2–3
Ingredients:

- 2 lbs. chicken tenders
- 1 cup cherry tomatoes
- 2 tbsp. olive oil
- 3 dill sprigs
- 1 large zucchini

For topping:

- 2 tbsp. feta cheese, crumbled
- 1 tbsp. fresh dill, chopped
- 1 tbsp. olive oil
- 1 tbsp. fresh lemon juice

Directions:

1. Preheat the air fryer to 370°F.
2. Spray the air fryer basket with cooking spray.
3. Add chicken, zucchini, dill, and tomatoes into the air fryer basket. Drizzle with olive oil and season with salt.
4. Cook chicken for 24 min.
5. Meanwhile, in a small bowl, stir together all topping ingredients.
6. Place chicken on the serving plate, top with veggies, and discard dill sprigs.
7. Sprinkle topping mixture on top of chicken and vegetables.
8. Serve and enjoy.

Nutrition: Calories: 388 kcal; **Fat:** 12.8 g; **Fiber:** 11.9 g; **Carbs:** 58.4 g; **Protein:** 18.6 g

370. Quail in White Wine Sauce

Preparation Time: 12 hrs.
Cooking Time: 90 min; **Servings:** 2–3
Ingredients:

- 4 large quail
- 1 bottle dry white wine
- 1 tsp. sweet paprika
- 1 tsp. hot paprika
- ½ package fresh sage, chopped or 2 tbsp. dehydrated sage
- 1 head garlic, minced

- ¼ tsp. virgin olive oil
- 1.7 oz. butter
- Salt, to taste
- 4 rosemary sprigs

Directions:

1. The recipe is very easy; it should only be prepared well in advance.
2. Wash the quail well. Boil salted water in a skillet enough to cover the quail.
3. When the water boils, place the quail in the pan and cover for 5 min.
4. Drain and let cool. Put a little minced garlic inside each quail; place the quail in a large bowl, and top with white wine. Then, add sweet bell pepper, hot pepper, olive oil, and sage. Marinate in the seasoning in the refrigerator for at least 12 hours. Remove the quail from the seasoning and place it in a pan with butter.
5. Take the preheated air fryer to about 200°F and bake for 90 min.
6. Open the oven every 15 minutes, turn the quails, and sprinkle with the marinade.

Nutrition: Calories: 319 kcal; **Fat:** 19 g; **Fiber:** 16.1 g; **Carbs:** 78 g; **Protein:** 21.1 g

371. Stuffed Turkey Breast

Preparation Time: 35 min
Cooking Time: 30 min; **Servings:** 2–3
Ingredients:

- 3 lb. turkey breast
- ¼ lb. banana with raisins
- 1 ¼ cup water
- 3 ½ oz. sugar
- 5 ¼ oz. fresh tamarind
- Parsley, chopped, salt and black pepper, freshly ground, to taste

Directions:

1. Open the turkey breast and place the raisin bananas lengthwise inside. Wrap and tie with string. Wrap in foil and bake in the air fryer, preheating at 400°F for approximately 30 minutes.
2. Remove from the air fryer and, with the help of a fork, check that the inside of the turkey is hot. If not, return it to the air fryer.
3. Discard the shell and core of tamarind.
4. In a saucepan, dilute the sugar in the water, add the pulp of the fruit and simmer for at least 30 min or until you get a thick and shiny sauce. Remove from heat and strain.
5. Cut the turkey breast and put it on the plates with the tamarind sauce.

Nutrition: Calories: 310 kcal; **Fat:** 10.6 g; **Fiber:** 18.5 g; **Carbs:** 71 g; **Protein:** 15.9 g

372. Grilled Chicken and Radish Mix Recipe

Preparation Time: 20 min
Cooking Time: 40 Min; **Servings:** 4
Ingredients:

- 4 chicken things, bone-in
- Salt and black pepper, to taste
- 1 tbsp. olive oil
- 3 carrots, cut into thin sticks
- 2 tbsp. chives, chopped
- 1 cup chicken stock
- 1 cup sugar
- 6 radishes, halved

Directions:

1. Start by heating a container that accommodates your air fryer over medium warmth, including stock, carrots, sugar, and radishes; mix delicately,
2. Reduce warmth to medium, spread pot somewhat, and permit to stew for 20 min.
3. Coat the chicken with olive oil, season with salt and pepper, put in your air fryer, and cook at 350°F for 4 min.
4. Introduce the chicken to radish blend and hurl appropriately
5. Introduce everything in your air fryer, cook for 4 min more,
6. Share among plates and serve.

Nutrition: Calories: 314 kcal; **Fat:** 15.4 g; **Fiber:** 10.1 g; **Carbs:** 28.7 g; **Protein:** 22.4 g

373. Hawaiian Roasted Quail

Preparation Time: 20 min
Cooking Time: 30 min; **Servings:** 2–3
Ingredients:

- 1 cup champagne
- 1 cup water
- ½ tbsp. black pepper, ground
- 2 tsp. salt
- 3 tsp. curry
- 3 tsp. virgin olive oil
- 3 garlic, minced
- 3 ½ tsp. lemon vinegar
- 4 medium-size Hawaii pineapple slices
- 4 very clean quails, washed and dried
- 20 endive leaves, sliced

Directions:

1. Cut the pineapple curry slices. Reserve.
2. Heat 2 tablespoons of oil in a frying pan and brown the pineapple slices on both sides.
3. Chop them and fill the quail. Tie well. Place on the baking sheet. Season with champagne, water, salt, and garlic.

4. Bake in the air fryer for 40 min or until golden brown.
5. Arrange the quail on the plates. Add endive and reserve.
6. Mix the vinegar, remaining oil, pepper, endive water, pineapple, rosemary, and thyme leaves to decorate.

Nutrition: Calories: 287 kcal; **Fat:** 7.5 g; **Fiber:** 12.9 g; **Carbs:** 45.9 g; **Protein:** 18.5 g

374. Chicken Soup

Preparation Time: 30 min
Cooking Time: 1 hour; **Servings:** 2–3
Ingredients:

- 2 cups black beans salsa
- 1 lb chicken tenderloins
- 1 tsp. salt
- 2 tsp. Mexican spice
- 1 tsp. cumin, ground
- 4 cups water
- 2 cups corn, frozen
- 4.5-oz. green chilies
- 10-oz. tomatoes, diced
- 2 tbsp. fresh coriander
- 10-oz. black beans
- 1 tsp. black pepper
- Cheese and lime juice, for garnishing (optional)

Directions:

1. Rinse the chicken tenderloins. Sprinkle pepper and salt on them before putting them in the crockpot.
2. Put the salsa and the spices. Then cook for 4 hours on low heat.
3. Take out and shred the chicken. Put it back in the crockpot. Add water, additional beans, corn, tomatoes, coriander, and chilies. Cook for 2 more hours.
4. Garnish with cheese and coriander leaves. Add a dash of lime juice and serve.

Nutrition: Servings: 2–32 oz.: Calories: 375 kcal; **Carbohydrate:** 10 g; **Protein:** 22 g; **Fat:** 29 g; **Saturated Fat:** 22 g; **Cholesterol:** 53 mg; **Sodium:** 1283 mg; **Potassium:** 740 mg; **Fiber:** 2 g; **Sugar:** 5 g; **Vitamin A:** 29 IU; **Vitamin C:** 21 mg; **Calcium:** 38 mg; **Iron:** 3 mg

375. Chicken Chili with Jalapeño and Cheddar

Preparation Time: 10 min
Cooking Time: 40 min; **Servings:** 2–3
Ingredients:

- 1 cup carrots, diced
- 1 tbsp. cumin
- ½ cup pepper jack cheese, shredded
- ¼ cup low-fat cream cheese
- ½ cup chicken broth,
- 1 tsp. oregano
- 1 tbsp. chili powder
- ⅓ cup jarred Jalapeño slices, diced
- 1 lb. chicken breast, skinless, boneless

Directions:

1. Add some cooking oil to a pan and place on medium heat.
2. Add the diced chicken along with the diced Jalapeños. Cook until the chicken turns opaque.
3. Add oregano, chili powder, and cumin to the chicken and Jalapeños. Stir everything together so that it is well combined.
4. Mix in the carrots and chicken broth. Stir to combine. Bring to a boil. Once boiling, turn the heat down to low and cover.
5. Allow this mixture to simmer for 20 min until the carrots are soft.
6. Add in pepper jack and cream cheese. Stir until mixed well, and the cheese is melted. Allow it to simmer for 5 min more.
7. Divide evenly into bowls.
8. Serve and enjoy.

Nutrition: Calories: 450 kcal; **Fat:** 18.2 g; **Protein:** 61.7 g; **Carb:** 7.9 g

376. Greek Yogurt Chicken

Preparation Time: 10 min
Cooking Time: 45 min; **Servings:** 2–3
Ingredients:

- 1 tsp. Garlic powder
- ½ tsp. pepper,
- 1 ½ tsp. seasoning salt
- ½ cup Parmesan cheese,
- 1 cup Greek yogurt
- 4 chicken breasts, skinless, boneless

Directions:

1. Start by setting your oven to 375°F.
2. Mix the seasonings, cheese, and Greek yogurt.
3. Lay some tin foil on a baking sheet and spritz it with nonstick spray.
4. Spread the Ggeek yogurt mixture over the chicken breasts and lay them on the prepared baking sheet.
5. Slide them into the oven and let them cook for 45 min.

Nutrition: Cal: 266 kcal; **Fat:** 4 g; **Protein:** 46 g; **Carb:** 3 g

377. Herbed Turkey Breast

Preparation Time: 10 min
Cooking Time: 1 ½ - 2 hours + standing
Servings: 2–3
Ingredients:

- ½ cup butter, cubed

- ¼ cup lemon juice
- 2 tbsp. soy sauce, reduced-sodium
- 2 tbsp. green onions, finely chopped
- 1 tbsp. rubbed sage
- 1 tsp. thyme, dried
- 1 tsp. marjoram, dried
- ¼ tsp. pepper
- 1 turkey breast, bone-in (5-½ to 6 lb.)

Directions:

1. Mix all first 8 ingredients in a small saucepan; bring them to a boil. Remove yourself from the heat. Put the turkey in a shallow roasting pan; drizzle with the butter mixture.
2. Bake for 1-½ to 2 hours, uncovered, at 325°F, or until a thermometer reads 165°F, basting every 30 min. Until carving, let it stand for 10 min.

Nutrition: 5 oz. Cooked Turkey: Calories: 291 kcal; **Fat:** 11 g; **Saturated Fat:** 3 g; **Cholesterol:** 112 mg; **Sodium:** 192 mg; **Carbohydrate:** 1 g; **Sugars:** 0 g; **Fiber:** 0 g; **Protein:** 44 g

378. Thai Chili Chicken Wings

Preparation Time: 10 min
Cooking Time: 16 min
Servings: 2–3
Ingredients:

- ½ lb. chicken wings
- 1 tsp. paprika
- ⅓ cup Thai chili sauce
- 2 tsp. garlic powder
- 2 tsp. ginger powder
- 2 ½ tbsp. dry sherry
- Pepper
- Salt

Directions:

1. Toss chicken wings with dry sherry, paprika, garlic powder, ginger, pepper, and salt.
2. Add chicken wings into the air fryer basket and cook at 365°F for 16 min.
3. Serve with Thai chili sauce and enjoy.

Nutrition: Calories: 120 kcal; **Fat:** 2.9 g; **Carbohydrate:** 6 g; **Sugar:** 3.9 g; **Protein:** 11.2 g; **Cholesterol:** 34 mg

379. BBQ Chicken Wings

Preparation Time: 10 min
Cooking Time: 8 min; **Servings:** 2–3
Ingredients:

- 1 lb. chicken wings
- ½ cup BBQ sauce, sugar-free
- ¼ tsp. garlic powder
- Pepper

Directions:

1. Preheat the air fryer to 400°F.
2. Season chicken wings with garlic powder and pepper and place them into the air fryer basket.
3. Cook chicken wings for 15 min. Shake basket 3–4 times while cooking.
4. Transfer cooked chicken wings into a large mixing bowl. Pour BBQ sauce over chicken wings and toss to coat.

Nutrition: Calories: 263 kcal; **Fat:** 8.5 g; **Carbohydrate:** 11.5 g; **Sugar:** 8 g; **Protein:** 32 g; **Cholesterol:** 100 mg

380. Chicken Jalapeño Poppers

Preparation Time: 10 min
Cooking Time: 10 min; **Servings:** 2–3
Ingredients:

- ½ cup chicken, cooked and shredded
- 6 Jalapeños, halved and seed removed
- ¼ cup green onion, sliced
- ¼ cup Monterey jack cheese, shredded
- ¼ tsp. garlic powder
- 4 oz. cream cheese
- ¼ tsp. oregano, dried
- ¼ tsp. basil, dried
- ¼ tsp. salt

Directions:

1. Preheat the air fryer to 370°F.
2. Spray the air fryer basket with cooking spray.
3. Mix all ingredients in a bowl except Jalapeños.
4. Spoon 1 tbsp. mixture into each Jalapeño halved and place into the air fryer basket.
5. Cook Jalapeño for 20 min.
6. Serve and enjoy.

Nutrition: Calories: 105 kcal; **Fat:** 8.5 g; **Carbohydrate:** 1.5 g; **Sugar:** 0.7 g; **Protein:** 6.3 g; **Cholesterol:** 35 mg

381. Mexican Chicken Burgers

Preparation Time: 10 min
Cooking Time: 5 min; **Servings:** 2–3
Ingredients:

- 1 Jalapeño pepper
- 1 tsp. cayenne pepper
- 1 tbsp. mustard powder
- 1 tbsp. oregano
- 1 tbsp. thyme
- 1 tbsp. paprika, smoked
- 1 beaten egg
- 1 small head cauliflower
- 3 chicken breasts

Directions:

1. Preparing the Ingredients. Ensure your Air fryer oven is preheated to 350°F.
2. Add seasonings to a blender. Slice cauliflower into florets and add to blender.

3. Pulse till the mixture resembles that of breadcrumbs.
4. Take out ¾ of the cauliflower mixture and add to a bowl. Set to the side. In another bowl, beat your egg and set it to the side.
5. Remove skin and bones from chicken breasts and add to blender with remaining cauliflower mixture. Season with pepper and salt.
6. Take out the mixture and form it into burger shapes. Roll each patty in cauliflower crumbs, then the egg, and back into crumbs again.
7. Air Frying. Place coated patties into the Air fryer oven. Set temperature to 350°F, and set time to 10 min.
8. Flip over at the 10-minute mark. They are done when crispy!

Nutrition: Calories: 234 kcal; **Fat:** 18 g; **Protein:** 24 g; **Sugar:** 1 g

382. Crispy Honey Garlic Chicken Wings

Preparation Time: 10 min
Cooking Time: 25 min; **Servings:** 2–3
Ingredients:

- ⅛ cup water
- ½ tsp. salt
- tbsp. garlic, minced
- ¼ cup vegan butter
- ¼ cup raw honey
- ¾ cup almond flour
- 6 chicken wings

Directions:

1. Preparing the Ingredients. Rinse off and dry chicken wings well.
2. Spray the air fryer rack/basket with olive oil.
3. Coat chicken wings with almond flour and add coated wings to the Air fryer oven.
4. Air Frying. Set temperature to 380°F, and set time to 25 min. Cook, shaking every 5 min.
5. When the timer goes off, cook 5–10 min at 400°F till the skin becomes crispy and dry.
6. As chicken cooks, melt butter in a saucepan and add garlic. Sauté garlic for 5 min. Add salt and honey, and simmer for 20 min. Make sure to stir every so often so the sauce does not burn. Add a bit of water after 15 min to ensure the sauce does not harden.
7. Take out chicken wings from the air fryer and coat them in the sauce. Enjoy!

Nutrition: Calories: 435 kcal; **Fat:** 19 g; **Protein:** 31 g; **Sugar:** 6 g

383. Minty Chicken-Fried Beef Chops

Preparation Time: 10 min
Cooking Time: 15 min; **Servings:** 2–3
Ingredients:

- 3 Medium-sized Beef chops, approximately 3.5 oz. each
- 1 cup breadcrumbs (Panko brand works well)
- 1 medium-sized egg
- Pinch salt and pepper
- ½ tbsp. of mint, either dried and ground; or fresh, rinsed and finely chopped

Directions:

1. Preparing the Ingredients. Cover the basket of the Air fryer oven with a lining of tin foil, leaving the edges uncovered to allow air to circulate through the basket. Preheat the Air fryer oven to 350°F.
2. In a bowl, beat the eggs until fluffy and until the yolks and whites are completely combined and set aside.
3. In a separate bowl, combine the crumbs, mint, salt, and pepper and set aside. One at a time, dip each raw Beef chop into the dry ingredient bowl, coat all sides, dip it into the wet ingredient bowl, then dip it back into the dry ingredients. This double layer will ensure cooler air. Place the breaded Beef chops on the oven rack in a single flat layer. Place the air fryer rack on the middle shelf of the fryer.
4. Air fry. Set the Air Fryer timer to 15 min. After 15 minutes, the Air Fryer oven will turn off, the beef should cook in the middle, and the bread layer should start to brown. Using tweezers, flip each piece of meat over to secure a full pair of pants. Return the fryer to 320°F for 15 min.
5. After 15 min, when the fryer is off, remove the fried Beef chops with tongs and place them in a source. Eat as fresh as you can, and enjoy!

Nutrition: Calories: 213 kcal; **Fat:** 9 g; **Protein:** 12 g; **Fiber:** 3 g

384. Garlic Honey Chicken

Preparation Time: 10 min
Cooking Time: 20–30 min; **Servings:** 2–3
Ingredients:

- ⅓ cup water
- ¼ cup low sodium soy sauce
- ¼ cup honey
- 2 garlic cloves, minced
- ¼ tsp. black pepper
- 1 ½-lb. medium-size boneless skinless chicken breasts
- 2 tsp. cornstarch

Directions:

1. Combine water, soy sauce, honey, garlic, chicken, and pepper in the air fryer.
2. Cook at High Pressure for 10 min.
3. In a bowl, mix 2 tsp. cornstarch and 1 tbsp. water.
4. Cook cornstarch mixture on Sauté mode for 2–3 min.
5. Dip sliced chicken in sauce.
6. Serve with rice and vegetable.

Nutrition: Calories: 267 kcal; **Fat:** 8.5 g; **Fiber:** 7.1 g; **Carbs:** 31.2 g; **Protein:** 12.6 g

385. Roasted Duck Breasts with Endives

Preparation Time: 20 min
Cooking Time: 35 min; **Servings:** 4–5
Ingredients:

- 2 duck breasts
- 1 tbsp. sugar
- Salt and black pepper, to the taste
- 1 tbsp. olive oil
- 6 endives, julienned
- 2 tbsp. cranberries
- 8 oz. white wine
- 1 tbsp. garlic, minced

Directions:

1. Score duck bosoms and season them with salt and pepper, place in the preheated air fryer, and cook at 350°F for 20 minutes, flipping them midway.
2. On the other hand, heat a skillet with the oil over medium warmth, including sugar and endives; blend and cook for 2 min.
3. Include salt, pepper, wine, garlic, cream, and cranberries; blend and cook for 3 min.
4. Divide duck bosoms between plates; spread the endives sauce all finished, and serve.

Nutrition: Calories: 314 kcal; **Fat:** 18.4 g; **Fiber:** 15.1 g; **Carbs:** 31 g; **Protein:** 29 g

386. Chicken Sausage with Nestled Eggs

Preparation Time: 20 min
Cooking Time: 17 min; **Servings:** 2–3
Ingredients:

- 6 eggs
- 2 bell peppers, seeded and sliced
- 1 tsp. oregano, dried
- 1 tsp. hot paprika
- 1 tsp. black pepper, freshly cracked
- 6 chicken sausages
- 1 tsp. sea salt
- 1 ½ shallot, cut into wedges
- 1 tsp. basil, dried

Directions:

1. Take 4 ramekins and divide chicken sausages, shallot, and bell pepper among those ramekins. Air fry at 315°F for about 12 min.
2. Now, crack an egg into each ramekin. Sprinkle the eggs with hot paprika, basil, oregano, salt, and cracked black pepper. Cook for 5 more min at 405°F.

Nutrition: Calories: 314 kcal; **Fat:** 18.4 g; **Fiber:** 19.8 g; **Carbs:** 27 g; **Protein:** 19.1 g

387. Mozzarella Turkey Rolls

Preparation Time: 15 min
Cooking Time: 10–15 min; **Servings:** 4
Ingredients:

- 4 slices turkey breast
- 4 chive shoots (for tying rolls)
- 1 tomato, sliced
- ½ cup basil, fresh, chopped
- 1 cup mozzarella, sliced

Directions:

1. Preheat your air fryer to 390°F.
2. Place the slices of mozzarella cheese, tomato, and basil onto each slice of turkey.
3. Roll up and tie with chive shoot.
4. Place into the air fryer and cook for 10-min. Serve warm.

Nutrition: Calories: 245 kcal; **Fat:** 5.7 g; **Fiber:** 9.1 g; **Carbs:** 28.6 g; **Protein:** 12.8 g

388. Thai Chicken Satay

Preparation Time: 20 min
Cooking Time: 20–30 min; **Servings:** 2–3
Ingredients:

- ½ cup crunchy peanut butter
- ⅓ cup chicken broth
- 3 tbsp. low-sodium soy sauce
- 2 tbsp. lemon juice
- 2 garlic cloves, minced
- 2 tbsp. olive oil
- 1 tsp. curry powder
- 1 lb chicken tenders

Directions:

1. Set to 390°F the Grill. In a medium bowl, combine the peanut butter, chicken broth, soy sauce, lemon juice, garlic, olive oil, and curry powder, and mix well with a wire whisk until smooth. Remove 2 tablespoons of this mixture to a small bowl. Put the remaining sauce into a serving bowl and set aside.
2. Add the chicken tenders to the bowl with the 2 tbsp. sauce and stir to coat. Let stand for a few min to marinate, then run a bamboo skewer through each chicken tender lengthwise.

3. Put the chicken in the air fryer basket and cook in batches for 6 to 9 min or until the chicken reaches 165°F on a meat thermometer. Serve the chicken with the reserved sauce.

Nutrition: Calories: 299 kcal; **Fat:** 7.5 g; **Fiber:** 8.1 g; **Carbs:** 29.5 g; **Protein:** 12.4 g

389. Butter and Orange Fried Chicken

Preparation Time: 20 min
Cooking Time: 13 min; **Servings:** 2–3
Ingredients:

- ½ tbsp. Worcestershire sauce
- 1 tsp. orange zest, finely grated
- 2 tbsp. butter, melted
- ½ tsp. paprika, smoked
- 4 chicken drumsticks, rinsed and halved
- 1 tsp. sea salt flakes
- 1 tbsp. cider vinegar
- ½ tsp. mixed peppercorns, freshly cracked

Directions:

1. Firstly, pat the chicken drumsticks dry. Coat them with melted butter on all sides. Toss the chicken drumsticks with the other ingredients.
2. Transfer them to the air fryer cooking basket and roast for about 13 min at 345°F.

Nutrition: Calories: 314 kcal; **Fat:** 11.4 g; **Fiber:** 12.1 g; **Carbs:** 29.7 g; **Protein:** 24.1 g

390. Lemon-Pepper Chicken Wings

Preparation Time: 10 min
Cooking Time: 10 min; **Servings:** 2–3
Ingredients:

- whole chicken wings
- Juice of ½ lemon
- ½ tsp. garlic powder
- 1 tsp. onion powder
- Salt
- Pepper
- ¼ cup low-fat buttermilk
- ½ cup all-purpose flour
- Cooking oil

Directions:

1. Place the wings in a sealed plastic bag. Drizzle the wings with lemon juice. Season the wings with garlic powder, onion powder, and salt and pepper to taste.
2. Seal the bag. Shake thoroughly to combine the seasonings and coat the wings.
3. Pour the buttermilk and the flour into separate bowls large enough to dip the wings.
4. Spray the Oven rack/basket with cooking oil.
5. One at a time, dip the wings in the buttermilk and then the flour.
6. Air Frying. Place the wings in the Oven rack/basket. It is okay to stack them on top of each other. Spray the wings with cooking oil and spray the bottom layer. Place the tray rack on the middle shelf of the Air fryer oven. Set temperature to 360°F and cook for 5 min.
7. Remove the basket and shake it to ensure all pieces will cook fully.
8. Return the basket to the Air fryer oven and continue to cook the chicken. Repeat shaking every 5 min until a total of 20 min has passed.
9. Cool before serving.

Nutrition: Calories: 347 kcal; **Fat:** 12 g; **Protein:** 46 g; **Fiber:** 1 g

391. Honey and Wine Chicken Breasts

Preparation Time: 5 min
Cooking Time: 8 min; **Servings:** 2–3
Ingredients:

- 3 chicken breasts, rinsed and halved
- 1 tbsp. melted butter
- A pinch of salt and ½ tsp. pepper, freshly ground, to taste
- ¾ tsp. sea salt, or to taste
- 1 tsp. paprika
- 1 tsp. rosemary, dried
- 2 tbsp. dry white wine
- 1 tbsp. honey

Directions:

1. Firstly, pat the chicken breasts dry. Lightly coat them with melted butter.
2. Then, add the remaining ingredients.
3. Air Frying. Transfer them to the air fryer rack/basket; bake for about 15 min at 330°F. Serve warm and enjoy

Nutrition: Cal: 189 kcal; **Fat:** 14 g; **Prot:** 11 g; **Sugar:** 1 g

392. Asian Chicken Noodles

Preparation Time: 20 min
Cooking Time: 30–35 min; **Servings:** 2–3
Ingredients:

- 1 tbsp. olive oil
- 1 onion, diced
- 3 garlic cloves, minced
- ½ tbsp. pepper
- 4 oz. extra-wide egg noodles
- ¼ cup flat-leaf parsley, minced
- 5 carrots, sliced into ½-inch chunks
- 2 celery sticks, sliced into ½-inch pieces

- 1 whole (5-lb.) chicken, giblets removed and discarded
- 2 tbsp. soy sauce
- 8 cups water
- ½ tbsp. salt

Directions:

1. Cook onion in olive oil at Sauté for 2–3 minutes.
2. Add garlic, carrots, celery, and sauté for 1 minute.
3. Add whole chicken, soy sauce, 2 teaspoons of salt, and several turns of freshly ground pepper in Pot.
4. Cook at High Pressure for 20 min and remove.
5. Turn the Air fryer back to Sauté and let the chicken broth come to a boil.
6. Add egg noodles and let cook for about 5 min.
7. Once noodles are cooked, add shredded chicken and fresh parsley and serve.

Nutrition: Calories: 261 kcal; **Fat:** 8.4 g; **Fiber:** 4.5 g; **Carbs:** 21.9 g; **Protein:** 6.5 g

393. Sweet and Sour Chicken

Preparation Time: 15 min
Cooking Time: 20–30 min; **Servings:** 2–3
Ingredients:

- 6 chicken drumsticks
- 3 tbsp. lemon juice, divided
- 3 tbsp. low-sodium soy sauce, divided
- 1 tbsp. peanut oil
- 3 tbsp. honey
- 3 tbsp. brown sugar
- 2 tbsp. ketchup
- ¼ cup pineapple juice

Directions:

1. Set to 350°F. Sprinkle the drumsticks with 1 tablespoon of lemon juice and 1 tablespoon of soy sauce. Place in the air fryer basket and drizzle with the peanut oil. Toss to coat. Bake for 18 min or until the chicken is almost done.
2. Meanwhile, in a 6-inch bowl, combine the remaining 2 tablespoons of lemon juice, the remaining 2 tablespoons of soy sauce, honey, brown sugar, ketchup, and pineapple juice.
3. Add the cooked chicken to the bowl and stir to coat the chicken well with the sauce.
4. Place the metal bowl in the basket. Cook for 5 to 7 min or until the chicken is glazed and registers 165°F on a meat thermometer.

Nutrition: Calories: 277 kcal; **Fat:** 12.5 g; **Fiber:** 10.9 g; **Carbs:** 31.9 g; **Protein:** 12 g

394. Easy General Tso's Chicken

Preparation Time: 15 min
Cooking Time: 14 min; **Servings:** 2–3
Ingredients:

- 1 tbsp. sesame oil
- 1 tsp. garlic, minced
- ½ tsp. ginger, ground
- 1 cup chicken broth
- 4 tbsp. soy sauce, divided
- ½ tsp. sriracha, plus more for serving
- 2 tbsp. hoisin sauce
- 4 tbsp. cornstarch, divided
- 4 chicken breasts, boneless, skinless, cut into 1-inch pieces
- Olive oil spray
- 2 medium scallions, sliced, green parts only
- Sesame seeds, for garnish

Directions:

1. In a small saucepan over low heat, combine the sesame oil, garlic, and ginger and cook for 1 minute.
2. Add the chicken broth, 2 tablespoons of soy sauce, the sriracha, and hoisin. Whisk to combine.
3. Whisk in 2 tablespoons of cornstarch and continue cooking over low heat until the sauce starts to thicken for about 5 min. Remove the pan from the heat, cover it, and set it aside.
4. Insert the crisper plate into the basket and the basket into the unit. Preheat the unit by selecting BAKE, setting the temperature to 400°F, and setting the time to 3 min. Select START/STOP to begin.
5. In a medium bowl, toss the chicken, the remaining 2 tablespoons of soy sauce, and the remaining 2 tablespoons of cornstarch.
6. Once the unit is preheated, spray the crisper plate with olive oil. Place the chicken into the basket and spray it with olive oil.
7. Select BAKE, set the temperature to 400°F, and set the time to 9 min. Select START/STOP to begin.
8. After 5 min, remove the basket, shake, and spray the chicken with more olive oil. Reinsert the basket to resume cooking.
9. When the cooking is complete, a food thermometer inserted into the chicken should register at least 165°F. Transfer the chicken to a large bowl and toss it with the sauce. Garnish with the scallions and sesame seeds, and serve.

Nutrition: Calories: 298 kcal; **Fat:** 11.4 g; **Fiber:** 12.1 g; **Carbs:** 21.7 g; **Protein:** 19.5 g

404 Rosemary Lamb Chops

IPH BOOKS
Healthy Lifestyle
407 Juicy and Tender Lemon Mustard Lamb Chops

419 Creamy Beef Stroganoff with Mushrooms

391 Honey and Wine Chicken Breasts

395. BBQ Lamb

Preparation Time: 90 min
Cooking Time: 8 min; **Servings:** 2–3
Ingredients:

- 4 lb. leg lamb, boneless, cut into 2-inch chunks
- 2-½ tbsp. herb salt
- 2 tbsp. olive oil

Directions:

1. Preheat the PowerXL Air Fryer Grill by selecting air fryer mode.
2. Adjust the temperature to 390°F and set the time to 5 min.
3. Season the meat with salt and olive oil.
4. Arrange on the Air fryer baking tray.
5. Transfer to the PowerXL Air Fryer Grill.
6. Air fry for 15 min, flipping halfway through.
7. Serve and enjoy.

Serving Suggestions: Serve with marinara sauce.
Directions and Cooking Tips: work in batches.
Nutrition: Calories: 341 kcal; **Fat:** 16 g; **Carb:** 1 g; **Protein:** 26 g

396. Lamb Meatballs

Preparation Time: 15 min
Cooking Time: 8 min
Servings: 2–3
Ingredients:

- 1 lb. lamb, ground
- ½ cup breadcrumbs
- 1 lemon, juiced and zested
- ¼ cup milk
- 2 egg yolks
- 1 tsp. cumin, ground
- 1 tsp. oregano, dried
- ½ tsp. salt
- 1 tsp. coriander, ground
- ½ tsp. black pepper
- 3 garlic cloves, minced
- ¼ cup fresh parsley, chopped
- ½ cup crumbled feta cheese

Directions:

1. Preheat the PowerXL Air Fryer Grill by selecting Broil mode.
2. Adjust the temperature to 390°F and set the time to 5 min.
3. Combine all the ingredients in a bowl.
4. Form into 12 balls.
5. Arrange on the Air fryer baking tray.
6. Transfer to the PowerXL Air Fryer Grill.
7. Cook for 12 min.
8. Serve and enjoy.

Serving Suggestions: Serve with tzatziki sauce.
Directions and Cooking Tips: Rub olive oil on your hand when forming the meatballs.
Nutrition: Calories: 129 kcal; **Fat:** 6.4 g; Carb: 4.9 g; **Protein:** 25 g

397. Glazed Lamb Chops

Preparation Time: 30 min
Cooking Time: 8 min; **Servings:** 2–3
Ingredients:

- 4 (4-oz.) lamb loin chops
- 1 tbsp. Dijon mustard
- 1 tsp. honey
- ½ tbsp. fresh lime juice
- ½ tsp. olive oil
- Salt and black pepper, ground, as required

Directions:

1. Preheat the PowerXL Air Fryer Grill by selecting air fryer mode.
2. Adjust the temperature to 390°F and set the time to 5 minutes.
3. Combine all the ingredients in a bowl.
4. Add the Beef chops and toss to coat.
5. Arrange on the Air fryer baking tray.
6. Transfer to the PowerXL Air Fryer Grill.
7. Air fry for 15 min, flipping halfway through.
8. Serve and enjoy.

Serving Suggestions: Serve while still hot.

Directions and Cooking Tips: Leave to marinate for a few min.
Nutrition: Cal: 224 kcal; **Fat:** 4 g; **Carb:** 2 g; **Protein:** 19 g

398. Garlic Lamb Shank

Preparation Time: 15 min
Cooking Time: 24 min
Servings: 2–3
Ingredients:

- 17 oz. lamb shanks
- 2 tbsp. garlic, peeled, and coarsely chopped
- tsp. kosher salt
- ½ cup chicken stock
- 2 tbsp. parsley, dried
- 1 tsp. rosemary, dried
- 4 oz. chive stems, chopped
- 1 tsp. butter
- 1 tsp. nutmeg
- ½ tsp. black pepper, ground

Directions:

1. Make the cuts in the lamb shank and fill the cuts with the chopped garlic.
2. Sprinkle the lamb shank with kosher salt, dried parsley, rosemary, nutmeg, and ground black pepper.
3. Stir the spices on the lamb shank gently.
4. Preheat the PowerXL Air Fryer Grill by selecting air fry mode.
5. Adjust the temperature to 380°F and set the time to 5 min
6. Put the butter, chives, and chicken stock in the air fryer baking tray.
7. Add the lamb shank and air fry the meat for 24 min.
8. Serve and enjoy

Serving Suggestions: Serve with the cooking liquid
Directions and Cooking Tips: Add spices to taste
Nutrition: Calories: 205 kcal; **Fat:** 8.2 g; **Carb:** 3 g; **Proteins:** 28 g

399. Indian Meatball with Lamb

Preparation Time: 10 min
Cooking Time: 14 min
Servings: 2–3
Ingredients:

- 1 lb. lamb, ground
- 1 garlic clove, minced
- 1 egg
- 1 tbsp. butter
- 4 oz. chive stems, grated
- ¼ tbsp. turmeric
- ⅓ tsp. cayenne pepper
- ¼ tsp. bay leaf
- 1 tsp. coriander, ground
- 1 tsp. salt
- 1 tsp. black pepper, ground

Directions:

1. Combine all the ingredients in a bowl.
2. Preheat the PowerXL air fryer by selecting the air fry mode.
3. Adjust the temperature to 390°F and set the time to 5 min.
4. Put the butter in the Air fryer baking tray and melt it.
5. Form the meatballs.
6. Place them in the air fryer baking tray.
7. Transfer to the PowerXL Air Fryer Grill.
8. Cook the dish for 14 min.
9. Stir the meatballs twice during the cooking.

Serving Suggestions: Serve with salad and sauce.
Directions and Cooking Tips: Use an ice-cream scooper to form the balls.
Nutrition: Calories: 300 kcal; **Fat:** 13 g; **Carb:** 19 g; **Protein:** 21 g

400. Roasted Lamb

Preparation Time: 60 min
Cooking Time: 13 min; **Servings:** 2–3
Ingredients:

- 2-½ lb. lamb leg roast, slits carved
- 2 tbsp. olive oil
- 3 garlic cloves, sliced into smaller slithers
- 1 tbsp. rosemary, dried

- Himalayan rock salt cracked; and peppercorns, cracked, to taste

Directions:

1. Make the cuts in the lamb roast and insert them with garlic.
2. Sprinkle the lamb roast with kosher salt, rosemary, and ground black pepper.
3. Brush with oil.
4. Preheat the PowerXL Air Fryer Grill by selecting air fry mode.
5. Adjust the temperature to 380°F and set the time to 5 min.
6. Place the lamb roast on the Baking Pan.
7. Transfer to the PowerXL Air Fryer Grill.
8. Air fry for 1 hour 15 min.
9. Serve and enjoy.

Serving Suggestions: Serve with mushroom sauce.

Directions and Cooking Tips: Leave to marinate for some min.

Nutrition: Cal: 246 kcal; **Fat:** 7 g; **Carb:** 9 g; **Protein:** 33 g

401. Lemon Lamb Rack

Preparation Time: 30 min

Cooking Time: 5 min; **Servings:** 2–3

Ingredients:

- ¼ cup olive oil
- 3 tbsp. garlic, minced
- ⅓ cup dry white wine
- 1 tbsp. lemon zest, grated
- 2 tbsp. lemon juice
- 1-½ tsp. oregano, dried and crushed
- 1 tsp. thyme leaves, minced
- Salt and black pepper
- 4 lamb rack
- 1 lemon, sliced

Directions:

1. Preheat the PowerXL Air Fryer Grill by selecting air fryer mode.
2. Adjust the temperature to 370°F and set the time to 5 min.
3. Whisk all the ingredients together in a bowl.
4. Pour into the air fryer baking tray.
5. Add the lamb rack.
6. Top with lemon.
7. Transfer to the PowerXL Air Fryer Grill.
8. Air fry for 30 min, flipping halfway through.
9. Serve and enjoy.

Serving Suggestions: Serve with juice.

Directions and Cooking Tips: Leave to marinate for a few min.

Nutrition: Cal: 288 kcal; **Fat:** 7 g; **Carb:** 5 g; **Protein:** 16 g

402. Juicy and Savory Lamb Chops

Preparation Time: 10 min

Cooking Time: 5 min; **Servings:** 3–4

Ingredients:

- ⅓ lb. lamb chop
- 1 tbsp. mixed fresh herbs, chopped
- ½ tbsp. olive oil
- ½ tbsp. Dijon mustard
- Pepper
- Salt

Directions:

1. Season lamb chop with pepper and salt.
2. In a small bowl, mix oil, mustard, and mixed herbs.
3. Brush lamb chop from both sides with the oil mixture.
4. Place lamb chop into the air fryer basket and cook at 375°F for 10 min. Turn halfway through.

Nutrition: Calories: 350 kcal; **Fat:** 18.5 g; **Carbohydrate:** 1.2 g; **Sugar:** 0.1 g; **Protein:** 43 g; **Cholesterol:** 136 mg

403. Lamb Patties

Preparation Time: 10 min

Cooking Time: 15 min; **Servings:** 4–5

Ingredients:

- 1 lb. lamb meat, ground
- 1 egg, lightly beaten
- ½ tbsp. garlic, minced
- 1 spring onion, chopped
- ¼ cup almond flour
- 1 tbsp. basil, chopped
- 1 tbsp. cilantro, chopped
- Pepper
- Salt

Directions:

1. Spray the air fryer basket with cooking spray.
2. Add all ingredients into the bowl and mix until well combined.
3. Make small patties from the meat mixture, place them into the air fryer basket, and cook at 390°F for 30 min. Turn patties halfway through.
4. Serve and enjoy.

Nutrition: Calories: 260 kcal; **Fat:** 17 g; **Carbohydrate:** 1.1 g; **Sugar:** 0.2 g; **Protein:** 23 g; **Cholesterol:** 121 mg

404. Rosemary Lamb Chops

Preparation Time: 10 min
Cooking Time: 12 min; **Servings:** 4–5
Ingredients:

- 4 lamb chops
- 2 tsp. ginger garlic paste
- 2 tsp. olive oil
- 1 tsp. rosemary, chopped
- Pepper
- Salt

Directions:

1. Add lamb chops, ginger garlic paste, oil, rosemary, pepper, and salt into the zip-lock bag.
2. Seal the bag, shake well, and place it in the refrigerator for 1 hour.
3. Add marinated lamb chops into the air fryer basket and cook at 360°F for 12 min. Turn halfway through.
4. Serve and enjoy.

Nutrition: Calories: 461 kcal; **Fat:** 22.3 g; **Carbohydrate:** 3.4 g; **Sugar:** 0 g; **Protein:** 64.2 g; **Cholesterol:** 203 mg

405. Dijon Garlic Lamb Chops

Preparation Time: 10 min
Cooking Time: 17 min; **Servings:** 3–4
Ingredients:

- 8 lamb chops
- 1 tsp. cayenne pepper
- 1 tsp. cumin powder
- 1 tsp. garlic, minced
- 1 tsp. soy sauce
- 2 tsp. olive oil
- 2 tsp. Dijon mustard
- ¼ tsp. salt

Directions:

1. Add lamb chops and remaining ingredients into the zip-lock bag. Seal the bag, shake well, and place it in the refrigerator for 30 min.
2. Place marinated lamb chops into the air fryer basket and cook at 350°F for 17 min. Turn lamb chops halfway through.
3. Serve and enjoy.

Nutrition: Calories: 445 kcal; **Fat:** 19.1 g; **Carbohydrate:** 0.9 g; **Sugar:** 0.1 g; **Protein:** 63.6 g; **Cholesterol:** 203 mg

406. Flavorful Cumin Lamb

Preparation Time: 10 min
Cooking Time: 5 min; **Servings:** 4–5
Ingredients:

- 1 lb. lamb, cut into ½-inch pieces
- ¼ tsp. Swerve
- 12 red chili peppers, chopped
- 1 tbsp. garlic, minced
- 1 tbsp. soy sauce
- 2 tbsp. olive oil
- ½ tsp. cayenne
- 1 ½ tbsp. cumin, ground
- 1 tsp. kosher salt

Directions:

1. Add lamb pieces and remaining ingredients into the zip-lock bag. Seal the bag, shake well, and place it in the refrigerator for 30 min.
2. Place marinated lamb pieces into the air fryer basket and cook at 360°F for 10 min. Shake basket halfway through.
3. Serve and enjoy.

Nutrition: Calories: 291 kcal; **Fat:** 16 g; **Carbohydrate:** 3.3 g; **Sugar:** 0.8 g; **Protein:** 32.8 g; **Cholesterol:** 102 mg

407. Juicy and Tender Lemon Mustard Lamb Chops

Preparation Time: 10 min
Cooking Time: 8 min; **Servings:** 4–5
Ingredients:

- 8 lamb chops
- 1 tbsp. fresh lemon juice
- 1 tsp. tarragon
- ½ tsp. olive oil
- 2 tbsp. mustard
- Pepper
- Salt

Directions:

1. Preheat the cosori air fryer to 390°F.
2. Mix lemon juice, tarragon, oil, mustard, pepper, and salt in a small bowl.
3. Brush lamb chops from both sides with lemon juice mixture.
4. Place lamb chops into the air fryer basket, and cook for 15 min. Turn halfway through.
5. Serve and enjoy.

Nutrition: Calories: 451 kcal; **Fat:** 18.7 g; **Carbohydrate:** 2.1 g; **Sugar:** 0.5 g; **Protein:** 64.6 g; **Cholesterol:** 203 mg

408. Lamb Balls

Preparation Time: 10 min
Cooking Time: 12 min; **Servings:** 4–5
Ingredients:

- 1 lb. lamb, ground
- 1 lemon juice
- 1 tbsp. dill, dried
- 1 tbsp. rosemary, dried
- 1 egg, lightly beaten
- 1 lb. beef, ground
- Pepper
- Salt

Directions:

1. Spray the air fryer basket with cooking spray.
2. Add all ingredients into the mixing bowl and mix until well combined.
3. Make 1-inch balls from the mixture, place them into the air fryer basket, and cook at 350°F for 7 min.
4. Shake the basket and cook for 5 min more.
5. Serve and enjoy.

Nutrition: Calories: 297 kcal; **Fat:** 11.1 g; **Carbohydrate:** 0.9 g; **Sugar:** 0.2 g; **Protein:** 45.3 g; **Cholesterol:** 163 mg

409. Spicy Lamb Steak

Preparation Time: 10 min
Cooking Time: 8 min; **Servings:** 4–5
Ingredients:

- 1 lb. lamb sirloin steaks, boneless
- 1 tsp. cayenne pepper
- ½ tsp. cardamom, ground
- 1 tsp. cinnamon, ground
- 1 tsp. fennel, ground
- 1 tsp. garam masala
- 4 garlic cloves
- 1 tbsp. ginger
- ½ onion
- 1 tsp. kosher salt

Directions:

1. Add all ingredients except lamb steaks into the blender and blend until a smooth paste is formed.
2. Add lamb steaks and blended paste into the mixing bowl and mix well. Place in refrigerator for 30 min.
3. Spray the air fryer basket with cooking spray.
4. Place marinated lamb steaks into the air fryer basket, and cook at 330°F for 15 min. Turn halfway through.
5. Serve and enjoy.

Nutrition: Calories: 76 kcal; **Fat:** 2.3 g; **Carbohydrate:** 4.6 g; **Sugar:** 0.7 g; **Protein:** 9.7 g; **Cholesterol:** 0 mg

410. Lamb Roast

Preparation Time: 10 min
Cooking Time: 8 min; **Servings:** 4–5
Ingredients:

- 10 oz. lamb leg roast
- 1 tsp. thyme, dried
- 1 tsp. rosemary, dried
- 1 tbsp. olive oil
- Pepper
- Salt

Directions:

1. Preheat the cosori air fryer to 360°F.
2. Mix oil, rosemary, thyme, pepper, and salt in a small bowl and rub all over the lamb roast.
3. Place lamb roast into the air fryer basket and cook for 15 min.
4. Serve and enjoy.

Nutrition: Calories: 319 kcal; **Fat:** 16.6 g; **Carbohydrate:** 0.7 g; **Sugar:** 0 g; **Protein:** 40 g; **Cholesterol:** 123 mg

411. Mom's Sloppy Joes

Preparation Time: 10 min
Cooking Time: 15 min; **Servings:** 2–3
Ingredients:

- Nonstick cooking spray
- 1 ½ lb. supreme lean ground beef
- 1 cup onion, chopped
- 1 cup celery, chopped
- 1 (8-oz.) can tomato sauce
- ⅓ cup catsup (free of high-fructose corn syrup)
- 2 tbsp. white vinegar
- 2 tbsp. Worcestershire sauce
- 2 tbsp. Dijon mustard
- 1 tbsp. brown sugar

Directions:

1. Spray a large skillet with the cooking spray, and place it over medium heat. Add the beef and brown until it is no longer pink, about 10 min. Drain off any grease.
2. Mix in the onion and celery, and cook for 2 to 3 min.
3. Stir in the tomato sauce, catsup, vinegar, Worcestershire sauce, mustard, and brown sugar. Bring the liquid to a simmer, and reduce the heat to low. Cook for 15 min, or until the sauce has thickened
4. Spoon about ¾ cup of the sloppy Joe mixture onto each plate, and serve.

Nutrition per serving (¾ cup): Calories: 269 kcal; **Total Fat:** 5 g; **Protein:** 24 g; **Carbs:** 32 g; **Fiber:** 6 g; **Sugar:** 6 g; **Sodium:** 656 mg

412. Cranberry Meatballs

Preparation Time: 20 min
Cooking Time: 10 min; **Servings:** 2–3
Ingredients:

- 2 large eggs, lightly beaten
- 1 cup cornflake crumbs
- ⅓ cup ketchup
- 2 tbsp. onion, dried and minced
- 2 tbsp. soy sauce
- 1 tbsp. parsley flakes, dried
- ½ tsp. salt
- ¼ tsp. pepper
- 2 lb. beef, ground

Sauce:

- 1 can (14 oz.) cranberry sauce, jellied
- 1 cup ketchup

- 3 tbsp. brown sugar
- 1 tbsp. lemon juice

Directions:

1. Heat the oven to 35°F. Combine 8 ingredients first. Add beef; blend thoroughly but lightly. Shape yourself into 1-in, with meatballs. Place it on a 15x10x1-in, greased shelf. Uh, pan. Bake for 20–25 minutes until the thermometer reads 160°F. Drain paper towels with meatballs.
2. Cook and mix the sauce ingredients over medium heat in a large skillet until blended. Incorporate meatballs; heat through.

Nutrition: 1 meatball: Calories: 58 kcal; **Fat:** 2 g; **Cholesterol:** 16 mg; **Sodium:** 142 mg; **Carbohydrate:** 6 g; **Protein:** 3 g

413. Apricot Brown Sugar Ham

Preparation Time: 2 hours
Cooking Time: 2 hours; **Servings:** 2–3
Ingredients:

- 1 (10 lb.) spiral cut ham, fully-cooked
- ⅔ cup brown sugar
- ⅓ cup apricot jam
- 1 tsp. dry mustard powder

Directions:

1. Heat the oven to 275°F.
2. Set the cut side of the ham down on a sheet of aluminum foil. I love putting up the shiny side. In a bowl, blend the brown sugar, apricot jam, and mustard powder. Use a pastry or barbeque brush to brush on the ham. Reserve any glaze remaining. Enclose the foil and put it on a rimmed baking sheet around the ham.
3. In the preheated oven, roast for 2 hours, or if your ham is of a different size, weigh 14 min per lb. 20 min before the ham is finished, and apply the remaining glaze.

Nutrition: Calories: 801 kcal; **Protein:** 56.1 g; **Carbohydrate:** 14.4 g; **Fat:** 56.2 g; **Cholesterol:** 169.6 mg; **Sodium:** 3895.3 mg

414. Steak Fajitas

Preparation Time: 15 min
Cooking Time: 15 min; **Servings:** 2–3
Ingredients:
Salsa:

- 1 onion that has been sliced into strips
- 1 green bell pepper that has been sliced into strips
- ½ tsp. thyme, dried
- ½ tsp. mustard powder
- 1 tsp. black pepper
- 1 tsp. cumin
- 2 tsp. rosemary, dried
- 2 tsp. chili powder
- 2 packets natural sweetener
- 1 tbsp. paprika
- 1 tbsp. sea salt
- 1 lb. lean sirloin steak, cut into strips

Directions:

1. Place the salt, paprika, sweetener, chili powder, dried rosemary, cumin, pepper, mustard powder, and dried thyme into a bowl and mix well to combine. Take out 1 teaspoon of this mixture and reserve. Rub the steak slices well with the spice mixture that you just made. Cover the steak and allow it to marinate until you are ready to cook it.
2. Place a large skillet on the stove and heat to medium-high. Add the onion and pepper to the skillet and the spice mixture you set to the side earlier. You need to cook the onion and peppers until they have softened up and the onions turn translucent. Take off heat and place in a bowl. Cover to keep warm.
3. Into the same skillet, add half the seasoned steak and cook for about 2 min per side or until done to your liking. Place cooked steak onto a clean plate and cover until the rest of the steak gets done.
4. Once all the steak strips are done, add everything back into the skillet and warm everything up for a few min. Spoon onto plates and enjoy.

Nutrition: Calories: 663 kcal; **Fat:** 22.1 g; **Protein:** 104.7 g; **Carb:** 6 g

415. Taco Beef

Preparation Time: 15 min
Cooking Time: 8 hours; **Servings:** 2–3
Ingredients:

- 1 chipotle pepper in adobo sauce, minced
- 5 garlic cloves, minced
- 2 tsp. chili powder,
- 1 small white onion, diced
- 2 lb. chuck's tender roast
- 2 tbsp. tomato paste
- 1 cup beef broth, low sodium
- ½ tsp. paprika,
- 1 tsp. cumin
- 2 tsp. olive oil

Directions:

1. Place the paprika, cumin, and chili powder into a small bowl and mix everything. Rub this mixture into the chuck roast. Make sure that you cover the chuck roast well.
2. Set a large pan on top of the stove and warm it to medium-high. Add the olive oil and let it get hot. Place beef into the skillet and sear for 2 min. Turn the roast and sear every side. Take the beef out of the skillet and put it into the bottom of the slow cooker.

3. Add the diced onion into the skillet you seared the beef in and cook for 3 min until onions become soft and translucent. Mix in the garlic, cooking until fragrant. Pour the beef broth into the skillet and scrape with a wooden spoon to deglaze the pan.
4. Add the minced chipotle and tomato paste into the skillet, and, using a whisk, stir until everything is combined. Allow the mixture to come up to a boil, and then turn the heat down until it simmers. Let it simmer for 5 minutes or until it has thickened. Take off the heat and pour over the beef in the bottom of the slow cooker.
5. Place lid on the slow cooker and set on low. Cook for 8 hours until the beef will shred easily with a fork.
6. When beef is done, take it out of the cooker and shred it up. Mix it back into the juices so that it is well coated.
7. Use as you would any meat mixture in your favorite Mexican dishes or eat as is.

Nutrition: Calories: 292 kcal; **Fat:** 11.1 g; **Protein:** 42.3 g; **Carb:** 4 g

416. Chipotle Shredded Beef

Preparation Time: 10 min
Cooking Time: 6 hours; **Servings:** 2–3
Ingredients:

- 1 (7.5-oz.) can chipotle peppers in adobo sauce
- 1 ½ tbsp. apple cider vinegar
- 1 tbsp. cumin, ground
- 1 tbsp. oregano, dried
- Juice of 1 lime
- 2 lb. Beef shoulder, trimmed of excess fat

Directions:

1. Purée the chipotle peppers and adobo sauce using the blender, apple cider vinegar, cumin, oregano, and lime juice.
2. Place the Beef shoulder in the slow cooker, and pour the sauce over it.
3. Cover the slow cooker, and cook on low for 6 hours.
4. The finished Beef should shred easily. Use 2 forks to shred the beef in the slow cooker. If there is any additional sauce, allow the Beef to cook on low for 20 min more to absorb the remaining liquid.

Nutrition per serving (½ cup Beef): Calories: 260 kcal; **Total Fat:** 11 g; **Protein:** 20 g; **Carbs:** 5 g; **Fiber:** 2 g; **Sugar:** 2 g; **Sodium:** 705 mg

417. One-Pan Beef Chops with Apples and Red Onion

Preparation Time: 10 min
Cooking Time: 15 min; **Servings:**
Ingredients:

- 2 tsp. extra-virgin olive oil, divided
- 4 Beef thin chops, boneless center-cut
- 2 small apples, thinly sliced
- 1 small red onion, thinly sliced
- 1 cup low-sodium chicken broth
- 1 tsp. Dijon mustard
- 1 tsp. sage, dried
- 1 tsp. thyme, dried

Directions:

1. Place a large nonstick frying pan over high heat and add 1 teaspoon olive oil. When the oil is hot, add the Beef chops and reduce the heat to medium. Sear the chops for 3 min on one side, flip, and sear the other side for 3 min, 6 min total. Put the chops by the side.
2. In the same pan, add the remaining 1 teaspoon of olive oil. Add the apples and onion. Cook for 5 min or until tender, frequently stirring to prevent burning.
3. While the apples and onion cook, mix the broth and Dijon mustard in a small bowl.
4. Add the sage and thyme to the pan and stir to coat the onion and apples. Stir in the broth mixture and return the Beef chops to the pan. Cover the pan and simmer for 10 to 15 min.
5. Let Beef chops rest for 2 min before cutting.

Nutrition per serving (1 Beef chop): Calories: 234 kcal; **Total Fat:** 11 g; **Protein:** 20 g; **Carbs:** 13 g; **Fiber:** 3 g; **Sugar:** 9 g; **Sodium:** 290 mg

418. Slow Cooker Beef with Red Peppers and Pineapple

Preparation Time: 10 min
Cooking Time: 5 hours; **Servings:** 2–3
Ingredients:

- ¼ cup low-sodium soy sauce or Bragg Liquid Aminos
- Juice of ½ lemon
- 1 tsp. garlic powder
- 1 tsp. cumin, ground
- ½ tsp. cayenne pepper
- ¼ tsp. coriander, ground
- 1 ½ lb. Beef tenderloin, boneless
- 2 red bell peppers, thinly sliced
- 2 (20-oz.) cans pineapple chunks in 100% natural juice or water, drained

Directions:

1. Mix the soy sauce, lemon juice, garlic powder, cumin, cayenne pepper, and coriander in a small bowl.
2. Place the Beef tenderloin in the slow cooker and add the red bell pepper slices. Cover with the pineapple chunks and their juices. Pour the soy sauce mixture on top.
3. Cover the slow cooker and turn it on low for about 5 hours.

4. Shred the Beef with a fork and tongs and continue to cook on low for 20 min more, or until juices are absorbed.
5. Serve and enjoy!

Nutrition per serving (3 oz.): Calories: 131 kcal; Total **Fat:** 2 g; **Protein:** 17 g; **Carbs:** 11 g; **Fiber:** 2 g; **Sugar:** 8 g; **Sodium:** 431 mg

419. Creamy Beef Stroganoff with Mushrooms

Preparation Time: 10 min
Cooking Time: 15 min; **Servings:** 2–3
Ingredients:

- Nonstick cooking spray
- 1 ½ lb. extra-lean beef sirloin, cut into ½-inch strips
- 1 tsp. extra-virgin olive oil
- 1 medium onion, chopped
- ½ lb. mushrooms, sliced
- 2 tbsp. whole-wheat flour
- 1 cup low-sodium beef broth
- 1 cup water
- 1 tsp. Worcestershire sauce
- ½ tsp. thyme, dried
- ½ tsp. dill, dried
- ½ cup low-fat plain Greek yogurt
- 2 tbsp. fresh parsley, finely chopped, for garnish

Directions:

1. Coat a medium pan with the cooking spray and place over medium-high heat. Add the beef. Cook, frequently stirring, until browned, about 5 min. Transfer to a bowl and set aside.
2. In the same pan, heat the olive oil over medium-high heat. Add the onion and cook until tender, 1 to 2 min.
3. Add the mushrooms and cook until tender, about 3 min.
4. Mix in the flour and stir to coat the onion and mushrooms.
5. Stir in the broth, water, Worcestershire sauce, thyme, and dill. Bring to a boil, cover the pan, and cook for about 10 min, stirring frequently.
6. Stir in the yogurt. Mix in the beef. Serve garnished with parsley.

Nutrition per serving (4 oz.): Calories: 351 kcal; **Total Fat:** 9 g; **Protein:** 31 g; **Carbs:** 30 g; **Fiber:** 5 g; **Sugar:** 5 g; **Sodium:** 418 mg

420. Italian Beef Sandwiches

Preparation Time: 10 min
Cooking Time: 7 hours; **Servings:** 2–3
Ingredients:

- 1 cup water
- 1 tbsp. balsamic vinegar
- ¾ tsp. garlic powder
- ¾ tsp. onion powder
- 1 ½ tsp. parsley, dried
- ¾ tsp. oregano, dried
- ¼ tsp. thyme, dried
- ½ tsp. basil, dried
- ¼ tsp. black pepper, freshly ground
- 1 ½ lb. beef chuck roast, boneless and fat trimmed
- 1 medium onion, sliced
- 1 red bell pepper, cut into strips
- 6 sprouted-grain hot dog buns or sandwich thins
- 1 (16-oz.) jar pepperoncini (optional)

Directions:

6. Mix the water, balsamic vinegar, garlic powder, onion powder, parsley, oregano, thyme, basil, and black pepper in a small bowl.
1. Place the beef in the slow cooker and add the onion and bell pepper.
2. Pour the sauce over the roast. Cover the slow cooker and cook on low for 7 hours. The meat should be tender and cooked through.
3. Carefully transfer the roast to a cutting board.
4. Thinly slice the roast.
5. Toast the buns or sandwich thins.
6. Layer each bun with the beef and top with the au jus, pepper, and onion. Serve with pepperoncini (if using).

Nutrition per serving (1 sandwich): Calories: 351 kcal; **Total Fat:** 9 g; **Protein:** 31 g; **Carbs:** 30 g; **Fiber:** 5 g; **Sugar:** 5 g; **Sodium:** 418 mg

421. Flavorful Beef Meatballs

Preparation Time: 10 min
Cooking Time: 5 min; **Servings:** 2–3
Ingredients:

- 2 eggs, lightly beaten
- 2 tbsp. capers
- ½ lb. Beef, ground
- 3 garlic cloves, minced
- 2 tbsp. fresh mint, chopped
- ½ tbsp. cilantro, chopped
- 2 tsp. red pepper flakes, crushed
- 1 ½ tbsp. butter, melted
- 1 tsp. kosher salt

Directions:

1. Preheat the air fryer to 395°F.
2. Add all ingredients into the mixing bowl and mix until well combined.
3. Spray the air fryer basket with cooking spray.
4. Make small balls from the meat mixture and place them into the air fryer basket.

5. Cook meatballs for 10 min. Shake basket halfway through.
6. Serve and enjoy.

Nutrition: Calories: 159 kcal; **Fat:** 8.7 g; **Carbohydrate:** 1.9 g; **Sugar:** 0.3 g; **Protein:** 18.1 g; **Cholesterol:** 135 mg

422. Crumbly Beef Meatballs

Preparation Time: 8 min
Cooking Time: 10 min; **Servings:** 2–3
Ingredients:

- 2 lb. beef, ground
- 3 large eggs
- 1-¼ cup panko breadcrumbs
- ¼ cup fresh parsley, chopped
- 1 tsp. oregano, dried
- ¼ cup Parmigianino Reggiano, grated
- 1 small garlic clove, chopped
- salt and pepper, to taste
- 1 tsp. vegetable oil

Directions:

1. Thoroughly mix beef with eggs, crumbs, parsley, and the rest of the ingredients.
2. Make small meatballs out of this mixture and place them in the basket.
3. Place the basket inside the Air Fryer toaster oven and close the lid.
4. Select the Air Fry mode at 350°F temperature for 13 min.
5. Toss the meatballs after 5 min and resume cooking.
6. Serve fresh.

Nutrition: Calories: 221 kcal; **Cal Protein:** 25.1 g; **Carbs:** 11.2 g; **Fat:** 16.5 g

423. Steak Nuggets

Preparation Time: 10 min
Cooking Time: 8 min; **Servings:** 2–3
Ingredients:

- 1 lb. beef steak, cut into chunks
- 1 large egg, lightly beaten
- ½ cup Beef rind, crushed
- ½ cup Parmesan cheese, grated
- ½ tsp. salt

Directions:

1. Add egg into a small bowl.
2. In a shallow bowl, mix beef rind, cheese, and salt.
3. Dip each steak chunk in egg, coat with beef rind mixture, and place on a plate. Place in refrigerator for 30 min.
4. Spray the air fryer basket with cooking spray.
5. Preheat the air fryer to 400°F.
6. Place steak nuggets in an air fryer basket and cook for 15-18 min or until cooked. Shake after every 4 min.
7. Serve and enjoy.

Nutrition: Calories: 609 kcal; **Fat:** 38 g; **Carbohydrate:** 2 g; **Sugar:** 0.4 g; **Protein:** 63 g; **Cholesterol:** 195 mg

424. Juicy Meatballs

Preparation Time: 10 min
Cooking Time: 14 min; **Servings:** 2–3
Ingredients:

- 1 lb. beef, ground
- 1 tsp. garlic powder
- 1 egg, lightly beaten
- ½ onion, diced
- ¼ tsp. pepper
- 1 tsp. salt

Directions:

1. Spray the air fryer basket with cooking spray.
2. Preheat the air fryer to 390°F.
3. Add all ingredients into the bowl and mix until well combined.
4. Make balls from the meat mixture and place them into the air fryer basket.
5. Cook meatballs for 14 min. Shake basket 3–4 times while cooking.
6. Serve and enjoy.

Nutrition: Calories: 259 kcal; **Fat:** 18 g; **Carbohydrate:** 3 g; **Sugar:** 0.5 g; **Protein:** 17 g; **Cholesterol:** 95 mg

425. Bacon Jalapeño Poppers

Preparation Time: 10 min
Cooking Time: 8 min; **Servings:** 2–3
Ingredients:

- 10 Jalapeño peppers, cut in half and remove seeds
- ⅓ cup cream cheese softened
- 5 turkey bacon strips, cut in half

Directions:

1. Preheat the air fryer to 370°F.
2. Stuff cream cheese into each Jalapeño half.
3. Wrap each Jalapeño half with half bacon strip and place in the air fryer basket.
4. Cook for 6–8 min.
5. Serve and enjoy.

Nutrition: Calories: 83 kcal; **Fat:** 7.4 g; **Carbohydrate:** 1.3 g; **Sugar:** 0.5 g; **Protein:** 2.8 g; **Cholesterol:** 9 mg

426. Pepperoni Chips

Preparation Time: 2 min
Cooking Time: 8 min; **Servings:** 2–3
Ingredients:

- 6 oz pepperoni slices

Directions:

1. Place 1 batch of pepperoni slices in the air fryer basket.
2. Cook for 8 min at 360°F.

3. Cook remaining pepperoni slices using the same steps.
4. Serve and enjoy.

Nutrition: Calories: 51 kcal; **Fat:** 1 g; **Carbohydrate:** 2 g; **Sugar:** 1.3 g; **Protein:** 0 g; **Cholesterol:** 0 mg

427. Cheese Bacon Jalapeño Poppers

Preparation Time: 10 min
Cooking Time: 5 min
Servings: 2–3
Ingredients:

- 10 fresh Jalapeño peppers, cut in half and remove seeds
- 2 turkey bacon slices, cooked and crumbled
- ¼ cup Cheddar cheese, shredded
- 6 oz. cream cheese, softened

Directions:

1. In a bowl, combine bacon, cream cheese, and Cheddar cheese.
2. Stuff each Jalapeño half with bacon cheese mixture.
3. Spray the air fryer basket with cooking spray.
4. Place stuffed Jalapeño halved in the air fryer basket and cook at 370°F for 5 min.
5. Serve and enjoy.

Nutrition: Calories: 195 kcal; **Fat:** 17.3 g; **Carbohydrate:** 3.2 g; **Sugar:** 1 g; **Protein:** 7.2 g; **Cholesterol:** 52 mg

428. Air Fry Bacon

Preparation Time: 5 min
Cooking Time: 5 min; **Servings:** 2–3
Ingredients:

- 11 turkey bacon slices

Directions:

1. Place half bacon slices in the air fryer basket.
2. Cook at 400°F for 10 min.
3. Cook the remaining half bacon slices using the same steps.
4. Serve and enjoy.

Nutrition: Calories: 103 kcal; **Fat:** 7.9 g; **Carbohydrate:** 0.3 g; **Sugar:** 0 g; **Protein:** 7 g; **Cholesterol:** 21 mg

429. Beef Stuffed Dumplings

Preparation Time: 15 min
Cooking Time: 12 min; **Servings:** 2–3
Ingredients:

- 1 tsp. canola oil
- 2 cups book Choy, chopped
- 1 tbsp. fresh ginger, chopped
- 1 tbsp. garlic, chopped
- 3 oz. Beef, ground
- ¼ tsp. red pepper, crushed
- 18 dumpling wrappers
- Cooking spray
- 2 tbsp. rice vinegar
- 2 tsp. lower-sodium soy sauce
- 1 tsp. sesame oil, toasted
- ½ tsp. packed light sugar
- 1 tbsp. scallions, finely chopped

Directions:

1. In a greased skillet, sauté Bok choy for 8 min, then add ginger and garlic. Cook for 1 minute.
2. Transfer the Bok choy to a plate.
3. Add Beef and red pepper, then mix well. Place the dumpling wraps on the working surface and divide the Beef fillings on the dumpling wraps.
4. Wet the edges of the wraps and pinch them together to seal the filling.
5. Place the dumpling in the Air Fryer basket.
6. Set the Air Fryer basket inside the Air Fryer toaster oven and close the lid.
7. Select the Air Fry mode at 375°F temperature for 12 min.
8. Flip the dumplings after 6 min, then resume cooking.
9. Serve fresh.

Nutrition: Calories: 172 kcal; **Cal Protein:** 2.1 g; **Carbs:** 18.6 g; **Fat:** 10.7 g

430. Crunchy Bacon Bites

Preparation Time: 5 min
Cooking Time: 5 min; **Servings:** 2–3
Ingredients:

- 4 turkey bacon strips, cut into small pieces
- ½ cup Beef rinds, crushed
- ¼ cup hot sauce

Directions:

1. Add bacon pieces into a bowl.
2. Add hot sauce and toss well.
3. Add crushed Beef rinds and toss until bacon pieces are well coated.
4. Transfer bacon pieces into the air fryer basket and cook at 350°F for 10 minutes.
5. Serve and enjoy.

Nutrition: Calories: 112 kcal; **Fat:** 9.7 g; **Carbohydrate:** 0.3 g; **Sugar:** 0.2 g; **Protein:** 5.2 g; **Cholesterol:** 3 mg

431. Bacon Poppers

Preparation Time: 10 min
Cooking Time: 8 min; **Servings:** 2–3
Ingredients:

- Strips turkey bacon, crispy cooked

Dough:

- ⅔ cup water
- 2 tbsp. butter
- 1 tbsp. bacon fat

- 1 tsp. kosher salt
- ⅔ cup all-purpose flour
- 2 eggs
- 2 oz. Cheddar cheese, shredded
- ½ cup Jalapeño peppers
- A pinch pepper
- A pinch black pepper

Directions:

1. Whisk butter with water and salt in a skillet over medium heat. Stir in flour, then stir and cook for about 3 min.
2. Transfer this flour to a bowl, then whisk in eggs and the rest of the ingredients.
3. Fold in bacon and mix well. Wrap this dough in a plastic sheet and refrigerate for 30 min. Make small balls out of this dough.
4. Place these bacon balls in the Air Fryer toaster oven and close the lid.
5. Select the Air Fry mode at 390°F temperature for 15 min. Flip the balls after 7 minutes, then resume cooking. Serve warm.

Nutrition: Calories: 240 kcal; **Cal Protein:** 14.9 g; **Carbs:** 7.1 g; **Fat:** 22.5 g

432. Beef Rinds

Preparation Time: 5 min
Cooking Time: 5 min; **Servings:** 2–3
Ingredients:

- ½ tsp. black pepper
- 1 tsp. chili flakes
- ½ tsp. sea salt, fine
- 1 tsp. olive oil
- 1 lb. beef rinds

Directions:

1. Start by heating your air fryer to 365°F, then spray it with olive oil.
2. Place your Beef rinds in your air fryer basket, and sprinkle with your seasoning. Mix well, and then cook for 7 min.
3. Shake gently, and then serve cooled.

Nutrition: Calories: 329 kcal; **Protein:** 36.5 g; **Fat:** 20.8 g; **Net Carbs:** 0.1 g

433. Baked Potatoes with Bacon

Preparation Time: 5 min
Cooking Time: 15 min; **Servings:** 2–3
Ingredients:

- 4 potatoes, scrubbed, halved, cut lengthwise
- 1 tbsp. olive oil
- Salt and black pepper to taste
- 4 oz. turkey bacon, chopped

Directions:

1. Preheat the air fryer to 390°F. Brush the potatoes with olive oil and season with salt and pepper. Arrange them in the greased frying basket, cut-side down.
2. Bake for 15 minutes, flip them, top with bacon, and bake for 12–15 minutes or until potatoes are golden and bacon is crispy. Serve warm.

Nutrition: Calories: 280 kcal; **Fat:** 5.7 g; **Fiber:** 12.1 g; **Carbs:** 40.7 g; **Protein:** 12.9 g

DESSERTS

434. Grilled Stone Fruit with Greek Yogurt

Preparation Time: 5 minutes
Cooking Time: 5 minutes; **Servings:** 2–3
Ingredients:

- Nonstick cooking time spray
- 3 large fresh peaches, halved and pitted
- 1 tsp. extra-virgin olive oil
- 6 oz. low-fat, honey-flavored
- Greek yogurt
- ¼ cup sliced almonds
- Cinnamon for garnishing

Directions:

1. Ground some cinnamon for garnishing
2. Spray your grill (or a pan on the stovetop) with cooking time spray.
3. Heat the grill or grill pan to high heat, about 500°F.
4. Brush each peach half with olive oil.
5. Place the cut fruit on the grill flesh-side down, and grill for 2 minutes.
6. Using tongs, turn the fruit over and cook for another 2 minutes.
7. Transfer to a serving dish. Serve the fruit with Greek yogurt, and garnish with almonds and cinnamon.

Nutrition: Calories: 78 kcal; **Total Fat:** 3 g; **Protein:** 4 g; **Carbohydrate:** 11 g; **Fiber:** 2 g; **Sugar:** 8 g; **Sodium:** 8 mg

435. Almond Strawberry Chia Seed Pudding

Preparation Time: 10 minutes + 4 hours to chill
Cooking Time: 0 minutes; **Servings:** 2–3
Ingredients:

- 2 cups almond milk
- 1 (16 oz.) package fresh strawberries, hulled
- ½ cup chia seeds
- ¼ cup honey
- 1 tsp. vanilla extract

Directions:

1. In a blender, purée the almond milk and strawberries until smooth; pour them into a bowl. In the strawberry purée, stir the chia seeds, butter, and vanilla extract.
2. Cover the bowl with plastic wrap and freeze it for 4 hours until set.

Nutrition: Calories: 209 kcal; **Protein:** 3.7 g; **Carbohydrate:** 37.2 g; **Fat:** 6.3 g; **Sodium:** 84.9 mg.

436. Blueberry Muffins

Preparation Time: 7 minutes
Cooking Time: 18 minutes; **Servings:** 2–3
Ingredients:

- 1 ¾ cup whole flour
- ⅓ cup stevia
- 2 ½ tsp. baking powder
- ½ tsp. salt
- ¾ cup milk
- 1 egg, lightly beaten
- ⅓ cup butter, softened
- 1 cup blueberries, fresh or frozen

Directions:

1. Heat oven to 400°F.
2. Mix salt, baking powder, stevia, and flour in a medium bowl, then set aside.
3. In a large bowl, beat butter and stevia until creamy; add egg and milk.
4. Add flour mixture to butter mixture and stir until the dry ingredients are moistened and a few lumps remain; fold in blueberries.
5. Spoon batter into 12 greased muffin cups; bake at 400°F for 18 minutes, or until a toothpick can be inserted in the center and come out clean.

Nutrition: Calories: 162.8 kcal; **Total Fat:** 3.4 g; **Total Carbohydrate:** 11.2 g; **Protein:** 7.5 g

437. Choco Frosty

Preparation Time: 5 minutes
Cooking Time: 5 minutes
Servings: 2–3
Ingredients:

- 1 tsp. vanilla
- 8 drops liquid stevia
- 2 tbsp. unsweetened cocoa powder
- 1 tbsp. almond butter
- 1 cup heavy cream

Directions:

1. Add all ingredients into the mixing bowl and beat with an immersion blender until soft peaks form.
2. Place in refrigerator for 30 minutes.
3. Add frosty mixture into the piping bag and pipe in serving glasses.
4. Serve and enjoy.

Nutrition: Calories: 240 kcal; **Fat:** 25 g; **Carbohydrate:** 4 g; **Sugar:** 3 g; **Protein:** 3 g; **Cholesterol:** 43 mg

438. Cheesecake Fat: Bombs

Preparation Time: 10 minutes
Cooking Time: 5 minutes; **Servings:** 2–3
Ingredients:

- 8 oz. cream cheese
- 1 ½ tsp. vanilla
- 2 tbsp. erythritol
- 4 oz. coconut oil
- 4 oz. heavy cream

Directions:

1. Add all ingredients into the mixing bowl and beat using the immersion blender until creamy.
2. Pour batter into the mini cupcake liner and place in the refrigerator until set.
3. Serve and enjoy.

Nutrition: Calories: 90 kcal; **Fat:** 9.8 g; **Carbohydrate:** 1.4 g; **Sugar:** 0.1 g; **Protein:** 0.8 g; **Cholesterol:** 17 mg

439. Matcha Ice Cream

Preparation Time: 5 minutes
Cooking Time: 5 minutes; **Servings:** 2–3
Ingredients:

- ½ tsp. vanilla
- 2 tbsp. swerve
- 1 tsp. matcha powder
- 1 cup heavy whipping cream

Directions:

1. Add all ingredients into the glass jar.
2. Seal the jar with a lid and shake for 4–5 minutes until the mixture doubles.
3. Place in refrigerator for 3–4 hours.
4. Servings chilled and enjoy.

Nutrition: Calories: 215 kcal; **Fat:** 22 g; **Carbohydrate:** 3.8 g; **Sugar:** 0.2 g; **Protein:** 1.2 g; **Cholesterol:** 82 mg

440. Moist Avocado Brownies

Preparation Time: 10 minutes
Cooking Time: 35 minutes; **Servings:** 2–3
Ingredients:

- 2 avocados, mashed
- 2 eggs
- 1 tsp. baking powder
- 2 tbsp. swerve
- ⅓ cup chocolate chips, melted
- 4 tbsp. coconut oil, melted
- ⅔ cup cocoa powder, unsweetened

Directions:

1. Preheat the oven to 325°F.
2. In a mixing bowl, mix all dry ingredients.
3. In another bowl, mix avocado and eggs until well combined.
4. Slowly add the dry mixture to the wet along with melted chocolate and coconut oil. Mix well.
5. Pour batter into a greased baking pan and bake for 30–35 minutes.
6. Slice and serve.

Nutrition: Calories: 207 kcal; **Fat:** 18 g; **Carbohydrate:** 11 g; **Sugar:** 3.6 g; **Protein:** 3.8 g; **Cholesterol:** 38 mg

441. Mix Berry Sorbet

Preparation Time: 10 minutes
Cooking Time: 5 minutes; **Servings:** 2–3
Ingredients:

- ½ cup raspberries, frozen
- ½ cup blackberries, frozen
- 1 tsp. liquid stevia
- 6 tbsp. water

Directions:

1. Add all ingredients into the blender and blend until smooth.
2. Pour the blended mixture into the container and place it in the refrigerator until hardened.
3. Servings chilled and enjoy.

Nutrition: Calories: 63 kcal; **Fat:** 0.8 g; **Carbohydrate:** 14 g; **Sugar:** 6 g; **Protein:** 1.7 g; **Cholesterol:** 0 mg

442. Chia Almond Pudding

Preparation Time: 5 minutes
Cooking Time: 5 minutes; **Servings:** 2–3
Ingredients:

- 2 tbsp. almonds, toasted and crushed
- ⅓ cup chia
- ½ tsp. vanilla
- 4 tbsp. erythritol
- ¼ cup cocoa powder, unsweetened
- 2 cups almond milk, unsweetened

Directions:

1. Add almond milk, vanilla, sweetener, and cocoa powder into the blender and blend until well combined.
2. Pour the blended mixture into the bowl.
3. Add chia seeds and whisk for 1-2 minutes.
4. Pour pudding mixture into the serving bowls and place in the fridge for 1-2 hours.
5. Top with crushed almonds and serve.

Nutrition: Calories: 170 kcal; **Fat:** 12 g; **Carbohydrate:** 12 g; **Sugar:** 1 g; **Protein:** 7 g; **Cholesterol:** 35 mg

443. Poached Spiced Apples and Pears

Preparation Time: 5 minutes
Cooking Time: 7–8 hours on low; **Servings:** 2–3
Ingredients:

- 2 apples, peeled and halved
- 2 pears, peeled and halved
- 2 tbsp. cloves
- 1 tsp. allspice
- 1 cinnamon stick

Directions:

1. Turn the slow cooker to a low setting.
2. Peel half the apples and pears.
3. Poke the cloves into the flesh of the fruits evenly.
4. Place into the slow cooker and cover with water.
5. Add the allspice and cinnamon stick. Mix.
6. Cover and cook for about 7–8 hours.
7. Remove the cinnamon stick before serving. The juices will have caramelized and formed a delicious sauce to serve with the fruits. Add Fat-free Greek yogurt if desired.

Nutrition: Calories: 84 kcal; **Protein:** 1 g; **Carbohydrate:** 23 g; **Fat:** 0 g; **Sugar:** 15 g; **Sodium:** 2 mg; **Potassium:** 175 mg; **Phosphorus:** 18 mg; **Calcium:** 15 mg; **Fiber:** 4 g

444. Chia Raspberry Pudding

Preparation Time: 5 minutes
Cooking Time: 5 minutes; **Servings:** 2–3
Ingredients:

- ¼ tsp. vanilla
- ¾ cup almond milk, unsweetened
- 1 tbsp. erythritol
- 2 tbsp. protein collagen peptides
- ¼ cup chia
- ½ cup raspberries, mashed

Directions:

1. Add all ingredients into the bowl and stir until well combined.
2. Place in refrigerator overnight.
3. Servings chilled and enjoy.

Nutrition: Calories: 102 kcal; **Fat:** 6 g; **Carbohydrate:** 13 g; **Sugar:** 1.4 g; **Protein:** 4 g; **Cholesterol:** 0 mg.

445. Smoked Tofu Quesadillas

Preparation Time: 6 minutes
Cooking Time: 5 minutes; **Servings:** 12
Ingredients:

- 1 lb. extra firm tofu, sliced
- 12 tortillas
- 2 tbsp. coconut oil
- 6 slices Cheddar cheese
- 2 tbsp. tomatoes, sundried
- 1 tbsp. cilantro
- 5 tbsp. sour cream

Directions:

1. Lay 1 tortilla flat, fill with tofu, tomato, and cheese, and top with oil. Repeat for as many as you need.
2. Bake for 5 minutes and remove from flame.
3. Top with sour cream.

Nutrition: Net Carbs: 13 g; **Fiber:** 3 g; **Fat:** 6 g; **Sugar:** 3 g; **Calories:** 136 kcal

446. Strawberry Frozen Yogurt Squares

Preparation Time: 8 hours
Cooking Time: 0 minutes; **Servings:** 2–3
Ingredients:

- 1 cup barley, wheat cereal
- 3 cup fat-free strawberry yogurt
- 10 oz. strawberries, frozen
- 1 cup fat-free milk
- 1 cup topping, whipped

Directions:

1. Set parchment paper on the baking tray.
2. Spread cereal evenly over the bottom of the tray.
3. Add milk, strawberries, and yogurt to the blender and process into a smooth mixture.
4. Use the yogurt mixture to top cereal, wrap with foil, and freeze until firm (about 8 hours).
5. Slightly thaw, slice into squares, and serve.

Nutrition: Net Carbs: 43.4 g; **Fiber:** 4 g; **Fat:** 3 g; **Sugar:** 7 g; **Calories:** 188 kcal

447. Chocolate Almond Ginger Mousse

Preparation Time: 10 minutes
Cooking Time: 15 minutes
Servings: 2–3
Ingredients:

- 325 ml milk, skim and cold
- 1 instant pudding package, Fat-free and sugar-free
- 250 ml cool whip lite, thawed out
- ¼ tsp. ginger, dried
- 1 tbsp. almonds, sliced

Directions:

1. Pour cold milk into a mixing bowl. Beating steadily with a wire whisk, add the pudding mix and dried ginger. Keep whisking for 2 minutes. Fold in the cool whip topping.
2. Spoon into 5 pudding cups, and refrigerate until needed. Garnish with sliced almonds just before servings.

Nutrition: (1 g) Calories: 310 kcal; **Carbohydrate:** 21 g; **Protein:** 3.9 g; **Fat:** 26.4 g; **Saturated Fat:** 9.5 g; **Polyunsaturated Fat:** 16.9 g; **Sodium:** 90 mg; **Fiber:** 10.2 g; **Sugar:** 7.1 g

448. Bella's Apple Crisp

Preparation Time: 20 minutes
Cooking Time: 10 minutes; **Servings:** 2–3
Ingredients:

- 4 apples, hard and crisp, cored and sliced
- ½ lemon
- 2 tbsp. water
- 2 tbsp. agave nectar or one tbsp. honey

Ingredients for toppings:

- 200 g old-fashioned rolled oats
- 2 tbsp. butter, cold
- ½ tsp. cinnamon
- 125 g walnuts, chopped

Directions:

1. Heat oven to 350°F.
2. Place sliced apples in the bottom of an 8-inch pie plate or square cake pan.
3. Drizzle the water, lemon juice, and syrup over the apples.
4. In a mixing bowl, stir together the oats and cinnamon. Use a pastry cutter or 2 knives to cut in the butter mixture until it resembles coarse breadcrumbs.
5. Stir in the chopped nuts.
6. Sprinkle the mixture over the apples covering them completely.
7. Cover pan with tin foil and slide into the middle of the oven for 20 minutes.
8. Remove tin foil from the pan and continue to bake for another 10 to 15 minutes until the topping is golden brown.

Nutrition: Calories: 424 kcal; **Carbohydrate:** 74.3 g; **Protein:** 14.6 g; **Fat:** 9.4 g; **Saturated Fat:** 2 g; **Polyunsaturated Fat:** 7.4 g; **Cholesterol:** 94 mg; **Sodium:** 572 mg; **Fiber:** 11.3 g; **Sugar:** 24.2 g

449. Red Energy Wonders

Preparation Time: 15 minutes
Cooking Time: 8 minutes; **Servings:** 2–3
Ingredients:

- 75 g almond butter
- 325 g coconut, shredded and divided into a 225 g portion and a 100 g portion
- 125 g oats, rolled
- 125 g strawberries
- 125 g almonds
- 4 dates Medrol, pit-less

Directions:

1. Place the 225 g portion of coconut and all the rest of the ingredients in a food processor. At high speed, process until smooth and fully mixed.
2. Pour the remaining coconut onto a plate. With a spoon, scoop 1 tablespoon of the mixture and form it into a ball. Roll this ball around the coconut, then place it on a plate lined with parchment paper. Repeat until all of the mixtures are used.
3. Place the plate in the fridge for at least 2 hours before servings. Keep energy wonders in an airtight container in the fridge.

Nutrition: Calories: 191 kcal; **Carbohydrate:** 17.9 g; **Protein:** 6.3 g; **Fat:** 12 g; **Saturated Fat:** 5.4 g; **Polyunsaturated Fat:** 6.6 g; **Cholesterol:** 7 mg; **Sodium:** 101 mg; **Fiber:** 2.8 g; **Sugar:** 8.6 g

450. Chocolate Protein Pudding Pops

Preparation Time: 5 minutes
Cooking Time: 4 hours to freeze; **Servings:** 2–3
Ingredients:

- 1 (3.9-oz.) package chocolate-flavored instant pudding
- 2 cups cold low-fat milk
- 2 scoops chocolate protein powder

Directions:

1. Whisk the pudding mix, milk, and protein powder for at least 2 minutes.
2. Spoon into ice pop molds or paper cups. Insert an ice pop stick into the center of each mold or cup.
3. Freeze for 4 hours, or until firm. Remove from the molds or cups before servings.

Nutrition: Calories: 215 kcal; **Total Fat:** 2 g; **Protein:** 12 g; **Carb:** 36 g; **Fiber:** 0 g; **Sugar:** 27 g; **Sodium:** 480 mg.

451. Lemon Mousse

Preparation Time: 15 minutes
Cooking Time: 4 hours to chill; **Servings:** 2–3
Ingredients:

- 1 ½ cup boiling water
- 1 (6-oz.) package sugar-free lemon-flavored gelatin
- 2 cups ice cubes
- 1 ½ cup whipped topping
- Fresh fruit, for servings (optional)

Directions:

1. In a large bowl, combine the boiling water and gelatin. Stir for at least 2 minutesutes or until the gelatin is completely dissolved. Add the ice cubes, and stir until melted. Refrigerate until thickened, 5 to 10 minutes.
2. Fold in the whipped topping. Divide into 4 portions and refrigerate until firm, about 4 hours.
3. Garnish with fresh fruit before serving (if desired).

Nutrition: Calories: 85 kcal; **Total Fat:** 6 g; **Protein:** 1 g; **Carbohydrate:** 6 g; **Fiber:** 0 g; **Sugar:** 3 g; **Sodium:** 45 mg

452. Watermelon-Basil Granita

Preparation Time: 10 minutes
Cooking Time: 3–4 hours to freeze; **Servings:** 2–3
Ingredients:

- Juice of 2 limes
- ½ medium watermelon, peel removed, roughly chopped (about 8 to 9 cups)
- ¼ cup sugar (or sugar substitute)
- 1 cup fresh basil leaves, finely chopped

Directions:

1. In a blender, combine the watermelon chunks, lime juice, and sugar (if used). Blend on high until smooth.
2. Pour the watermelon mixture into a 9-x-13-inch baking dish, and stir in the basil leaves.
3. Freeze for 1 hour.
4. Remove from the freezer, and using a fork, scrape the frozen areas until broken apart.
5. Return the dish to the freezer, and continue this process every half hour for at least 2 to 3 hours, or until the granita resembles coarse crystals.
6. Before servings, scrape the frozen mixture again with a fork.

Nutrition: Calories: 76 kcal; **Total Fat:** 0 g; **Protein:** 1 g; **Carb:** 20 g; **Fiber:** 1 g; **Sugar:** 16 g; **Sodium:** 2 mg

453. Strawberry Yogurt

Preparation Time: 5 minutes
Cooking Time: 5 minutes; **Servings:** 2–3
Ingredients:

- 1 lb. strawberries, frozen
- 1 cup non-fat yogurt
- 1 tsp. liquid stevia

Directions:

1. Add all ingredients into the blender and blend until smooth.
2. Pour the blended mixture into the container.
3. Cover and place in the refrigerator for 2–3 hours.
4. Serve and enjoy.

Nutrition: Calories: 87 kcal; **Fat:** 0 g; **Carbohydrate:** 19.8 g; **Sugar:** 12 g; **Protein:** 1.8 g; **Cholesterol:** 2 mg

454. Chia Seed Pudding

Preparation Time: 5 minutes
Cooking Time: 5 minutes
Servings: 2–3
Ingredients:

- ½ cup chia seeds
- 1 tsp. liquid stevia
- 1 ½ tsp. pumpkin pie spice
- ½ cup pumpkin purée
- ¾ cup coconut milk, unsweetened
- ¾ cup full-fat coconut milk

Directions:

1. Add all ingredients into the mixing bowl and whisk well to combine.
2. Pour into the serving bowls, and place them in the refrigerator for 2 hours.
3. Serve and enjoy.

Nutrition: Calories: 275 kcal; **Fat:** 24.5 g; **Carbohydrate:** 9.9 g; **Sugar:** 3.3 g; **Protein:** 5.3 g; **Cholesterol:** 0 mg

455. Strawberry and Peach Crumble

Preparation Time: 10 minutes
Cooking Time: 6–7 hours on low; **Servings:** 2–3
Ingredients:

- 2 cups strawberries, sliced
- 2 cups peaches, sliced
- 1 tbsp. lemon zest, grated
- 1 cup gluten-free oats
- 1 tbsp. chia seeds, milled
- ½ tsp. cinnamon, ground

Directions:

1. Mix the strawberries, peaches, and lemon zest, and place them in the slow cooker.
2. Mix the oats with the milled chia seeds and ground cinnamon, and top over the fruits.
3. Set the slow cooker high for 2–3 hours or low for 6–7 hours.
4. The crumble is ready when the fruits are bubbling, and the topping turns golden brown.

Nutrition: Calories: 138 kcal; **Protein:** 4 g; **Carbohydrate:** 26 g; **Fat:** 3 g; **Sugar:** 8 g; **Sodium:** 3 mg; **Potassium:** 296 mg; **Phosphorus:** 142 mg; **Calcium:** 52 mg; **Fiber:** 6 g

456. Sugar-free Applesauce

Preparation Time: 5 minutes
Cooking Time: 1 hour on high
Servings: 2–3
Ingredients:

- 8 large apples, peeled, cored, and diced
- 2 cups water
- juice ¼ lemon
- 1 tsp. cinnamon, ground

Directions:

1. Add all the ingredients into the slow cooker.
2. Set the slow cooker to high for 1 hour.
3. Stir a couple of times during the cooking time.
4. Mash the stewed apples with a fork for chunkier applesauce, or blend them for smooth applesauce.

Nutrition: Calories: 66 kcal; **Protein:** 0.5 g; **Carbohydrate:** 15 g; **Fat:** 0 g; **Sugar:** 11 g; **Sodium:** 1 mg; **Potassium:** 116 mg; **Phosphorus:** 12 mg; **Calcium:** 9.5 mg; **Fiber:** 2.5 g

457. Oat and Fruit Parfait

Preparation Time: 11 minutes
Cooking Time: 0 minute; **Serving**: 2
Ingredients:

- 1/2 cup whole-grain rolled oats
- 1/2 cup walnut pieces
- 1 teaspoon honey
- 1 cup sliced fresh strawberries
- 11/2 cups (12 ounces) vanilla low-fat Greek yogurt
- Fresh mint leaves for garnish

Direction:

1. Preheat the oven to 300°F.
2. Spread the oats and walnuts in a single layer on a baking sheet.
3. Toast the oats and nuts just until you begin to smell the nuts, 10 to 12 minutes. Pull out the pan from the oven and set aside.
4. In a small microwave-safe bowl, heat the honey just until warm, about 30 seconds. Add the strawberries and stir to coat.
5. Place 1 tablespoon of the strawberries in the bottom of each of 2 dessert dishes or 8-ounce glasses. Add a portion of yogurt and then a portion of oats and repeat the layers until the containers are full, ending with the berries. Serve.

Nutrition: 108 calories, 10g fats, 3g protein

458. Zucchini Strips with Marinara Dip

Preparation Time: 1 hour and 10 minutes
Cooking Time: 15 minutes; **Servings:** 2–3
Ingredients:

- 2 zucchinis, sliced into strips
- Salt to taste
- 1 ½ cup all-purpose flour
- 2 eggs, beaten
- 2 cups bread crumbs
- 2 tsp. onion powder
- 1 tbsp. garlic powder
- ¼ cup Parmesan cheese, grated
- ½ cup marinara sauce

Directions:

1. Season zucchini with salt.
2. Let sit for 15 minutes.
3. Pat dry with paper towels.
4. Add flour to a bowl.
5. Add eggs to another bowl.
6. Mix the remaining ingredients except for marinara sauce in a third bowl.
7. Dip zucchini strips in the first, second, and third bowls.
8. Cover with foil and freeze for 45 minutes.
9. Add a crisper plate to the air fryer basket inside the Power XL Grill.
10. Select the air fry function.
11. Preheat to 360°F for 3 minutes.
12. Add zucchini strips to the crisper plate.
13. Air fry for 20 minutes.
14. Flip and cook for another 10 minutes.
15. Serve with marinara dip.

Nutrition: Calories: 364 kcal; **Fat:** 35 g; **Saturated Fat:** 17 g; **Trans Fat:** 0 g; **Carbohydrate:** 8 g; **Fiber:** 1.5 g; **Sodium:** 291 mg; **Protein:** 8 g

459. Roasted Garlic Dip

Preparation Time: 10 minutes
Cooking Time: 10 minutes
Servings: 2–3
Ingredients:

- 1 head garlic
- ½ tbsp. olive oil

Directions:

1. Slice the top off the garlic.
2. Drizzle with olive oil.
3. Add to the air fryer.
4. Set it to roast.
5. Cook at 390°F for 20 minutes.
6. Peel the garlic.
7. Transfer to a food processor.
8. Pulse until smooth.

Nutrition: Calories: 207 kcal; **Carbs:** 17 g; **Protein:** 9 g; **Fat:** 12 g

460. Kohlrabi Chips

Preparation Time: 10 minutes
Cooking Time: 10 minutes; **Servings:** 4–5
Ingredients:

- 1 lb. kohlrabi, peel and slice thinly
- 1 tsp. paprika
- 1 tbsp. olive oil
- 1 tsp. salt

Directions:

1. Preheat the air fryer to 320°F.
2. Add all ingredients into the bowl and toss to coat.
3. Transfer kohlrabi into the air fryer basket and cook for 20 minutes. Toss halfway through.
4. Serve and enjoy.

Nutrition: Calories: 108 kcal; **Fat:** 1.4 g; **Carbohydrate:** 17.4 g; **Sugar:** 2.4 g; **Protein:** 7.3 g; **Cholesterol:** 0 mg

461. Daikon Chips

Preparation Time: 10 minutes
Cooking Time: 16 minutes; **Servings:** 4–5
Ingredients:

- 15 oz. Daikon, slice into chips
- 1 tbsp. olive oil
- 1 tsp. chili powder
- ½ tsp. pepper
- 1 tsp. salt

Directions:

1. Preheat the air fryer to 375°F.
2. Add all ingredients into the bowl and toss to coat.
3. Transfer sliced the daikon into the air fryer basket and cook for 16 minutes. Toss halfway through.
4. Serve and enjoy.

Nutrition: Calories: 207 kcal; **Carbs:** 17 g; **Protein:** 9 g; **Fat:** 12 g

462. Jalapeño Cheese Dip

Preparation Time: 10 minutes
Cooking Time: 16 minutes; **Servings:** 4–5
Ingredients:

- 1 ½ cup Monterey jack cheese, shredded
- ½ cup Cheddar cheese, shredded
- 1 Jalapeño pepper, minced
- 1 tsp. garlic powder
- ⅓ cup sour cream
- ⅓ cup mayonnaise
- 2 oz. cream cheese, softened
- Pepper and salt, to taste

Directions:

1. Preheat the air fryer to 325°F.
2. Add all ingredients into the bowl and mix until combined.
3. Transfer bowl mixture into the air fryer baking dish, place in the air fryer and cook for 16 minutes.
4. Serve and enjoy.

Nutrition: Cal: 227 kcal; **Carbs:** 27 g; **Prot:** 9 g; **Fat:** 10 g

463. Onion Dip

Preparation Time: 10 minutes
Cooking Time: 25 minutes; **Servings:** 4–5
Ingredients:

- 2 lb. onion, chopped
- ½ tsp. baking soda
- 2 tbsp. butter, softened
- Pepper and salt to taste

Directions:

1. Melt butter in a pan over medium heat.
2. Add onion and baking soda and sauté for 5 minutes.
3. Transfer the onion mixture into the air fryer baking dish.
4. Place in the air fryer and cook at 370°F for 25 minutes.
5. Serve and enjoy.

Nutrition: Calories: 143 kcal; **Fat:** 9 g; **Carbohydrate:** 8.1 g; **Sugar:** 5.7 g; **Protein:** 9 g; **Cholesterol:** 175 mg

464. Easy Carrot Dip

Preparation Time: 10 minutes
Cooking Time: 8 minutes; **Servings:** 4–5
Ingredients:

- 2 cups carrots, grated
- ¼ tsp. cayenne pepper
- 1 tbsp. butter, melted
- 1 tbsp. chives, chopped
- Pepper and salt to taste

Directions:

1. Add all ingredients into the air fryer baking dish and stir until well combined.
2. Place dish in the air fryer and cook at 380°F for 15 minutes.
3. Transfer cook carrot mixture into the blender and blend until smooth.
4. Serve and enjoy.

Nutrition: Calories: 211 kcal; **Fat:** 9 g; **Carbohydrate:** 7.2 g; **Sugar:** 3.4 g: **Protein:** 9 g; **Cholesterol:** 155 mg

465. Veggie Salsa Wraps

Preparation Time: 5 minutes
Cooking Time: 7 minutes; **Servings:** 2–3
Ingredients:

- 1 cup red onion, sliced
- 1 zucchini, chopped
- 1 poblano pepper, deseeded and finely chopped
- 1 head lettuce
- ½ cup salsa
- 8 oz. (227 g) Mozzarella cheese

Directions:

1. Place the red onion, zucchini, and poblano pepper in the air fryer basket. Select the Air Fry function and cook at 390°F (199°C) for 7 minutes, or until they are tender and fragrant.
2. Divide the veggie mixture among the lettuce leaves and spoon the salsa over the top. Finish off with Mozzarella cheese. Wrap the lettuce leaves around the filling.
3. Serve immediately.

Nutrition: Calories: 140 kcal; **Fat:** 4 g; **Fiber:** 3 g; **Carbohydrate:** 5 g; **Protein:** 7 g

466. Tilapia and Salsa

Preparation Time: 10 minutes
Cooking Time: 10 minutes; **Servings:** 2–3
Ingredients:

- 3 tilapia fillets, boneless
- 2 oz. tomatoes, canned and chopped
- 2 tbsp. green onions, chopped
- 2 tbsp. sweet red pepper, chopped
- 1 tbsp. balsamic vinegar
- 1 tbsp. olive oil
- A pinch salt and black pepper

Directions:

1. Arrange the tilapia on a baking sheet that fits the air fryer and season with salt and pepper.
2. Mix all the other ingredients in a bowl, toss, and spread over the fish. Introduce the pan into the fryer and cook at 350°F for 15 minutes.
3. Divide the mix between plates and serve.

Nutrition: Calories: 221 kcal; **Total Fat:** 12 g; **Saturated Fat:** 0 g; **Cholesterol:** 0 mg; **Sodium:** 0 mg; **Total Carbs:** 5 g; **Fiber:** 2 g; **Sugar:** 0 g; **Protein:** 14 g

467. Panko Tofu with Mayo Sauce

Preparation Time: 10 Minutes
Cooking Time: 10 minutes; **Servings:** 2–3
Ingredients:

- 8 tofu cutlets

For the Marinade:

- 1 tbsp. sesame oil, toasted
- ¼ cup soy sauce
- 1 tsp. rice vinegar
- ½ tsp. garlic powder
- 1 tsp. ginger, ground

Make the Tofu:

- ½ cup vegan mayo
- 1 cup panko breadcrumbs
- 1 tsp. sea salt

Directions:

1. Whisk the marinade ingredients in a bowl and add tofu cutlets. Mix well to coat the cutlets. Cover and marinate for 1 hour.

2. Meanwhile, whisk crumbs with salt and mayo in a bowl. Coat the cutlets with the crumbs mixture. Place the tofu cutlets in the Air Fryer basket. Set the basket inside the Air Fryer toaster oven and close the lid.
3. Select the Air Fry mode at 370°F temperature for 20 minutes. Flip the cutlets after 10 minutes, then resume cooking. Serve warm.

Nutrition: Calories: 151 kcal; **Cal Protein:** 1.9 g; **Carbs:** 6.9 g; **Fat:** 8.6 g

468. Spicy Dip

Preparation Time: 5 minutes
Cooking Time: 5 minutes; **Servings:** 4–5
Ingredients:

- 12 oz. hot peppers, chopped
- 1 ½ cup apple cider vinegar
- Pepper and salt to taste

Directions:

1. Add all ingredients into the air fryer baking dish and stir well.
2. Place dish in the air fryer and cook at 380°F for 5 minutes.
3. Transfer pepper mixture into the blender and blend until smooth.
4. Serve and enjoy.

Nutrition: Cal: 207 kcal; **Carbs:** 17 g; **Prot:** 9 g; **Fat:** 12 g

469. Kale Dip

Preparation Time: 10 minutes
Cooking Time: 12 minutes; **Servings:** 4–5
Ingredients:

- 1 lb. kale, washed and chopped
- 1 cup heavy cream
- 1 onion, diced
- 1 tsp. butter
- 2 oz. Parmesan cheese, shredded
- ¼ tsp. pepper
- 1 tsp. salt

Directions:

1. Add all ingredients into the air fryer baking dish and stir well.
2. Preheat the air fryer to 250°F.
3. Place dish in the air fryer and cook for 12 minutes.
4. Serve and enjoy.

Nutrition: Calories: 117 kcal; **Carbs:** 27 g; **Protein:** 11 g; **Fat:** 12 g

470. Brussel Sprouts, Mango, Avocado Salsa Tacos

Preparation Time: 25 minutes
Cooking Time: 8 minutes; **Servings:** 2–3
Ingredients:

- 4 taco shells
- 8 oz. Brussels sprouts, diced
- Half a mango, diced
- Half of an avocado, diced
- ½ cup black beans, cooked
- 2 tbsp. onions, chopped
- ¼ cup cilantro, chopped
- 1 tbsp. Jalapeño, chopped
- Lime juice
- Olive oil
- 1 tbsp. taco seasoning
- Salt and Pepper

Directions:

1. Preheat the Power XL Air Fryer Grill at 230°C or 400°F.
2. Mix the sprouts with taco seasoning, olive oil, and salt and pepper on the pan.
3. Roast for 15 minutes. Turn every 5 minutes.
4. To make the salsa, combine the mango, avocado, black beans, lime juice, cilantro, onion, Jalapeño, salt, and pepper.
5. Cook taco shells and fill them with sprouts and salsa.

Nutrition: Calories: 407 kcal; **Carbs:** 63.20 g; **Protein:** 11.4 g; **Fat:** 13.9 g

471. Cod Tacos with Salsa

Preparation Time: 5 minutes
Cooking Time: 8 minutes; **Servings:** 4
Ingredients:

- 2 eggs
- 1 ¼ cup Mexican beer
- 1 ½ cup coconut flour
- 1 ½ cup almond flour
- ½ tbsp. chili powder
- 1 tbsp. cumin
- Salt, to taste
- 1 lb. (454 g) cod fillet, slice into large pieces
- 4 corn tortillas, toasted
- 4 large lettuce leaves, chopped
- ¼ cup salsa
- Cooking spray

Directions:

1. Spritz the air fry basket with cooking spray.
2. Break the eggs in a bowl, then pour in the beer. Whisk to combine well.
3. Combine the almond flour, coconut flour, cumin, chili powder, and salt in a separate bowl. Stir to mix well.
4. Dunk the cod pieces in the egg mixture, shake the excess, and dredge into the flour mixture to coat well. Arrange the cod in the basket.

5. Place the basket in the air fry position.
6. Select Air Fry, set the temperature to 375°F (190°C), and set Time to 15 minutes. Flip the cod halfway through the cooking time.
7. When cooking is complete, the cod should be golden brown.
8. Unwrap the toasted tortillas on a large plate, then divide the cod and lettuce leaves on top. Baste with salsa and wrap to serve.

Nutrition: Calories: 133 kcal; **Fat:** 19 g; **Protein:** 8 g

472. Cod Fish Tacos with Mango Salsa

Preparation Time: 15 minutes
Cooking Time: 17 minutes; **Servings:** 6
Ingredients:

- 1 egg
- 5 oz. Mexican beer
- ¾ cup all-purpose flour
- ¾ cup cornstarch
- ¼ tsp. chili powder
- ½ tsp. cumin, ground
- ½ lb. cod, cut into large pieces
- 6 corn tortillas
- Cooking spray

Salsa:

- 1 mango, peeled and diced
- ¼ red bell pepper, diced
- ½ small Jalapeño, diced
- ¼ red onion, minced
- Juice half a lime
- Pinch fresh cilantro, chopped
- ¼ tsp. salt
- ¼ tsp. black pepper, ground

Directions:

1. Spritz the perforated pan with cooking spray.
2. Whisk the egg with a beer in a bowl. Combine the flour, cornstarch, chili powder, and cumin in a separate bowl.
3. Dredge the cod in the egg mixture first, then in the flour mixture to coat well. Shake the excess off.
4. Arrange the cod in the perforated pan and spritz with cooking spray.
5. Select Air Fry. Set temperature to 380°F (193°C) and set time to 17 minutes. Press Start to begin preheating.
6. Once preheated, place the pan into the oven. Flip the cod halfway through the cooking time.
7. When cooked, the cod should be golden brown and crunchy.
8. Meanwhile, combine the ingredients for the salsa in a small bowl. Stir to mix well.
9. Unfold the tortillas on a clean work surface, divide the fish on the tortillas, and spread the salsa on top. Fold to serve.

Nutrition: Calories: 126 kcal; **Total Fat:** 12.1 g; **Total Carbohydrate:** 2.8 g; **Protein:** 2.1 g

473. Bacon and Egg Wraps with Salsa

Preparation Time: 15 minutes
Cooking Time: 5 minutes; **Servings:** 3; **Ingredients**:

- 3 corn tortillas
- 3 slices turkey bacon, cut into strips
- 2 scrambled eggs
- 3 tbsp. salsa
- 1 cup Pepper Jack cheese, grated
- 2 tbsp. cream cheese, divided
- Cooking spray

Directions:

1. Spritz the perforated pan with cooking spray.
2. Unfold the tortillas on a clean work surface, divide the bacon and eggs in the middle of the tortillas, then spread with salsa and scatter with cheeses. Fold the tortillas over.
3. Arrange the tortillas in the pan.
4. Select Air Fry. Set temperature to 390°F (199°C) and 10 minutes. Press Start to begin preheating.
5. Once the oven has preheated, place the pan into the oven. Flip the tortillas halfway through the cooking time.
6. When cooking is complete, the cheeses will be melted, and the tortillas will be lightly browned.
7. Serve immediately.

Nutrition: Calories: 290 kcal; **Total Fat:** 10.5 g; **Total Carbohydrate:** 23.2 g; **Protein:** 27.3 g

474. Grilled Tomato Salsa

Preparation Time: 15 minutes
Cooking Time: 5 minutes; **Servings:** 2–3
Ingredients:

- 1 onion, sliced
- 1 jalapeño pepper, sliced in half
- 5 tomatoes, sliced
- 2 tbsp. oil
- Salt and pepper to taste
- 1 cup cilantro, trimmed and sliced
- 1 tbsp. lime juice
- 1 tsp. lime zest
- 2 tbsp. ground cumin
- 3 garlic cloves, peeled and sliced

Directions:

1. Coat onion, Jalapeño pepper, and tomatoes with oil.

2. Season with salt and pepper.
3. Add grill grate to your Power XL Grill.
4. Press grill setting.
5. Choose max temperature and set it to 10 minutes.
6. Press start to preheat.
7. Add vegetables to the grill.
8. Cook for 5 minutes per side.
9. Transfer to a plate and let cool.
10. Add vegetable mixture to a food processor.
11. Stir in the remaining ingredients.
12. Pulse until smooth.

Nutrition: Calories: 369 kcal; **Fat:** 16 g; **Carbohydrate:** 37 g; **Fiber:** 5 g; **Protein:** 14 g

475. Zucchini Parmesan Dip

Preparation Time: 1 hour and 10 minutes
Cooking Time: 15 minutes
Servings: 2–3
Ingredients:

- 2 zucchinis, sliced into strips
- Salt to taste
- 1 ½ cup all-purpose flour
- 2 eggs, beaten
- 2 cups bread crumbs
- 2 tsp. onion powder
- 1 tbsp. garlic powder
- ¼ cup Parmesan cheese, grated
- ½ cup marinara sauce

Directions:

1. Season the zucchinis with salt.
2. Let them sit for 15 minutes.
3. Pat dry with paper towels.
4. Add flour to a bowl.
5. Add eggs to another bowl.
6. Mix the remaining ingredients except for marinara sauce in a third bowl.
7. Dip zucchini strips in the first, second, and third bowls.
8. Cover with foil and freeze for 45 minutes.
9. Add a crisper plate to the air fryer basket inside the Power XL Grill.
10. Select the air fry function.
11. Preheat to 360°F for 3 minutes.
12. Add zucchini strips to the crisper plate.
13. Air fry for 20 minutes.
14. Flip and cook for another 10 minutes.
15. Serve with marinara dip.

Nutrition: Calories: 364 kcal; **Fat:** 35 g; **Saturated Fat:** 17 g; **Trans Fat:** 0 g; **Carbohydrate:** 8 g; **Fiber:** 1.5 g; **Sodium:** 291 mg; **Protein:** 8 g

476. Easy Corn and Black Bean Salsa

Preparation Time: 10 minutes
Cooking Time: 5 minutes; **Serves:** 2
Ingredients:

- ½ (15-oz.) can corn, drained and rinsed
- ½ (15-oz.) can black beans, drained and rinsed
- ¼ cup chunky salsa
- 2 oz. reduced-fat cream cheese, softened
- ¼ cup reduced-fat Cheddar cheese, shredded
- ½ tsp. paprika
- ½ tsp. cumin, ground
- Salt and black pepper, freshly ground, to taste

Directions:

1. Combine the corn, black beans, Cheddar cheese, cream cheese, salsa, cumin, and paprika in a medium bowl. Sprinkle with salt and pepper and stir until well blended.
2. Pour the mixture into a baking dish.
3. Place the baking dish in the air fryer grill.
4. Select Air Fry, set the temperature to 325°F (163°C) and set the time to 10 minutes.
5. When cooking is complete, the mixture should be heated through. Rest for 5 minutes and serve warm.

Nutrition: Calories: 108 kcal; **Fat:** 1.4 g; **Carbohydrate:** 17.4 g; **Sugar:** 2.4 g; **Protein:** 7.3 g; **Cholesterol:** 0 mg

477. Turkey Fritters and Sauce

Preparation Time: 10 minutes
Cooking Time: 15 minutes; **Servings:** 2–3
Ingredients:

- 2 garlic cloves, minced
- 1 egg
- 1 red onion, chopped
- 1 tbsp. olive oil
- ¼ tsp. red pepper flakes
- 1 lb. turkey meat, ground
- ½ tsp. oregano, dried
- Cooking spray

For the sauce:

- 1 cup Greek yogurt
- 1 cucumber, chopped
- 1 tbsp. olive oil
- ¼ tsp. garlic powder
- 2 tbsp. lemon juice
- ¼ cup parsley, chopped

Directions:

1. Heat a pan with 1 tbsp. oil over medium heat, add the onion and the garlic, sauté for 5 minutes, cool down and transfer to a bowl.
2. Add the meat, turkey, oregano, and pepper flakes, and stir and shape medium patties out of this mix.

3. Heat another pan greased with cooking spray over medium-high heat, add the turkey patties, and brown for 5 minutes on each side.
4. Introduce the pan into the oven and bake the patties at 375°F for 15 minutes more.
5. Meanwhile, in a bowl, mix the yogurt with the cucumber, oil, garlic powder, lemon juice, and parsley and whisk well.
6. Divide the fritters between plates, spread the sauce, and serve for lunch.

Nutrition: Calories: 364 kcal; **Fat:** 16.8 g; **Fiber:** 5.5 g; **Carbs:** 26.8 g; **Protein:** 23.4 g

478. Spaghetti in Clam Sauce

Preparation Time: 5 minutes
Cooking Time: 45 minutes; **Servings:** 2–3
Ingredients:

- 8 oz. spaghetti
- 2 tbsp. olive oil
- 2 garlic cloves, minced
- 2 tomatoes, peeled and diced
- 1 cup cherry tomatoes, halved
- 1 lb fresh clams, cleaned and rinsed
- 2 tbsp. white wine
- 1 tsp. sherry vinegar

Directions:

1. Heat the oil in a heavy saucepan and add the garlic. Cook for 30 seconds until fragrant, then add the tomatoes, wine, and vinegar. Bring to a boil and cook for 5 minutes, then stir in the clams and continue cooking for 10 more minutes.
2. In the meantime, bring a large pot of water to a boil with a pinch of salt and add the spaghetti. Cook them for 8 min just until al dente. Drain well and mix with the clam sauce.
3. Serve the dish right away.

Nutrition: Calories: 305 kcal; **Fat:** 8.8 g; **Carbs:** 48.3 g; **Protein:** 8.1 g

479. Duck Breast with Apricot Sauce

Preparation Time: 10 minutes
Cooking Time: 10 minutes; **Servings:** 2–3
Ingredients:

- 4 duck breasts, boneless
- Salt and black pepper to taste
- ¼ tsp. cinnamon, ground
- ¼ tsp. coriander, ground
- 5 tbsp. apricot preserves
- 3 tbsp. chives, chopped
- 2 tbsp. parsley, chopped
- A drizzle olive oil
- 3 tbsp. apple cider vinegar
- 2 tbsp. red onions, chopped
- 1 cup apricots, chopped
- ¾ cup blackberries

Directions:

1. Season duck breasts with salt, pepper, coriander, and cinnamon, place them on a preheated grill pan over medium-high heat, cook for 2 minutes, flip them and cook for 3 minutes more.
2. Flip duck breasts again, add 3 tbsp. apricot preserves, cook for 1 minute, transfer them to a cutting board, leave aside for 2–3 minutes, and slice.
3. Heat a pan over medium heat, add vinegar, onion, and 2 tbsp. apricot preserves, apricots, blackberries, and chives, stir, and cook for 3 minutes.
4. Divide sliced duck breasts between plates and serve with apricot sauce drizzled on top.

Nutrition: Calories: 275 kcal; **Fat:** 4 g; **Fiber:** 4 g; **Carbs:** 7 g; **Protein:** 12 g

480. Duck and Orange Sauce

Preparation Time: 10 minutes
Cooking Time: 5 hours
Servings: 2–3
Ingredients:

- 2 medium ducks, fat trimmed
- 1 tbsp. olive oil
- 1 cup water
- Salt and black pepper to taste
- 2 tomatoes, chopped
- 2 carrots, chopped
- 2 celery stalks, chopped
- 1 leek, chopped
- 2 garlic cloves, minced
- 1 yellow onion, chopped
- 2 bay leaves
- 3 tbsp. white flour
- 1 tsp. thyme, dried
- 2 tbsp. tomato paste
- 1-quart chicken stock
- Juice 2 oranges
- 3 oranges, peeled and cut into segments
- ⅓ cup sugar
- 2 tbsp. currant jelly
- ⅓ cup cider vinegar
- 2 tbsp. cold butter

Directions:

1. Pierce the duck skin, and season all over with salt and pepper. Arrange them in a roasting pan, add the water, and bake in the oven at 450°F for 20 minutes.

2. Reduce heat to 350°F, turn the ducks and bake them for 30 minutes more.
3. Turn ducks again and roast them for 30 minutes more. Meanwhile, heat a pan with the oil over high heat, add carrots, celery, leek, tomatoes, garlic, onion, thyme, and bay leaves, stir and cook for 10 minutes.
4. Add tomato paste, flour, the wine, and the stock gradually, bring to a boil, and reduce heat to medium-low, simmer for 50 minutes, take off the heat and strain the sauce into a bowl.
5. Heat a small pan over medium-high heat, add vinegar and sugar, stir and cook for 4 minutes.
6. Add orange juice and currant jelly, stir and bring to a boil. Add strained sauce, salt, and pepper, stir and cook for 8 minutes.
7. Add butter gradually and stir well again. Take ducks out of the oven, turn them, place them in the oven again and cook for 40 minutes. Take ducks out of the oven again, place them under preheated broiler and broil them for 3 minutes.
8. Transfer ducks to a platter and keep them warm.
9. Heat juices from the pan in a saucepan over medium heat, take them off and strain them into a bowl.
10. Add this to the orange sauce and stir. Arrange the orange segments next to the ducks and serve with orange sauce on top.

Nutrition: Calories: 342 kcal; **Fat:** 13 g; **Fiber:** 4 g; **Carbs:** 17 g; **Protein:** 12 g

481. Seafood Sauce

Preparation Time: 10 minutes
Cooking Time: 5 minutes; **Servings:** 4–5
Ingredients:

- 1 ½ cup catsup (free of high-fructose corn syrup)
- 2 tbsp. horseradish, grated
- Juice 1 lemon
- 1 tbsp. Worcestershire sauce
- 1 tsp. chili powder
- ¼ tsp. freshly ground black pepper

Post-Op:

- ¼ cup

Directions:

1. Mix the catsup, horseradish, lemon juice, Worcestershire sauce, chili powder, and pepper in a small bowl. Refrigerate and cover for at least 30 minutes overnight to let the flavors meld.
2. Serve with shrimp cocktail, oysters, grilled scallops, or other seafood.

Nutrition per serving (¼ cup): Calories: 56 kcal; **Total Fat:** 0 g; **Protein:** 0 g; **Carbs:** 14 g; **Fiber:** 0 g; **Sugar:** 10 g; **Sodium:** 445 mg

482. Creamy Peppercorn Ranch Dressing

Preparation Time: 10 minutes
Cooking Time: 5 minutes; **Servings:** 2–3
Ingredients:

- ¾ cup low-fat plain Greek yogurt
- ⅓ cup Parmigiano-Reggiano cheese, grated
- ¼ cup low-fat buttermilk (see here for a tip to make from scratch)
- Juice 1 lemon
- 2 tsp. black pepper, freshly ground
- ½ tsp. onion flakes
- ¼ tsp. salt

Post-Op:

- 2 tbsp.

Directions:

1. In a blender or food processor, purée the yogurt, cheese, buttermilk, lemon juice, pepper, onion flakes, and salt on medium-high speed until the dressing is completely smooth and creamy.

Nutrition per serving (tbsp.): Calories: 35 kcal; **Total Fat:** 1 g; **Protein:** 4 g; **Carbs:** 2 g; **Fiber:** 0 g; **Sugar:** 1 g; **Sodium:** 133 mg

483. Sweet Peach Jam

Preparation Time: 10 minutes
Cooking Time: 16 minutes; **Servings:** 2–3
Ingredients:

- 1 ½ lb. fresh peaches, pitted and chopped
- ½ tbsp. vanilla
- ¼ cup maple syrup

Directions:

1. Put all of the ingredients in the air fryer and stir well.
2. Seal pot and cook on high for 1 minute.
3. Once done, allow to release pressure naturally. Remove lid.
4. Set pot on sauté mode and cook for 15 minutes until jam thickens.
5. Pour it into the container and store it in the fridge.

Nutrition: Calories: 16 kcal; **Protein:** 0.1 g; **Fat:** 0 g; **Carbs:** 3.7 g

484. Warm Peach Compote

Preparation Time: 10 minutes
Cooking Time: 1 minutes; **Servings:** 2–3
Ingredients:

- 4 peaches, peeled and chopped
- 1 tbsp. water
- ½ tbsp. cornstarch
- 1 tsp. vanilla

Directions:

1. Add water, vanilla, and peaches into the air fryer basket.
2. Seal pot and cook on high for 1 minute.
3. Once done, allow to release pressure naturally. Remove lid.
4. Whisk together 1 tablespoon of water and cornstarch in a small bowl, pour into the pot, and stir well.
5. Serve and enjoy.

Nutrition: Calories: 66 kcal; **Protein:** 1.4 g; **Fat:** 0.4 g; **Carbs:** 15 g

485. Cherry-Choco Bars

Preparation Time: 7 minutes
Cooking Time: 8 minutes; **Servings:** 2–3
Ingredients:

- ¼ tsp. salt
- ½ cup almonds, sliced
- ½ cup chia
- ½ cup dark chocolate, chopped
- ½ cup cherries, dried and chopped
- ½ cup prunes, puréed
- ½ cup quinoa, cooked
- ¾ cup almond butter
- ⅓ cup honey
- 2 cups oats
- 2 tbsp. coconut oil

Directions:

1. Preheat the Smart Air Fryer Oven to 375°F.
2. In a bowl, combine the oats, quinoa, chia seeds, almond, cherries, and chocolate.
3. Heat the almond butter, honey, and coconut oil in a saucepan.
4. Pour the butter mixture over the dry mix, add salt and prunes, and mix until well combined.
5. Pour over a baking dish that can fit inside the air fryer.
6. Bake for 15 minutes.
7. Let it cool before slicing it into bars.

Nutrition: Calories: 378 kcal; **Fat:** 9 g; **Carbs:** 5 g; **Protein:** 4 g

486. Cherry Avocado Smoothie

Preparation Time: 5 minutes
Cooking Time: 2 minutes; **Servings:** 2–3
Ingredients:

- ½ ripe avocado, chopped
- 1 cup fresh cherries
- 1 cup coconut water, sugar-free
- 1 whole lime

Directions:

1. Peel the avocado and cut it in half. Remove the pit and chop it into bite-sized pieces. Reserve the rest in the refrigerator. Set aside.
2. Rinse the cherries under cold running water using a large colander. Cut each in half and remove the pits. Set aside.
3. Peel the lime and cut it in half. Set aside.
4. Now, combine avocado, cherries, coconut water, and lime in a blender. Pulse to combine and transfer to a serving glass.
5. Add a few ice cubes and refrigerate for 10 minutes before serving.

Nutrition: Net Carbs: 17 g; **Fiber:** 3.8 g; **Fat:** 6.8 g; **Sugar:** 3 g; **Calories:** 128 kcal

487. Lemon Avocado Salad Dressing

Preparation Time: 5 minutes
Cooking Time: 5 minutes; **Servings:** 2–3
Ingredients:

- 2 tbsp. olive oil
- 1 garlic clove, minced
- ½ tsp. seasoned salt
- 1 medium ripe avocado, peeled and mashed
- ¼ cup water
- 2 tbsp. sour cream
- 2 tbsp. lemon juice
- 1 tbsp. fresh dill, minced, or 1 tsp. dill weed
- ½ tsp. honey
- Salad greens, cherry tomatoes, sliced cucumbers, and sweet red and yellow pepper strips

Directions:

1. In a blender, combine the first 9 ingredients; cover and process until blended.
2. Serve with salad greens, tomatoes, cucumbers, and peppers. Store in the refrigerator.

Nutrition: Calories: 38.2 kcal; **Fat:** 2.6 g; **Cholesterol:** 1.2 mg; **Carbohydrate:** 3.6 g; **Fiber:** 1.0 g; **Protein:** 0.8 g

488. Creamy Avocado Cilantro Lime Dressing

Preparation Time: 20 minutes
Cooking Time: 5 minutes; **Servings:** 2–3
Ingredients:

- ¼ cup olive oil
- ¼ tsp. sea salt
- ½ cup cilantro, chopped
- ¼ cup plain goat yogurt
- Juice ½ lime
- 1 tsp. lime zest
- 1 avocado

- 1 garlic clove, peeled
- ½ Jalapeño, chopped
- ¼ tsp. pepper
- ½ tsp. cumin

Directions:

1. Place/put all the ingredients in a food processor or mixer and mix it until well balanced.

Nutrition: Calories: 123 kcal; **Protein:** 1 g; **Fat:** 12 g; **Carbohydrate:** 3.6 g

489. Creamy Avocado Dressing

Preparation Time: 5 minutes
Cooking Time: 5 minutes; **Servings:** 2–3
Ingredients:

- ¼ tsp. black pepper, ground
- Water, as needed
- 1 whole large avocado
- 1 garlic clove, peeled
- ½ tbsp. fresh lime or lemon juice
- 3 tbsp. olive oil or avocado oil
- ¼ tsp. Kosher salt

Directions:

1. Put the peeled garlic clove, lime or lemon juice, avocado, olive oil, salt, and pepper into a mini food processor.
2. Process till smooth, stopping a few times to scrape the sides down. Thin the salad dressing with water (¼ cup to ½ cup) before a perfect consistency is achieved.
3. Maintain/keep at least a week in an airtight container, but 3 to 4 days is best.

Nutrition: Calories: 38.2 kcal; **Fat:** 2.6 g; **Cholesterol:** 1.2 mg; **Carbohydrate:** 3.6 g; **Fiber:** 1.0 g

490. Southwestern Avocado Salad Dressing

Preparation Time: 5 minutes
Cooking Time: 1 hour; **Servings:** 2–3
Ingredients:

- 1 ripe avocado
- 1 cup buttermilk
- ½ tsp. garlic powder
- ½ tsp. chipotle chili powder
- ½ tsp. salt
- ¼ cup cilantro
- Juice of ½ lime
- 1 tsp. ranch seasoning powder homemade or store-bought

Directions:

1. Break the avocado in half, extract the pit from the flesh and scoop the skin.
2. Attach all the other ingredients to a mixer.
3. Blend in until creamy and smooth.
4. Before serving, refrigerate for one hour.
5. Keeps in the refrigerator for 3 days.

Nutrition: Calories: 61 kcal; **Fat:** 4 g; **Cholesterol:** 3 mg; **Carbohydrate:** 4 g; **Fiber:** 1 g; **Protein:** 1 g

491. Mango Salsa

Preparation Time: 15 minutes
Cooking Time: 8 minutes; **Servings:** 2–3
Ingredients:

- 1 avocado, peeled, pitted, and cubed
- 2 tbsp. fresh key lime juice
- 1 mango, peeled, pitted, and cubed
- 1 cup cherry tomatoes, quartered
- 1 tbsp. fresh cilantro, chopped
- Sea salt, as needed

Directions:

1. In a bowl, add avocado cubes and lime juice and mix well.
2. In the bowl, add the remaining ingredients and stir to combine.
3. Serve immediately.

Nutrition: Calories: 108 kcal; **Fat:** 1.4 g; **Cholesterol:** 0 mg; **Carbohydrate:** 12.5 g; **Fiber:** 3.5 g; **Protein:** 1.4 g

492. Zoodles with Basil and Avocado Sauce

Preparation Time: 10 minutes
Cooking Time: 0 minutes; **Servings:** 2–3
Ingredients:

- 2 zucchinis, spiralized into noodles
- 2 avocados, peeled, pitted
- ½ cup walnuts
- 2 cups basil leaves
- 24 cherry tomatoes, sliced

Extra:

- ⅓ tsp. salt
- 4 tbsp. key lime juice
- ½ cup spring water

Directions:

1. Prepare the sauce, place all the ingredients except for zucchini noodles and tomatoes in a food processor and then pulse until smooth.
2. Take a large bowl, place zucchini noodles, add tomato slices, pour in the prepared sauce, and then toss until coated.

Nutrition: Calories: 330 kcal; **Fat:** 20.7 g; **Protein:** 7.1 g; **Carbohydrate:** 35.3 g; **Fiber:** 7.8 g;

493. Avocado Mayo

Preparation Time: 10 minutes
Cooking Time: 5 minutes; **Servings:** 2–3
Ingredients:

- Juice from half of a lime
- 1 avocado
- ¼ cup cilantro
- ½ tbsp. sea salt
- ½ tbsp. onion powder
- 2–4 tbsp. olive oil
- Pinch cayenne powder
- Blender or hand mixer

Directions:

1. Remove the pit of the avocado and scoop the insides into a blender.
2. Add the rest of the ingredients and blend at high speed.
3. For hand mixers, add all other ingredients except the oil, which should be added slowly until the desired consistency is reached.

Nutrition: Calories: 45 kcal; **Fat:** 4.5 g; **Sodium:** 100 mg; **Carbohydrate:** 0.5 g

494. Applesauce

Preparation Time: 5 minutes
Cooking Time: 5 minutes; **Servings:** 2–3
Ingredients:

- 3 tbsp. agave
- ⅛ tsp. cloves
- 3 cups apples peeled, chopped
- 1 tsp. Sea moss gel
- 1 tsp. lime juice
- ½ cup strawberries
- ⅛ tsp. sea salt
- Spring water

Equipment:

- Blender

Directions:

1. In addition to cloves, salt, lime juice, and agave, apply sliced apples to the blender.
2. Pulse to obtain the optimal quality using the blender.
3. Pulse through the strawberries just until combined.
4. If it doesn't mix well, apply 1 tablespoon of spring water.
5. Serve and relax! Preserve the leftover food in the freezer.

Nutrition: Calories: 294 kcal; **Fat:** 12 g; **Fiber:** 2 g; **Carbohydrate:** 8 g; **Protein:** 45 g

495. Beef Roasted Wine Sauce

Preparation Time: 10 minutes
Cooking Time: 45 minutes; **Servings:** 2–3
Ingredients:

- 3 lb. beef roast
- Carrot, chopped
- 3 oz. red wine
- ½ tsp. paprika, smoked
- 5 potatoes, chopped
- ½ tsp. salt
- 1 yellow onion, chopped
- 4 garlic cloves, pressed
- 17 oz. beef stock
- ½ tsp. chicken salt

Directions:

1. Preheat the air fryer to 360°F.
2. Add salt, paprika, and chicken salt to a bowl, and stir. Rub the beef with the mixture and transfer to a plan that will fit into the air dryer.
3. Add the remaining ingredients and cook for 45 minutes.
4. Enjoy and serve.

Nutrition: Calories: 304 kcal; **Fat:** 20 g; **Carb:** 18 g; **Protein:** 32 g

496. Beet Salad Dressing

Preparation Time: 15 minutes
Cooking Time: 15 minutes; **Serving:** 2
Ingredients:

- Black pepper and salt
- 1 garlic clove
- 2 tbsp. balsamic vinegar
- 4 beets
- 2 tbsp. capers
- 1 bunch parsley, chopped
- 1 tbsp. olive oil

Directions:

1. Place bets on the Power XL Air Fryer Grill pan.
2. Set the Power XL Air Fryer Grill to the air fry function.
3. Set timer and temperature to 15 minutes and 360°F.
4. Mix pepper, garlic, capers, salt, and olive oil in another bowl. Mix well
5. Remove the beets from the Power XL Air Fryer Grill and place them on a flat surface.
6. Peel and put it in the salad bowl
7. Serve with vinegar.

Serving Suggestions: Dress with parsley mixture.
Directions and Cooking Tips: Rinse beets before cooking.
Nutrition: Calories: 185 kcal; **Fat:** 16 g; **Carb:** 11 g; **Protein:** 8 g

497. Short Ribs and Beer Sauce

Preparation Time: 15 minutes
Cooking Time: 43 minutes; **Servings:** 2–3
Ingredients:

- 4 lb. short ribs, cut into small pieces
- 1 dried Portobello mushroom
- 1 yellow onion, chopped
- 1 cup chicken stock
- 6 thyme sprigs, chopped
- ¼ cup tomato paste
- 1 bay leaf
- 1 cup dark beer
- Salt and pepper, to taste

Directions:

1. Preheat the air fryer to 350°F.
2. Heat oil over medium heat in a pan that fits into your air fryer. Add onion, stock, tomato paste, beer, mushroom, bay leaf, and thyme. Simmer for 3–5 minutes.
3. Add the rib and transfer to the air fryer; cook for 40 minutes.
4. Bon appetite!

Nutrition: Calories: 300 kcal; **Fat:** 7 g; **Carb:** 18 g; **Protein:** 23 g

498. Short Ribs and Special Sauce

Preparation Time: 10 minutes
Cooking Time: 26 minutes; **Servings:** 2–3
Ingredients:

- 4 lb. short ribs
- ½ cup soy sauce
- 3 garlic cloves, pressed
- ½ cup water
- 2 tbsp. sesame oil
- ¼ cup rice wine
- 3 ginger slices
- ¼ cup pear juice
- 1 tsp. vegetable oil
- 2 green onions, chopped

Directions:

1. Preheat the air fryer to 350°F.
2. Heat oil in a pan, put green onions, garlic, and ginger, stir and cook for 1 minute.
3. Add the rib and the remaining ingredients, transfer to the air fryer, and cook for 35 minutes.
4. Serve and enjoy.

Nutrition: Calories: 321 kcal; **Fat:** 12 g; **Carb:** 20 g; **Protein:** 14 g

499. Beef Patty in Mushroom Sauce

Preparation Time: 15 minutes
Cooking Time: 22 minutes
Servings: 2–3
Ingredients:

- 2 lb. beef, ground
- ¾ cup flour
- 1 tbsp. onion flakes
- ½ tsp. garlic powder
- ¼ cup beef stock
- 1 tbsp. parsley, chopped
- 1 tbsp. soy sauce
- Salt and pepper to taste
- ½ cup beef stock
- ½ tsp. soy sauce
- 2 cups mushroom, sliced
- 2 tbsp. butter
- 1 cup yellow onion, chopped
- ¼ cup sour cream
- Salt and black pepper, to taste

Directions:

1. Preheat the air fryer to 350°F.
2. Mix beef, pepper, salt, garlic powder, and 1 tablespoon in a bowl. soy sauce, ¼ cup beef stock, parsley, onions flakes, and flour. Stir and shape six patties. Move it into the air fryer and cook for 14 minutes.
3. While the patties are still cooking, heat butter in a pan on medium heat, add the mushroom, and cook for 4 minutes with constant stirring. Add onions and cook for another 4 minutes; add the soy sauce and sour cream, and simmer. Remove from heat.
4. Serve patties with mushroom sauce.

Nutrition: Calories: 235 kcal; **Fat:** 23 g; **Carb:** 6 g; **Protein:** 32 g

500. Beef Brisket and Onion Sauce

Preparation Time: 10 minutes
Cooking Time: 2 hours; **Servings:** 2–3
Ingredients:

- 4 lb. beef brisket
- 1 lb. yellow onion, chopped
- ½ lb. celery, chopped
- 1 lb. carrot, chopped
- 4 cups water
- 8 earl gray tea bags
- Salt and black pepper, to taste
- 4 lb. beef brisket

- 1 lb. yellow onion, chopped
- ½ lb. celery, chopped
- 1 lb. carrot, chopped
- 4 cups water

Directions:

1. Preheat the air fryer to 300°F.
2. Put water in a pan that fits into the air fryer. Add the onions, celery, carrots, salt, and pepper. Stir and allow to simmer over medium-high heat.
3. Add the beef brisket, 8 earl grey tea bags, and stir. Put it into the air fryer, then cook for 1 hour and 30 minutes.
4. Meanwhile, place a pan over medium-high heat, add vegetable oil, and heat until shimmering. Add the sweet onion and sauté for 10 minutes and the remaining sauce ingredients, and cook for 10 minutes. Remove and discard the teabags.
5. Cut and serve the beef brisket with the onion sauce.

Nutrition: Calories: 400 kcal; **Fat:** 12 g; **Carb:** 26 g; **Protein:** 34 g

501. Turkey Wraps with Sauce

Preparation Time: 10 minutes
Cooking Time: 16 minutes
Servings: 2–3
Ingredients:
Wraps:

- 4 large collard leaves, stems removed
- 1 medium avocado, sliced
- ½ cucumber, thinly sliced
- 1 cup mango, diced
- 6 large strawberries, thinly sliced
- 6 (200 g) turkey breasts, grilled and diced
- 24 mint leaves

Dipping Sauce:

- 2 tbsp. almond butter
- 2 tbsp. coconut cream
- 1 bird eye chili, finely chopped
- 2 tbsp. applesauce, unsweetened
- ¼ cup fresh lime juice
- 1 tsp. sesame oil
- 1 tbsp. apple cider vinegar
- 1 tbsp. tahini
- 1 garlic clove, crushed
- 1 tbsp. fresh ginger, grated
- ⅛ tsp. sea salt

Directions:
For the chicken breasts:

1. Start by setting your air fryer toast oven to 350°F.
2. Lightly coat the basket of the air fryer toast oven with oil.
3. Season the turkey with salt and pepper, arrange the red basket directions, and air fry for 8 minutes on each side.
4. Once done, remove from the air fryer toast oven and set on a platter to cool slightly, then dice them up.

For the wraps:

1. Divide the veggies and diced turkey breasts equally among the 4 large collard leaves; fold the bottom edges over the filling, and then both sides and roll very tightly up to the end of the leaves; secure with toothpicks and cut each in half.

Make the sauce:

1. Combine all the sauce ingredients in a blender and blend until very smooth. Divide between bowls and serve with the wraps.

Nutrition: Calories: 389 kcal; **Carbs:** 11.7 g; **Fat:** 38.2 g; **Protein:** 26 g

502. Cod Steaks and Plum Sauce

Preparation Time: 10 minutes
Cooking Time: 30 minutes
Servings: 2–3
Ingredients:

- 1 tbsp. plum sauce
- ½ tsp. garlic powder
- 3 large cod steaks
- Cooking spray
- ½ tsp. ginger powder
- Black pepper and salt
- ¼ tsp. turmeric powder

Directions:

1. Drizzle the cod steaks with cooking spray.
2. Add pepper, ginger powder, salt, turmeric powder, and garlic powder.
3. Place the coated cod steaks in the Power XL Air Fryer Grill.
4. Set the function to Air fryer/Grill.
5. Grill for about 20 minutes at 360°F.
6. Flip while cooking for uniformity.
7. Heat plum sauce over medium heat for 2 minutes at reheat function.
8. Divide the cod steaks and serve immediately

Serving Suggestions: Serve with plum sauce
Directions and Cooking Tips: Allow the coated shrimps to rest for some minutes before grilling.
Nutrition: Calories: 330 kcal; **Fat:** 3 g; **Carb:** 25 g, **Protein:** 30 g

8 + 1 WEEK MEAL PLAN (28 days)

	BREAKFAST	SNACKS	LUNCH	SNACKS	DINNER	SNACKS
PRE-OP						
Day 1	Almond Tea	Simply Vanilla Frozen Greek Yogurt	Lush Roasted Vegetable Salad	Everything Parmesan Crisps	Creamy Broccoli Soup	Caprese Salad Bites
Day 2	Kiwi Sorbet	Caprese Salad Bites	Seitan Bites	Edamame Hummus	Beef, White Bean, and Spinach Soup	Kale, Butternut Squash, and Sausage Pasta
Day 3	Chicken Bone Broth	Greek Chop-Chop Salad	Sloppy Joes in Lettuce	Chia Chocolate Pudding	Spaghetti Squash Casserole with Ground Beef	Lemon Juice Salmon with Quinoa
Day 4	Pineapple and Mango Water	Roasted Garden Vegetables	Spaghetti Squash Noodles	Spicy Roasted Chickpeas	Ham and Bean Soup	Asian Peanut Cabbage Slaw
Day 5	Honeydew and Kiwi Infused Water	Asian Cabbage Salad	Super Veg Chili	Mashed Cauliflower	Potato Broccoli Soup	Cinnamon Fried Bananas
Day 6	Sweet and Sour Lychee Infused Water	Southwest Deviled Eggs	Tempeh and Avocado Lettuce Wraps	Pickle Roll-Ups	Creamy Chicken Vegetable Soup	Spinach and Artichoke Dip
Day 7	Kiwi and Kale Detox Water	Rajun' Cajun Roll-Ups	Seven-Layer Mexican Salad	Italian Eggplant Pizzas	Cucumber and Basil Gazpacho	
POST-OP						
WEEK 1						
Day 8	Watermelon and Lemon Water	Strawberry Juice	Refreshing Watermelon Pops	Turmeric Tea	Fennel and Ginger Herbal Tea	Almond Tea
Day 9	Mango and Ginger Infused Water	Grape Juice	Raspberry Watermelon Pops	Basil Tea	Ginger and Cinnamon Herbal Tea	Kiwi Sorbet
Day 10	Lavender and Blueberry Infused Water	Mango Juice	Raspberry Grapefruit Ice Pops	Strawberry-Infused Water	Ginger and Lime Herbal Tea	Chicken Bone Broth
Day 11	Pina Colada Infused Water	Apple and Kale Juice	Delicious Cherry Lime Pops	Peanut Tea	Linden Herbal Tea	Pineapple and Mango Water
Day 12	Watermelon Juice	Watermelon and Strawberries Drink	Watermelon Sorbet	Beef Bone Broth	Raspberry Herbal Tea	Honeydew and Kiwi Infused Water

Day 13	Ginger Tea	Clear Vegetable Stock	Apple Basil Lime Infused Water	Carrot and Red Apple Tea	Anise and Cinnamon Herbal Tea	Sweet and Sour Lychee Infused Water
Day 14	Orange Juice	Strawberry Limeade	Cinnamon Tea	Banana Pops	Grape Juice	Kiwi and Kale Detox Water
WEEK 2						
Day 15	Piña Colada Smoothie	Potato Mash	Pureed Kale Curry	Herbed Chicken Purée	Cauliflower Soup	Protein Spinach Shake
Day 16	Green Mango Smoothie	Shrimp and Parsnip Bisque	Pureed General Tso's Chicken Thigh	Matcha Mango Smoothie	Avocado Milk Whip	Fresh Lemon Cream Shake
Day 17	Peachy Greek Yogurt Panna Cotta	Salmon Curry	Rustic Beef Ragu Puree	Ricotta Peach Fluff	Banana and Kale Smoothie	Avocado Banana Smoothie
Day 18	Nutty Creamy Wheat Bowl	Coconut and Cornmeal Porridge	Cheesy Grits	Simple Applesauce	Beef Purée	Banana Cherry Smoothie
Day 19	Baked Cinnamon-Apple Ricotta	Coconut Pudding	High-Protein Porridge	Split Pea and Carrot Soup	Blueberry and Spinach Smoothie	Squash Soup
Day 20	Decadent Tomato-Basil Soup	Pimento Berry and Cornmeal Porridge	Mushroom and Wild Rice Soup	Herb And Melon Kefir Smoothie	Broccoli Purée	Creamy Avocado Soup
Day 21	Easy Green Pea And Ham Soup	Clam Chowder	Black Bean and Pumpkin Soup	Kefir And Yogurt Banana Flaxseed Shake	Easy Chocolate and Orange Pudding	Celery Soup
WEEK 3						
Day 22	Best Chocolate Porridge	Ham and Swiss Sandwich	Carrot Pudding	Cheesy Tomato Omelet	Tropical Porridge	Egg White Scramble
Day 23	Chocolate Chia Pudding	Egg Salad Sandwich	Fancy Scrambled Eggs	Colorful Scrambled Eggs	Delicious Mugastrone	Ham and Swiss Eggs
Day 24	Lemon-Blackberry Frozen Yogurt	Easy Baked Tomatoes	Yogurt Crème Brulee Custard	Corn Meal Mush with Polish Sausage	Porridge with Berries	Peanut Butter Cup Smoothies
Day 25	Creamy Cauliflower Dish	Black Bean Chipotle Hummus	BBQ'd Baked Beans	Chunky Mediterranean Tomato Soup	Strawberries with Whipped Yogurt	Berry Cheesecake Smoothies
Day 26	Beetroot and Butterbean Hummus	Finely Crispy Wok Veggies	Pumpkin Pancakes	Fried Deli Turkey Mushroom Sandwich	Gazpacho	Tropical Porridge

Day 27	Raisin and Oats Mug Cakes	Tomato Omelet	Vegan Porridge	Denver Sandwich	Cream of Chicken Soup	Delicious Mugastrone
Day 28	No-Bake Peanut Butter Protein Bites and Dark Chocolate	Stuffed Avocado	Chicken Sausage and Egg "Pizza"	Curried Chicken Salad Sandwich	Mushroom Soup with Brie	Porridge with Berries
WEEK 4						
Day 29	Cheese-Filled Acorn Squash	Everything Parmesan Crisps	Vegetable Low Mein	Tomato, Basil, and Cucumber Salad	Power Pesto Zoodles	Roasted Root Vegetables
Day 30	Cheesy Spinach Bake	Edamame Hummus	Spiced Okra Curry	Caprese Salad Bites	Spinach With Chickpeas and Lemon	Tomato and Mozzarella Bites
Day 31	Greek Yogurt, Granola, and Berry Parfait	Chia Chocolate Pudding	Baked Portobello Mushrooms	Green Beans Greek Style	Mushroom Sauce	Homemade Potato Chips
Day 32	Eggs Florentine	Spicy Roasted Chickpeas	Chard and Lime Pasta	Italian Herb Muffins	Vegetable Fajitas	Brie with Apricot Topping
Day 33	Mexican Scrambled Eggs	Mashed Cauliflower	Roasted Squash and Apples	Kale, Butternut Squash, and Sausage Pasta	Chickpea and Mushroom Curry	Chocolate Peanut Butter Protein Balls
Day 34	Spinach Omelet	Pickle Roll-Ups	Mushroom Steak	Lemon Juice Salmon with Quinoa	Crispy Zucchini Wedges	Hummus
Day 35	Open-Face Feta and Basil Omelet	Italian Eggplant Pizzas	Chayote Mushroom Stew	Asian Peanut Cabbage Slaw	Tomatoes and Basil Mix	Cheese Chips
WEEK 5						
Day 36	Ricotta and Spinach Frittata	Roasted Root Vegetables	Baked Halibut with Tomatoes and White Wine	Spinach and Artichoke Dip	Caramelized Salmon Fillet	Caprese Salad Bites
Day 37	Hearty Whole-Grain Breakfast Burrito	Tomato and Mozzarella Bites	Baked Cod with Fennel and Kalamata Olives	Slow Cooker Boston Beans	Salmon Butter Crumbed	Kale, Butternut Squash, and Sausage Pasta
Day 38	Turkey, Cheese, and Hash Brown Mini-Bake	Homemade Potato Chips	Shrimp, Zucchini and Cherry Tomato Sauce	Low Cholesterol Scalloped Potatoes	Cajun Shrimp	Lemon Juice Salmon with Quinoa
Day 39	Smoothie Bowl with Greek Yogurt and Fresh Berries	Brie with Apricot Topping	Monkfish with Olives and Capers	Green Beans Greek Style	Vegetable Egg Halibut	Asian Peanut Cabbage Slaw
Day 40	High-Protein Pancakes	Chocolate Peanut Butter Protein Balls	Baked Garlic Scallops	Marinated Mushrooms	Deep-Fried Prawns	Cinnamon Fried Bananas

Day 41	Baked Egg, Parm, and Spinach Cup	Hummus	Ranch Tilapia	Moch Mashed Potatoes	Salmon with Pistachio Bark	Spinach and Artichoke Dip
Day 42	Pumpkin Muffins with Walnuts and Zucchini	Cheese Chips	Easy Crab Sticks	No Dish Summer Medley	Vegetable Egg Halibut	Lemon Juice Salmon with Quinoa
WEEK 6						
Day 43	Wisconsin Scrambler with Aged Cheddar Cheese	Kale, Butternut Squash, and Sausage Pasta	Greek-Style Chicken	Maple-Mashed Sweet Potatoes	Dry-Rubbed Chicken Wings	Pickle Roll-Ups
Day 44	Andrea's Hangry Eggs with Cauliflower	Lemon Juice Salmon with Quinoa	Quail in White Wine Sauce	Garlic-Parmesan Cheesy Chips	Herbed Roast Chicken	Italian Eggplant Pizzas
Day 45	Southwestern Scrambled Egg Burritos	Asian Peanut Cabbage Slaw	Stuffed Turkey Breast	Cheesy Baked Radish Chips	Zaatar Chicken	Tomato, Basil, and Cucumber Salad
Day 46	Farmer's Egg Casserole with Broccoli, Mushroom, and Onions	Cinnamon Fried Bananas	Grilled Chicken and Radish Mix Recipe	Savory Cheese Biscuits	Spicy Asian Chicken	Slow Cooker Boston Beans
Day 47	Blueberry Greek Yogurt Pancakes	Spinach and Artichoke Dip	Hawaiian Roasted Quail	Italian Herb Muffins	Turkey Loaf	Low Cholesterol Scalloped Potatoes
Day 48	Egg White Porridge with Strawberries and Peanut Butter	Slow Cooker Boston Beans	Chicken Soup	Cheesy Cauliflower Tots	Cheesy Turkey Calzone	Green Beans Greek Style
Day 49	Hearty Shakshouka	Low Cholesterol Scalloped Potatoes	Chicken Chili with Jalapeno and Cheddar	Mozzarella Mushroom Caps	Korean Chicken Wings	Marinated Mushrooms
WEEK 7						
Day 50	Protein-Packed Breakfast Bars	Marinated Mushrooms	Italian Beef Sandwiches	Caprese Salad Bites	Caribbean Chicken Thighs	Savory Cheese Biscuits
Day 51	Lox, Egg White, and Avocado Scramble	Moch Mashed Potatoes	Chipotle Shredded Beef	Cinnamon Fried Bananas	Coconut Chicken Meatballs	No Dish Summer Medley
Day 52	Make-Ahead Breakfast Burritos	No Dish Summer Medley	One-Pan Beef Chops with Apples and Red Onion	Pureed Classic Egg Salad	Whole Roasted Turkey	Pureed Classic Egg Salad
Day 53	Magic Hot Cereal	Pureed Classic Egg Salad	Slow Cooker Beef with Red Peppers and Pineapple	Simply Vanilla Frozen Greek Yogurt	Sundried Tomato and Goat Cheese Turkey Roll	Maple-Mashed Sweet Potatoes

Day 54	Baked Broccoli and Eggs	Maple-Mashed Sweet Potatoes	Creamy Beef Stroganoff with Mushrooms	Caprese Salad Bites	Creole Cornish Hen	Garlic-Parmesan Cheesy Chips
Day 55	Broccoli and Tofu Quiche	Garlic-Parmesan Cheesy Chips	Italian Beef Sandwiches	Greek Chop-Chop Salad	Caribbean Chicken Thighs	Cheesy Baked Radish Chips
Day 56	Sunday Morning Special	Cheesy Baked Radish Chips	Flavorful Beef Meatballs	Roasted Garden Vegetables	Thanksgiving Turkey with Mustard Gravy	Savory Cheese Biscuits
WEEK 8						
Day 57	Very Berry Muesli	Savory Cheese Biscuits	Crumbly Beef Meatballs	Asian Cabbage Salad	Curry Chicken Wings	Italian Herb Muffins
Day 58	Strawberry and Mushroom Breakfast Sandwich	Cheesy Cauliflower Tots	Grilled Sardines	Rajun' Cajun Roll-Ups	Taco Beef	Cheesy Cauliflower Tots
Day 59	Shakshuka Egg Bake	Mozzarella Mushroom Caps	Rangoon Crab Dip	Everything Parmesan Crisps	Lamb Roast	Mozzarella Mushroom Caps
Day 60	Ricotta Baked in The Oven	Almond-Crusted Mozzarella Sticks	Perfect Crab Dip	Edamame Hummus	Mom's Sloppy Joes	Almond-Crusted Mozzarella Sticks
Day 61	Poached Eggs Italian Style	Almond Light-as-Air Cookies	Herb-Crusted Salmon	Chia Chocolate Pudding	Cranberry Meatballs	Almond Light-as-Air Cookies
Day 62	Denver Egg Muffins with Ham Crust	Strawberry Gelatin Tea	Shrimp Kabobs	Spicy Roasted Chickpeas	Apricot Brown Sugar Ham	Strawberry Gelatin Tea
Day 63	Cheesy Slow Cooker Egg Casserole	Subtly Sweet Coconut Milk "Flan"	Crab Mushrooms	Mashed Cauliflower	Steak Fajitas	Subtly Sweet Coconut Milk "Flan"

10-Days Gastric Sleeve Pouch Reset

What is a pouch reset?

A pouch reset is a diet that lasts 10 days, and whose purpose is to recharge your body and your mind for a successful weight loss post-bariatric surgery. The plan will begin with a liquid diet, followed by a pureed diet, and then back to solid foods.

It is a non-invasive way to shrink your stomach after stretching, and this will give you an opportunity to regain control of your eating habits and get back onto your weight loss path.

The real difference between the gastric sleeve surgery post-op diet and the pouch reset diet is duration: The post-surgery diet can last as long as ten, or more, weeks, while the pouch reset usually lasts for ten days.

How gastric sleeve pouch reset diet does it works?

Day 1: The first day of a gastric sleeve reset diet is similar to the early days of your post-operation diet; you'll consume nothing but clear liquids, such as water, broth, green tea, and non-carbonated sugar-free drinks.

Days 2-3: you can take protein shakes and can also incorporate thin soups into your diet, as well as yogurt, applesauce, and other soft foods with high liquid content.

Days 4-5-6: you can introduce soft and pureed foods into your diets, such as cottage cheese, scrambled eggs, and hummus.
Days 7-8-9: you can start eating soft foods like steamed vegetables, soft cereal, lean ground meat, and mashed fruit.
Day 10: the last day of the diet is the beginning of the diet you'll maintain for the rest of your life. The focus is on lean proteins, vegetables, fruit (minimal), and other healthy foods.

Bear in mind that poor eating habits can cause your stomach to stretch after the procedure, and this can lead to weight gain. It's important not only to eat healthy food but also to eat small portions during the day and chew your food thoroughly, in order to prevent gas and help you realize when you're full.

INDEX RECIPES A-Z

Review this Book

Thank you for reading this far!
We worked hard for almost a year to complete this 500-recipes cookbook, even comparing ourselves with different doctors. Rachel put in all the effort she could, thanks in part to her experience with daddy troubles. We are very pleased with this book, but now **what matters most is your feedback!**

If you enjoyed this book, please take a few moments **to leave a review on Amazon** about this work, or rating (it takes less than 5 seconds) hoose your amazon marketplace below).

We appreciate your time!

Scan this QR code to review on Amazon.com

Scan this QR code to review on Amazon.co.uk

Scan this QR code to review on Amazon.co.au

Scan this QR code to review on Amazon.ca

MEASUREMENT CONVERSION

VOLUME EQUIVALENTS	U.S. STANDARD	U.S. STANDARD (OZ.)	METRIC (APPROXIMATE)
LIQUID	2 tbsp	1 fl. oz.	30 mL
	¼ cup	2 fl. oz.	60 mL
	½ cup	4 fl. oz.	120 mL
	1 cup	8 fl. oz.	240 mL
	1½ cups	12 fl. oz.	355 mL
	2 cups or 1 pint	16 fl. oz.	475 mL
	4 cups or 1 quart	32 fl. oz.	1 L
	1 gallon	128 fl. oz.	4 L
DRY	⅛ tsp	—	0.5 mL
	¼ tsp	—	1 mL
	½ tsp	—	2 mL
	¾ tsp	—	4 mL
	1 tsp	—	5 mL
	1 tbsp	—	15 mL
	¼ cup	—	59 mL
	⅓ cup	—	79 mL
	½ cup	—	118 mL
	⅔ cup	—	156 mL
	¾ cup	—	177 mL
	1 cup	—	235 mL
	2 cups or 1 pint	—	475 mL
	3 cups	—	700 mL
	4 cups or 1 quart	—	1 L
	½ gallon	—	2 L
	1 gallon	—	4 L

OVEN TEMPERATURES

F	CELSIUS (APPROXIMATE)
250°F	120°C
300°F	150°C
325°F	165°C
350°F	180°C
375°F	190°C
400°F	200°C
425°F	220°C
450°F	230°C

WEIGHT EQUIVALENTS

U.S. STANDARD	METRIC (APPROXIMATE)
½ oz.	15 g
1 oz.	30 g
2 oz.	60 g
4 oz.	115 g
8 oz.	225 g
12 oz.	340 g
16 oz. or 1 lb.	455 g

CONCLUSION

Gastric sleeve bariatric surgery is a type of weight-loss surgery that removes 75% or more of the stomach and connects it to the small intestine. The procedure limits the amount of food you can eat and causes you to feel full faster, which should reduce how many times you're hungry during an average day. Although gastric sleeve patients typically lose about 50% to 70% of their excess weight, because the body typically stores fats in different areas than carbs or protein, they should still be able to consume daily portions of other nutrients like protein and vegetables while losing weight slowly over time. Keeping yourself motivated after a gastric sleeve surgery to reduce additional weight and perform exercise can be very tricky and challenging. Numerous individuals get fit stall out regarding where they need to be and when they should stop after gastric sleeve medical procedure. The risk that one can put themselves at with this is of getting underweight or anorexic. It can become like a race to get down to objective weight, yet they do not know how to quit losing and stick inside range. Some fundamental advances that you can make to guarantee you do not put yourself in danger of being underweight are to ascertain your optimal weight territory. Stick with around a 10-lb. range that you permit yourself to remain between, for example, 150 to 160 lb. When you let yourself a degree, you remove a ton of the pressure of hitting a precise number, and you know not to drop down underneath that run as it is beneficial to stay within it.

At the point when you begin to slip on what are solid propensities, try giving motivational speeches yourself to refocus. You cannot generally have someone there to take you to the rec center, cook your nourishments for you, or remind you to take your nutrients. If you begin tumbling off course, do not excuse it and let yourself think it is alright, or you will slip into a problematic pattern of defending helpless practices. Similarly, if you at that point where you go on vacation for a couple of days, which turns into a couple of more weeks, a month, past a month. You will go again; however, perhaps some family gives come up, your back damaged, or you have a migraine. These things keep coming up, and you let them prevent you from getting out and being dynamic. It is significant that you build up an excellent mental demeanor and accomplish something by bouncing up, grinning into the mirror, and stately, "I am going to go for a run." This equivalent attitude becomes possibly the essential factor with diet and different everyday issues too. Remember that a gastric sleeve medical procedure is more a device than a total weight reduction arrangement. Some get all energized from the outset and need to get in shape as fast as could be expected under the circumstances. Thus, they drop a few lbs. until they arrive at their objective just to find that they do not have the foggiest idea of what to do from that point.

This occasionally prompts getting into negative behavior patterns and falling right back to where they were before they experienced gastric sleeve medical procedure in any case. Taking care of this issue is to understand that being solid is a basic framework, not a race to be won. After experiencing gastric sleeve medical procedures, numerous patients find that it gets exhausting to eat similar stuff, drink similar protein drinks, and go on the same walk or do a similar exercise schedule. Switch things up by concocting new plans to attempt through some accommodating sites. The equivalent goes for practices you do to keep yourself dynamic every day. You do not need to lift loads or run to be emotional, as those are only some famously advertised strategies for keeping genuinely active. You can do yoga, Pilates, tennis, ball, swimming, full-body cardio, and significantly more. However, if you cannot escape the house to go for a workout session, you can even go to YouTube, type in-home full-body cardio, gastric sleeve works out, etc.

One terrible propensity that should be halted for some individuals is keeping some snacks and fat-dense foods away from visual perception and reach in the kitchen. So, what would you be able to do to cure this issue? The appropriate response is just to throw away or lose the shoddy nourishment with the goal that you do not have the enticement gazing you in the face. If you cannot get the nourishments out of your home because of relatives or the craving to sometimes treat yourself, that is completely fine. Simply conceal the food where you will not see it often, for example, over your refrigerator or at the head of your washroom above eye level. At that point, place sound nourishments out where you see them promptly and at eye level in the bathroom. So, as opposed to snatching those chips or that sweet treat, you can get some blended nuts, baby carrots, possibly some apple cuts.

Ensure that you discover somebody who will get down on you about your helpless decisions or terrible practices. That individual will assist you with remaining on target and assist you with pushing ahead with your weight reduction and weight upkeep plan. If you get an empowering influence as a responsibility accomplice, you may not end up stuck at a weight recapture. This is an opportunity to be straightforward with yourself and be overly legitimate about your examples of conduct considering your wellbeing. Compose the solid feast plan, get the nutritious food, go for an exercise, and continue doing it again and again. The demonstration of rehearsing an action, again and again, makes it easy after some time since you become accustomed to doing it. On the first occasion, when you do anything, it is supposed to be troublesome. The more you make a move, the simpler it will get. Likewise, as the weight falls off, you will feel better moving in your body because there will be less to carry around.

You can be the cause of all your problems when glancing in the mirror. Quiet your inward pundit and have a go at rehashing positive certifications to yourself consistently. Additionally, abstain from contrasting yourself with others. Keep in mind that each weight reduction venture is unique.

There is a particular outcome that individuals need from making a move. This is likewise why inspiration is connected with defining and accomplishing objectives. Suppose by chance somebody accepts that it will take a ton of hard, predictable work to get to a particular outcome. In that case, they will probably maintain a strategic distance from the assignment and have low inspiration due to the envisioned or saw torment included (enthusiastic, physical, mental, and so on.) in getting to their ideal outcome or objective. So, as expected, they dawdle, and later, the errand feels more excellent, and thus, they accept they have low or no inspiration. So, in short, always consider your tasks easy to be achieved so you can get to your goal quickly.

Your weight reduction medical procedure is a viable method to lose abundance weight; however, it is anything but a marvel fix. You may hit a weight reduction level or recapture a little weight, yet do not let this perplex you. Be prepared for potential difficulties, and keep looking forward. Figure out how to give yourself a somewhat congratulatory gesture. Prize yourself with something pleasant like a back rub or a long shower. Make a point to maintain a strategic distance from any food-related prizes since that could prompt undesirable propensities.

Try not to race into a high-power exercise and anticipate quick outcomes, as that may prompt disappointment. After your medical procedure, you will have to moderate you're eating routine and physical movement levels. Simplicity into an agreeable schedule that fits with your way of life.

Ensure that your home and your environmental factors are helpful for your new way of life. Dispose of any enticing nourishments, and fill the washroom with more beneficial alternatives. Additionally, have a go at keeping your tennis shoes by the entryway to remind you to work out. By straightforwardly following your medical procedure, you will get in shape quickly; however, in the long run, this will back off. Show restraint toward yourself, set aside some effort to understand that your weight reduction medical procedure and way of life changes for wellbeing are a long-lasting responsibility to a superior and more advantageous you. After weight reduction medical procedure, there will be days while staying cheery and spurred will be hard. Your weight reduction medical procedure is the start of your excursion to a healthier life, so continue pushing ahead by making plans to discover things that make you cheerful and inspire you to be effective.

Thank you for your time and for reading this far!

Stay in touch with me, email me at rachelamy.meyer.author@ichnospublications.com, for whatever you want. If you are really interested in receiving:
- updates on upcoming editions.
- offers reserved only for members of our newsletter.p
- valuable content from the brain trust generated by our community.
you can specify it in the same email, otherwise I will only reply to the reason for your email.

I will publish more books on healthy diets and cookbooks for physical well-being and ***rediscovering the love of food without being addicted to it.*** *I cherish this book especially because of my dad's health problems. Your honest opinion is very important to me.*
Please, leave a review directly on this amazon link *(it takes less than 30seconds, it will be enough to just put stars.).*
Click Here (https://www.amazon.com/dp/1914409795)

Rachel Amy Meyer

Other Author's Works

by IPH Books – Healthy Lifestyle

Whole Food Plant Based Cookbook:

Clean Eating And Gain Vibrant Health With Over 600 WFPB Budget-Friendly & Easy Recipes That You Can Prepare Everyday | Including 30-Days Meal Plan Bonus

Would you like to turn your eating habits into more healthful, beneficial, and energizing ones that amongst all the effects, can reduce the risk of physical and cognitive diseases?
If the answer is "YES", this is the book for you.

We all know the importance of having a healthy diet to stay healthy and prevent diseases, but nowadays it has become pretty difficult to keep track of everything that we put inside our bodies.

The Whole Food Plant-Based diet is the best eating habit to keep eating delicious, natural, and rich meals while avoiding unhealthy levels of added sugar, sodium, and fat, which can be responsible for serious health issues.
Find Out More…
(please visit here https://www.amazon.com/dp/B09NRNPJ7J)

Or for your convenience, Scan this QR with your smartphone →

IPH BOOKS
Healthy Lifestyle

Printed in Great Britain
by Amazon

87749952R00102